Between Death and Life

by
Dolores Cannon

OZARK
MOUNTAIN
PUBLISHING

Library of Congress Cataloging-in-Publication Data

Cannon, Dolores, 1931- 2014

Between Death and Life: Conversations with a Spirit; previously titles:

Conversations with a Spirit: Between Death and Life by Dolores Cannon

What occurs between death and life, as revealed by numerous subjects through hypnotic past-life regression.

1. Hypnosis   2. Reincarnation   3. Past-life therapy 4. Life after death

1. Cannon, Dolores, 1931- 2014 II. Reincarnation III. Title

Library of Congress Catalog Card Number: 2013947641

ISBN: 9781940265001

Cover Design: Victoria Cooper Art

Book set in: Centaur & Times New Roman

Book Design: Tab Pillar

Published by:

PO Box 754

Huntsville, AR 72740

800-935-0045 or 479-738-2348 fax: 479-738-2448

WWW.OZARKMT.COM

Printed in the United States of America

TABLE OF CONTENTS

Books by Dolores Cannon

Conversations with Nostradamus, Volume I
Conversations with Nostradamus, Volume II
Conversations with Nostradamus, Volume III
Jesus and the Essenes
They Walked with Jesus
Keepers of the Garden
Between Death and Life
The Legend of Starcrash
A Soul Remembers Hiroshima
Legacy from the Stars
The Custodians
The Convoluted Universe - Book One
The Convoluted Universe - Book Two
The Convoluted Universe - Book Three
The Convoluted Universe - Book Four
Five Lives Remembered
The Three Waves of Volunteers & the New Earth

For more information
about any of the above titles, or other titles
in our catalog, write to:

Ozark Mountain Publishing, Inc.
PO Box 754
Huntsville, AR 72740
info@ozarkmt.com
479-738-2348 or 800-935-0045
www.ozarkmt.com

This book was originally written in the early 1990s and has stood the test of time. At that time the subject of life after death was not openly discussed because of the fear associated with it. Now people are more open to talking about it and exploring the unseen realm. In 2013 I decided to update this book because of the questions I have been asked over the years and the additional information that has come forth. Nothing I have written about since I first discovered this subject in 1968 has ever been contradicted. In my 45 years of working in this field only new information has been added as I continue my job as a reporter searching for lost knowledge.

Dolores Cannon

Death, be not proud, though some have called thee
Mighty and dreadful, for thou are not so;
For those whom thou think'st thou dost overthrow
Die not, poor Death; nor yet canst thou kill me.

John Donne
[1573-1631]
Sonnet: Death

Chapter I
The Death Experience

I HAVE BEEN ACCUSED of speaking to and communicating with the spirits of the dead, a definite "no-no" in religious circles. I had never thought of it in just that way, but I suppose it is true. With the exception that the dead with whom I speak are no longer dead, but are living again today and going about their daily lives. For, as you see, I am a regressionist. This is a popular term for a hypnotist that specializes in past-life regressions and historical research.

Many people still have difficulty accepting the idea that I am able to go back through time and talk to people as they relive other lives down through history. I soon became accustomed to this and found it fascinating. I have written books describing some of my adventures in this incredible field.

With most hypnotists, past-life work is strictly off limits. I don't really understand why, unless they are afraid of what they might find and would rather stick with known and familiar situations which they are positive they can handle. One such therapist confided in me, as though he had made a real breakthrough, "I have tried some regressions. I once took someone back to when he was a baby."

He was so serious, it was almost impossible for me to suppress a laugh as I answered, "Oh? That is where I *begin*."

Even among other regressionists who work regularly with past-life memories as therapy, I have found many who have their own fears about taking a hypnotized subject through the death experience, or venturing into the periods between lives when a person is supposedly "dead." They are afraid something physical might actually happen to the living body of the subject in trance.

That somehow they may be harmed by the reliving of these memories, especially if they are traumatic. After going through this experience with thousands of subjects, I know that there are no physical problems even if the regressed personality died in a horrible way. Of course, I always take special precautions to insure that there will be no physical effects. The welfare of my subject is always my most immediate concern. I feel that my technique completely safeguards the subject. I would not attempt this type of research otherwise.

To me the in-between life plane, the so-called "dead" state is the most exciting sphere of existence I have encountered, because I believe there is much information to be obtained there that can be of great benefit to humankind. I believe people can come to realize that death is nothing to fear. When they face that time in their life, they can see that it is not a new experience but one they are well acquainted with. They, themselves, have already performed it many times. They will not go into the great terrifying unknown, but to a familiar place they have already visited many, many times. A place that many call "home." I hope people can learn to see birth and dying as evolutional cycles that each person goes through many times and are thus a natural part of their soul's growth. After death there is life and existence in the other planes that is just as real as the physical world they see around them. It may be even more real.

Once while talking to a woman who considered herself "enlightened," I was trying to explain some of the things I have found. I told her I did research into what it is like to die and where you go afterwards. She asked excitedly, "Where do you go ... Heaven, Hell or Purgatory?"

I was disappointed. If those were the only choices her mind would accept, it was obvious the woman was not as enlightened as she thought.

Exasperated, I replied, "Neither!"

She was shocked. "You mean you stay in the dirt?"

THUS I REALIZED that in order to write this book, I must retrace my steps to where I stood when the door first opened and try to remember my beliefs and thoughts as they were before the light entered. No easy task, but necessary if I am to understand and relate to those still searching for that door and that light. For I must speak to them in terms they can understand and try to lead them gently down the path of awareness. Then they can live their lives to the fullest without fear of what tomorrow brings.

To many people the word "death" seems so forbidding, so final, so hopeless. A black void of mystery and confusion because it represents a cutting-off from the physical world, which is the only place they definitely know with certainty exists. Like many things in life, death is unknown, shrouded in mystery, folklore and superstition, and thus to be feared. Yet it is something that we know everyone must eventually experience. No matter how much we wish to push it to the back of our minds and not think about it, we know that the body is only mortal and will someday expire. What happens then? Will the personality that we consider to be ourselves also perish with the physical shell? Is this life all there is? Or is there something more, something rare and beautiful beyond what we know as life? Maybe the churches are correct when they preach about Heaven for the good and pious and Hell for the evil and damned. With my insatiable curiosity I am always searching for answers and I believe there are many others who also share this craving to know. It would make life so much easier if we could live out our time in happiness and love, not fearing what lies at the end.

When I first began my regression research I had no idea I would find the answers to any of these questions. Being a history enthusiast I mostly enjoyed going back through time and talking to people in different eras. I enjoyed reliving history as it was being made, and as it was seen through their eyes as they remembered their other lives. I wanted to write books about their versions of these historical periods, because each unknowingly corroborated the others' stories while in deep trance. There are patterns I did not expect to find. But then something unexpected occurred that opened up a whole new world for me to explore. I discovered the period between lives, the so-called "dead" state, the place where people went after they left a physical life here on Earth.

I can still remember the first time I stumbled through the door and spoke to the "dead." It was during a past-life regression and when the subject "died" on me, it happened so quickly and spontaneously that I was taken off guard. I was not fully aware of what had happened. I don't know what I expected would occur if someone were to go through a death experience. But as I said, it happened so quickly, there was not time to stop it. The person was looking down at their body and saying they looked just like any other corpse. I was amazed that the personality had definitely remained intact - it had not changed. This is important. This is a fear that some people have: that somehow the experience of dying will transform them or their loved ones into something different, strange or unrecognizable. Again, it is the fear of the unknown. Why else are we so afraid of ghosts and spirits? We think that somehow the process of crossing over will change them from the beloved person we knew into something evil and frightening. But I have discovered that the personality remains the same. Although on some occasions it experiences momentary confusion, it is still basically the same person.

When I overcame my shock and wonder of being able to speak with someone after they had died, my curiosity took over and I was filled with questions I had always wondered about. From that time forward, each time I found a subject who could go into the deeper states of hypnosis required for this type of research, I made a practice of asking some of the same questions. Religious beliefs or lack thereof seem to have no influence on what they reported. Their answers were basically identical each time. Although worded differently, they were all saying the same thing; a phenomenon in itself.

Since I began my work in 1979, I have had hundreds and hundreds of people go through the death experience. They have died in every conceivable manner: accidents, shooting, stabbing, fire, hanging, decapitation, drowning, and even in one case by death in an atomic explosion, which I reported in my book A *Soul Remembers Hiroshima*. They have also died naturally from heart attacks, disease, old age and peacefully in their sleep. Although there has been a great deal of diversity, there have also been definite patterns that have emerged. The manner of death may be different but what happens afterward is always the same. Thus I have come to the conclusion that there is really no reason to fear death. We subconsciously know what happens and what lies over there. We should; we have had so much practice at it. We have all gone through it countless times before. So in my study of death, I have found the celebration of life. It is far from being a morbid subject, but a most fascinating other world.

With death also comes wisdom. Something happens with the shedding of the physical body and a whole new dimension of knowledge opens up. Apparently the human being is limited and hampered by being in the physical. The personality or spirit that continues on is not hindered in this way and can perceive so much more than we can even imagine. Thus when I talked to these people after they had "died," I was able to obtain the answers to many puzzling and perplexing questions-questions that have haunted humankind since the beginning of time. What the spirit reported depended upon the personal spiritual growth of that spirit. Some had more knowledge than others and were able to express it clearer in terms that were easier for us mortals to grasp. I will attempt to describe what they experienced by letting them speak for themselves. This book is a compilation of what many people reported.

THE MOST COMMON DESCRIPTIONS I have found of the moment when death occurs is that there is a feeling of coldness and then suddenly the spirit is standing by the side of the bed (or wherever) looking at their body. They usually can't understand why the other people in the room are so upset because they feel so wonderful. The overall sensation is one of exhilaration rather than dread.

The following is a description of the moment of release by a woman in her 80s who was dying of old age. It is an example that is typical and constantly repeated.

D: *[Dolores] You lived a long time, didn't you.*
S: [Subject] Um, yes. I move slow, takes so long. *(Moaning)* There's not much joy any more. I am so tired.

Since she was obviously experiencing discomfort, I moved her ahead in time until the death was over. When I finished counting the subject's entire body jerked on the bed and she suddenly smiled. Her voice was full of life, nothing that even resembled the weary tones of only a moment before. "I feel free! I'm light!" She sounded so pleased.

D: *Can you see the body?*
S: *(Disgusted)* Ohh! That old thing? It's down there! Ohh! I had no *idea* I looked so *bad!* I was so wrinkled and shriveled. I feel too *good* to be that shriveled. It was all wore out. *(She was making sounds of delight.)* Oh, oh, I'm so glad I'm *here!*

I could hardly keep from laughing, her expression and tone of voice was quite a contrast.

D: *No wonder it was shriveled; that body lived many years. That's probably why it died. You said you are "here," where are you?*
S: I'm in the light, and oooh, it feels *good!* I feel intelligent... I feel peace ... I feel calm. I don't *need* anything.

6

D: *What are you going to do now?*

S: They tell me I've got to go and rest. Oh, I hate to rest when I've got so much to do.

D: *Do you have to rest if you don't want to?*

S: No, but I don't feel like I want to be *cramped* again. I want to grow and learn.

After this I was unable to get any more answers from her except that she was floating. I could tell by her expression and her breathing that she was in the resting place. When a subject goes there it is as if they have drifted into a deep sleep and they don't want to be disturbed. It is useless to try to question them because their answers will be incoherent.

This special place will be explained in further detail later in the book.

IN ANOTHER CASE a woman was reliving the birth of a baby at home. Her breathing and bodily movements showed that she was experiencing the physical symptoms of childbirth. This often occurs when the body remembers as well as the mind. In order not to cause the subject discomfort I moved her ahead in time to when the birth should have been over.

D: *Did you have the baby?*

S: No. I had a difficult time. It just wouldn't come. I was wore out, so I just left my body.

D: *Do you know what the baby was?*

S: No. It doesn't make any difference.

D: *Can you see your body?*

S: Yes. Everybody's upset.

D: *What are you going to do now?*

S: I think I'm going to rest. I've got to come back eventually, but I'm going to stay here awhile. I'm in the light. It's restful.

D: *Can you tell me where this light is?*

S: Where all knowledge and everything is known. Everything is pure and simple. There is more pure truth here. You don't have the things of the world to confuse you. You have the truth on Earth but you just don't see it.

D: *But you said you have to come back sometime. How do you know that?*

S: I was weak. I should have been able to tolerate the pain. I must learn to better withstand it. I could have stayed if I hadn't been so weak. I'm glad I can't remember the pain. I know I need to go back and I must become complete, whole. Pain is one thing I must overcome. I must overcome all the pains of the world.

D: *But experiencing pain is very human and it's always difficult to do when you're in the body. From the side you're on now, it's easier to look at it in a different way. Do you think that's a lesson you want to learn?*

S: I will, yes. It takes me awhile sometimes, but I can do anything. I think I should have been stronger. I would have done better, but I think I had a lot of fear from the illness I had when I was a child. I was afraid that *this* would be as bad. And ... I gave up. Pain ... when you deal with the higher conscious level of your mind and remove yourself to the pure light and the pure thought; the pain ceases to be. Pain is only a lesson. When we learn about pain on the human level, we get frantic and show outward concern for just the moment. By removing ourselves and concentrating and reaching deep and having patience, we can rise above it.

D: *Does pain have a purpose?*

S: Pain is a teaching tool. Sometimes it is used to humble certain people. Sometimes a haughty spirit can be brought down and taught to be more gracious through suffering. It may teach them that they must eventually learn to rise above the pain, and then they can deal with it. Sometimes just understanding pain and why we have it, lessens the pain.

8

D: *But like you said, people become frantic and they think they can't handle it.*

S: They become too self-centered. They need to rise above their own interests and what they're feeling at the moment to a more spiritual level and then they can deal with it. Now, some people, they bring the pain on because it's a shelter. They may have the pain as an excuse or as an "out," and that's the purpose. It varies with the individual. What is pain? It cannot touch you if you don't let it. If you admit that you will hurt, you're giving power to pain. Do not give it power. It's unnecessary to feel it. It's all connected to man. Reach into your spirit, your higher mind; it has no hold on you.

D: *People can separate themselves from pain?*

S: Of course, if they want to. They don't always want to. They want the sympathy and self-punishment and *all* sorts of things. People are funny. Everyone knows how to do these things if they take the time. They must find a way for themselves because they wouldn't believe it if you told them there was an easier way. They have to figure it out on their own. That's part of the lessons that get you there.

D: *People are so afraid of dying. Can you tell me what it is like when it happens?*

S: Well, when I'm in the body it feels heavy. It pulls on me. It's just uncomfortable. But when you die it's a lifting of weight. It's relaxing. People carry all those problems around. And it's like they are carrying around a weight because they are heavy and laden with all these other things. When you die it's like tossing them out the window and it feels good. It's a transition.

D: *I guess people are mostly afraid because they don't know what to expect.*

S: They fear the unknown. They must just have faith and just trust.

D: *What happens when somebody dies?*

9

S: You just rise up and leave it. You go up here. In the light.

D: *What do you do when you're there?*

S: Perfect all things.

D: *Where do you go if you have to go away from the light?*

S: Back to Earth.

D: *Is it unusual for us to speak to you through time like this?*

S: But time has no meaning. On this frame there is no time, all time is one.

D: *Then it doesn't bother you that we speak to you from another time or plane?*

S: Why should it?

D: *Well, we thought it might and I didn't want to disturb you.*

S: I find that it disturbs you more than it does I.

ANOTHER EXAMPLE concerns a little girl who died at the age of nine. When I first began speaking to her she was going on a hayrack ride to a school picnic in the late 1800's. There was a creek near where the picnic would be held and the others would be going swimming. She couldn't swim very well and was afraid of the water, but she didn't want the other children to know it for fear they would make fun of her. Since some of the others had fishing poles, she had decided she would pretend to fish so no one would know she couldn't swim. The little girl was really worrying about it and was not enjoying the hayride at all. I told her to move forward to an important day when she was older. When I finished counting, she announced happily, "I'm not there anymore. I'm in the light." This was a surprise, so I asked what had happened.

S: *(Sadly)* I couldn't swim. The dark just closed in on me. I felt my chest burning. And then I just came out into the light, and it didn't matter anymore.

D: *Do you think the creek was deeper than you thought?*

S: I don't think it was that deep. I got real scared. I think my knees just folded up and I couldn't stand up. I was just scared.

D: *Do you know where you are?*

S: *(Her voice was still childish.)* I'm in forever.

D: *Is anybody with you?*

S: They're working. They're all busy ... contemplating what they *have* to do. I'm trying to get the hang of everything.

D: *Do you think you've ever been to this place before?*

S: Yes, it's very peaceful here. But I'll go back. I must overcome fear. Fear is something you bring on and it is paralyzing. I don't really think the water was deep. I think I doubled up because of my fear. The worst thing that can happen usually isn't near as bad as what we fear. *(The voice was now more mature.)* It's a monster in man's mind and fear only affects those on Earth. It's the carnal mind. The spirit is left unaffected.

D: *Do you think when people are afraid of things that they draw it to them?*

S: Oh, yes! You bring those things upon yourself. Thought is energy; it is creative and it makes things happen. It's easy to see how another person's fears can be silly and unimportant and you think, "Why would they be afraid of that?" Yet when it's *your* fear, it's so *deep* and so *personal* and so *touching* that it just engulfs you. So if I can look at other people's fears and try to help them understand *theirs,* I think somewhere along those lines it would help me understand the ones I had.

D: *That makes a lot of sense. You know one of the biggest fears people have is that they are so afraid of dying.*

S: That's not so bad. That's the *easiest* thing I'll ever do. It's, like the end of all confusion, until you start all over again, and then it's more confusion.

D: *Then why do people keep coming back?*

S: You must complete the cycle. You must learn all and overcome all the things of the world so you can enter into perfection and everlasting life.

D: *That's a big order though, to try to learn everything.*

S: Yes. Sometimes it's very tiring.

D: *Seems like it would take a long time.*

11

S: Well, from where I am here it all seems so simple. I am in control. For instance, I can understand the fear, and the way I feel now; I feel like I couldn't be touched by it. Yet there's something about the human person. When you're *there,* it engulfs you. I mean, it becomes part of you and it touches you and it's not so easy to stand off and be objective.

D: *No, it's because you're emotionally involved. It's always easy for somebody else to look at it and say, "How simple."*

S: It's like looking at somebody else's fears. I must learn to endure and stay with a life and not leave until I can take as much as I possibly can from that life. I think if I had a life that I could stay with to go through many experiences; it would be much easier than going through so many short lives. I'm wasting a lot of time. So I will choose carefully to get one where I can experience many things and therefore limit my trips back. But I also think it will be harder. There are certain things you have to work out between people while interacting in a relationship. What you do comes around.

There has long been an expression in our culture, that when you are dying, your life "flashes before your eyes." This has occurred in some of the cases I have investigated. It happens more often after death when the deceased looks back over their life and analyzes it to see what they have learned from it. This is often done with the help of the masters on the other side, who are able to look at the life more objectively, with emotions removed.

One of my subjects was able to review her past life in an unconventional way. Although it's difficult to say what is conventional and what follows a set pattern when you're working in this field of regressive hypnotic research.

The woman had just relived a past lifetime through regression and had come to the point of death in that life. She died peacefully as an old woman, and watched as her body was taken to a hilltop near her home to be buried in a family cemetery. Then instead of going on to the other side, she decided to return to her home to try to complete some unfinished business. There she was startled to find herself appearing as a ghost, and having the ability to walk through walls. She saw herself as a fog or mist in the shape of a person, but she was amazed to discover that furniture and objects could be seen through her, as though she was transparent. It was very interesting to her to find herself in this strange condition, and she wandered through the house discovering what she was able to do. At one point she overheard the chambermaid's remark that the old woman was haunting the house, because they could hear her walking around.

After a while being a ghost became boring, because she knew no one could see or hear her, and she was unable to communicate. She soon discovered that she would not be able to accomplish whatever she had gone back to the house to do, because of her unsolid state. The instant she came to this revelation she was out of the house, and standing on a hill overlooking a valley. Her deceased husband had come to meet her, and was standing next to her. In that dimension they were young again, looking exactly as they had on the day of their marriage. As they stood arm-in-arm looking out over the valley, it became a "valley of lives, but it was more or less like a valley." life." She later described this as if a brightly colored pallet or quilt had been thrown over the valley, and it appeared as a collage of scenes and places from the life she had just left. Instead of her life passing before her eyes in linear fashion, one scene following the other, the whole thing was laid out before them.

She said, "We can see the cemetery, we can see the city, we can see the house, we can see the mountains. It's like we can see everything we've ever known all combined together. It's as if this was our life, and this is what we had together. And we can see that we shared it and we got through it together. We were glad we came through that life like we did. We had something intact when it was over with. It's peaceful. It's sort of like you stand there and survey. As if you had some great big fields and you had different things growing in them. Or if you had lots of flowers in a garden and you stand and survey it. You'd remember what you did to get the garden ready. You'd remember how things grew and developed. And this was the final result spread out before you. You look out over this valley of life, point to certain areas, and you say, 'Well, we really did have a good time *here,* and this was the great thing that we did together *here.'* You're admiring all the different parts of the garden, and you can see it all at once. All the different scenes of your life are laid out, and you can touch them. It was *literally* as though we were going through a scrapbook looking at our lives, but it was more or less like a valley."

This was very satisfying to her to look at the scenes, even though the hard parts of the life were difficult to review. There was also no judgment involved. There appeared to be a mental note-taking to remind them of what they wanted to change the next time around. This is undoubtedly not the only method of viewing the life that had just been departed, but it was a beautiful one.

IN ANOTHER CASE, I was speaking to a man who had just died in an avalanche. I asked him what it was like to die.

S: Have you ever dived into a deep pool ... to where it's dark and murky at the bottom? As you come back up towards the surface of the water it gets lighter and lighter. Then when you break through the surface of the water there's sunlight all around. Death was like that.
D: *Do you think it was like that because of the way you died, with the rocks falling on you?*
S: No, it was like that because I was going from the physical plane to the spiritual plane. As I left my body it was like coming up through the pool. Then when I reached the spiritual plane it was like breaking the surface of the water and coming out into sunlight. If you die in an accident, physically it is painful just before you lose consciousness of the physical plane because your body has been injured. But after you lose consciousness it is very easy and natural. It's as natural as anything else in life:

making love, walking, running, swimming. It is just another part of life. There's no such thing as dying. You just go on to a different stage of your life. Dying is pleasant. If people are worried about it, tell them to go to a place in the river that has a deep pool. Tell them to dive down to the bottom of the pool. And then, at the bottom push up vigorously with their feet and come plunging up to the surface. Tell them it is like that.

D: *I think many people are worried that death will be painful.*

S: Death is not painful unless that you have need of pain. For the most part there is no pain unless it is wished for. It can be extremely painful if you wish it to be or if you feel you have need of it in order to teach you a lesson. But you can separate yourself from that at all times. And this is available no matter how connected you are with what is going on. It is available to everyone, the separation of the body and soul during this time of pain.

D: *But the actual death itself, the leaving of the body, is that painful?*

S: No. The transition is one of ease rather than of duress. Pain comes from the body. The spirit feels no pain except remorse. That is really the only pain that a spirit can feel. A feeling that they could have done something ... more. This is painful. But physical pain no longer has meaning because that was left with the body.

D: *Is it possible to leave the body before actual death occurs and let the body suffer the pain?*

S: Yes. The person has that choice, whether or not they want to stay there and go through it or if they want to leave and just watch. That is an option that is open to everyone.

D: *I personally think it would be easier, especially if it was going to be a traumatic death.*

S: This is strictly up to the individual.

In my work I have come across examples of this. In one regression a young woman was being burned at the stake for her beliefs while the whole town watched. She was terrified but was also very angry at the bigoted people who were responsible for this. As the flames leaped higher, she decided she would not give them the satisfaction of seeing her suffer. So she left the body and watched from a hovering position above the scene. There, much to her chagrin and aggravation, she saw her body screaming as it went through the agonies of burning to death. In this case it was very obvious that the body and the spirit were two separate things.

I think it would be very reassuring and comforting to people who have lost loved ones in a violent, horrible way, to know that they probably did not even experience the most traumatic part of the death. It makes a great deal of sense to realize that the spirit would not want to remain in the body and experience all that pain. Therefore the spirit removes itself and the body is merely reacting spontaneously. Much in the same way that we react when we cut or burn ourselves accidentally. We yell and pull our hand away. This is not a conscious reaction but an involuntary one. Thus it would appear that during a horrible death the body is merely reacting while the real personality has vacated and is watching from the sidelines.

ANOTHER DESCRIPTION of death:

S: Imagine yourself naked, cold and bleeding, walking through the dark woods full of briers and wild animals and strange noises. You know that behind every bush is a beast ready to pounce and tear you apart. And then suddenly you walk into a clearing where there is grass growing and birds singing, clouds in the sky and a pleasant laughing brook that meanders on its way to its destination. Imagine the difference in these scenarios and you can see my analogy portraying what you would call life and death.

D: *But there are many people on Earth who are afraid of it.*

S: Many people who are in the forest are afraid, that is correct. Once they are out of the forest there is no fear. The fear is in the forest.

D: *Then there is nothing to be afraid of in the transition?*

S: There are some transitions which are more desirable than others. I will not mince words on this. However, a door is merely a door. No matter how many times you open it, it simply will not change from being a door.

ANOTHER DESCRIPTION:

S: People should not be afraid of dying. Death is no more to be feared than breathing. Dying is as natural and as painless as ... blinking your eyes. And that's almost the way it is. At one moment you're in one plane of existence and you blink your eyes, so to speak, and you're in another plane of existence. That's about the physical sensation you have, and it's as painless as that. Any pain you feel in the process is from physical damage, but spiritually there is no pain. Your memories are intact and you feel the same, as if your life is continuing. Sometimes it takes you a little bit to notice that you're no longer connected to your physical body, but usually that is noticed right away because your perceptions are broadened to where you can perceive the spiritual plane without the veil in the way. This is the clouded mirror, as some have likened it to. What happens is that at first there is a period of orientation. You are still very conscious of the physical plane but you are exploring and absorbing the sensations of being aware of the spiritual plane, until you get used to the fact that you're really on the spiritual plane and you are comfortable with it.

D: *Can you tell me, does your spirit include your soul when it leaves your body?*

S: Your spirit is your soul. The soul concept encompasses that energy which you would call your spirit, your identity, your reality. That is indeed your *true* self. You may call it your spirit or your soul depending on which perception you would choose to integrate into your reality.

D: *We've heard a lot about what is called the "silver cord." Is there any such thing?*

S: This is, as you might perceive it, a lifeline to your body which is very real in nature. In an energetic sense this is the cord which maintains a lifeline with your energies to your body. It is indeed a real device.

D: *Then at the point of death this cord is severed?*

S: That is accurate.

D: *Some people are afraid to have out-of-the-body experiences for fear that they might become separated from their body prematurely.*

S: It is possible to do this. However, it is almost certainly done intentionally and not through accident.

D: *You mean when they go out of the body the silver cord connects them so they can't become lost, so to speak?*

S: That is accurate. There should be no fear in experiencing astral travel, for were it not meant to happen it would never happen.

D: *But in many cases, it is not planned, it is spontaneous.*

S: That is accurate. It is "spontaneous."

In my work I have discovered that most people are not aware that everyone travels out of the body every night when they go to sleep. The body is the part that gets tired and must rest; the spirit or soul never requires sleep. It would be awfully boring for the "real" you, the spirit, to wait around for the body to wake up so it could continue its work. So while the body is sleeping, the real you is going off and having all kinds of adventures. It can travel all over the Earth, spend time on the spirit side or even go to other planets or dimensions. The person is normally not aware of this unless they remember dreams of flying or unusual places. You are always connected to your body by the silver cord, your lifeline, your umbilical.

And when it is time to return to the body you are more or less "reeled in," and the spirit reenters the body. I have been told by my clients that they sometimes experience temporary paralysis just before awakening. This occurs when the person is awakened suddenly (by a loud noise etc.) before the spirit is totally back in the body. The body/spirit connections have not been completed and temporary paralysis is the result. It usually passes quickly and is nothing to be feared.

D: *Is there any danger of someone staying out of the body?*

S: We perceive there is no danger. For were the individual not to return, it would be of his or her own choosing and not because some malevolent energy has come in behind and severed the cord.

D: *They couldn't become lost, in other words, and not find their way back?*

S: We do not perceive this as true.

D: *Then they are definitely connected with the body until the point of death, and then the cord is severed? It is like an umbilical, so to speak.*

S: That is entirely accurate.

D: *If death would occur during an out-of-body experience what would we say the body died of? Would it be a heart attack?*

S: You are asking what the physical symptoms would be. Sudden infant syndrome is often ascribed to this. There are also those who because of age simply choose not to return, and so they are found in their sleep.

D: *Is it a heart attack?*

S: That is not the case, because a heart attack is death induced by a real physical ailment, and is not what we refer to here. They would die in their sleep, and it would be called "from natural causes."

D: *If an autopsy were performed, they wouldn't find any cause at all?*

S: That is accurate.

D: *What about people who seem to die of spontaneous combustion? That is an unexplained mystery.*

S: This is due to an imbalance of what you would call "chemicals" within the system. It is because of the fact that human bodies do burn food, though through a very controlled and very slow process. Such a death is caused by the combustion of the body fluids. This is oftentimes due to hereditary factors which cause an imbalance in the chemical makeup of the body. For example, too much phosphorus in the body system.

When people are on the spirit side they make a plan before they reenter the karmic wheel called "Earth." It is a plan of what they hope to accomplish during the next life. They also make contracts with other souls that are going to be important for them to interact with during the upcoming lifetime. Also a part of this contract is their exit plan. Everyone plans the way they will leave or exit this present lifetime. I have found that no one ever dies until it is their time to die. There are no such things as accidents. It was just the manner chosen for the soul to exit. When the soul has completed what it came to accomplish it is time to move to the next phase of their existence. I have found that it is possible to delay the death for a short period of time, however when it is the appointed time, the spirit chooses to leave. Of course, the conscious mind of the person has no memory of this part of the plan, because when we come into this life the veil of forgetfulness comes down and all memory of the spirit side is removed. They said one time, "It would not be a test if you knew the answers." So we have to remain consciously oblivious to our soul plans.

D: *What about people who seem to die in groups? There are many cases such as train accidents, massacres, earthquakes, where several people die at one time. Did they all choose to go at the same time or did they have anything to say about it?*

S: You are aware of the concept of karma on an individual basis. There is indeed also what is called "group" karma. There have been, through many eons of time, instances where souls have tended to group together to perform certain tasks, or to establish changes, or to experience life in a group, much as you tend to experience on an individual basis. These "group deaths" are nothing more than individual souls who would come together at some certain points in their transition; that is, in their learning experience of dying. And in so doing find themselves at a juncture at which it would be most appropriate for them to depart simultaneously.

D: *Did they agree to do this before their entry into the life?*

S: That is accurate. For it is in this group transition that they find support. There is a sharing of the experience in that they are not alone in this transition. In many cases there have been multiple births and lives shared, so it is not uncommon to find multiple or shared deaths.

D: *Was this the case with the astronauts who passed over in the Challenger spaceship accident?*

S: Indeed this was one instance in which it was agreed that there would be that sharing of the death experience.

D: *But there was so much suffering for the families and people all over the country when this happened. If they were going to their destiny, why can't we be happy about it?*

S: Perhaps there is a short sightedness in seeing these events. You are thinking only of the individuals who departed. This is not the case. There are many other elements involved. In cases like this there was a coming together of the survivors, a sharing of the experience. In seeing that someone else is sharing the grief, it is much easier for an individual to experience this, knowing that there are others who are going through the same thing. Thus this was a group experience on many levels.

Many subjects describe the experience after leaving the physical body as journeying toward a bright dazzling light at the end of a tunnel or whatever. These descriptions have been duplicated in reports of NDES (Near Death Experiences). One of my subjects said that this white light was an intense energy field that served as the barrier between our physical world and the spiritual realm. In NDES the person will approach the light, but are pulled back into their body before entering it. They have actually been in a near death situation, but they did not complete the transition. They did not go far enough. When my subjects have relived the death experience, they pass through the white light, the barrier. At that point, the energy is so intense that it severs the "silver cord," the umbilical that attaches the spirit to the physical body. When this occurs, the spirit cannot cross back through the barrier and enter their body again. The two have been forever separated. Without this connection to its life force (the soul or spirit), the body quickly begins to deteriorate.

Chapter 2
The Greeters

AFTER DYING, there seems to be a period of confusion for some spirits. All do not experience this. Much of it depends upon the manner of death, whether it was natural or sudden and unexpected. The main thing that I found is the assurance that one is never alone after going through the death experience.

S: There's sometimes a period when you're not really sure where you are, whether you're on the physical plane or the spiritual plane because some of the sensations are similar, yet they're different. And you're trying to figure out what is going on and where you are. There is a period of orientation or reorientation, which can be confusing to some as they figure out where they should go from here. But they needn't worry because help is sent immediately. Usually a handful of souls will come that you have had close karmic connections with in former lifetimes. There's always one or two or even more on hand that are in-between incarnations themselves. They will be there to greet you. And the person will recognize them due to his connection with them in the immediate past lifetime. Another thing that causes confusion when you cross over to the spiritual planes is that your memory starts opening up to your past incarnations and your entire karmic picture. So you'll recognize those souls. First, initially in the relationship you knew them in the life you just left. Then you'll start remembering other relationships where you've known them. That's part of the process of remembering all of your karma while you're on that plane, so you can understand what you've just completed and what you still need to work out when you return to Earth again.

D: *Then it is true that someone always comes when people die*

S: Yes. If possible it's usually someone who was special to them during their life, if they have not reincarnated. Someone that they can identify with and the power of attraction is there to help them through the period of transition.

D: *But many times people die violently or suddenly. If they don't know they are dead, are they more apt to be confused?*

S: Yes, that is true. And the helper who is there has to explain to them what is going on, and to help them through it.

D: *When the spirit is met by other souls after it has died, where does it usually go?*

S: It goes to the plane where the learning takes place. There's no central location for it; it's just a state of being. And usually the spirit interacts with many other souls while it is doing this. After learning what it needs for its next lifetime, it consults with the spiritual masters and starts preparing for its next incarnation. It consults with the spiritual masters to see what kind of situation would be best for the spirit to come back into. There is also consultation about which souls would be best for it to interact with for the benefit of all.

D: *Have you ever heard of the resting place?*

S: Yes, if you are referring to what I am picturing, it is a special place for damaged souls or those who have died traumatically to go to rest and restore themselves before they can enter the company of other souls or enter the plane of incarnation again.

D: *Some people believe that the form of Jesus' spirit will contact you to guide you at the time that your spirit leaves your body.*

S: It is entirely possible; however, not mandatory or in all cases. It is sometimes done if the individual crossing over requests or desires to see this Jesus energy, and so it is in fact the Jesus energy which would manifest itself. For He has so stated that His help shall be a part of this process, and it is there for any who would so choose to open themselves up to this energy, be they incarnate or not. This is also true for people of other beliefs or religions. If they have a deep abiding belief in a particular entity, that spirit energy will be there for them to help ease the crossing, if this is what they desire.

D: *There is also a belief that there is a place in the spirit world where spirits sleep because they die believing that they have to rest until Jesus comes the second time and resurrects them.*

S: That which you expect to find or that reality you create, you do indeed find. Were they to expect to awaken into perhaps a carnival, then that would be what they would find. Anything is possible if they believe in it. There are so many different things that *can* happen after the death of what you would term "the physical body." When a *body* expires (the soul never does); if it is a gentle death then there is a feeling of relief, of wonder, of freedom. For the most part what the person expects to be there will be there. If they expect to meet guides or friends along the way to help them toward the light, this is what they shall see. If they were steeped in the belief of damnation and hellfire and if they believe that they deserve this, this is what they shall also perceive. Most of this is based upon the preparation of the individual soul prior to death. But usually, there are those who were close to them before they passed over to the other side. More times than not, another soul will come and guide them to a place of healing so they will lose their confusion and understand what has occurred. Perhaps the spirit is confused because it's been a long time since they've been to this side. The greeters will help them become unconfused and find where they want to

25

go and need to go. In this way, if it is someone they have known then they have no fear, for fear is what causes people to be in shock. Some people, if it is a traumatic death, go into a period of deep, deep resting until they can handle the experience of knowing that their body has ceased to exist. And the awakening will be very slow. We don't need people who are wandering around in a daze. They can cause themselves harm and others also.

D: *Do they do that sometimes?*

S: It has not been unknown to happen, yes. They don't know where they are. In their panic, they can hurt themselves by feeling, "I've got to get back, I've got to get back." And they tie themselves to wherever they died by the feeling that this can't be happening.

D: *It is better if they go and rest?*

S: Yes, because then they can be awakened slowly, knowing that what has happened is good and it is right and natural. The shock and trauma have been lost then.

D: *Do their loved ones come when there is a traumatic death also?*

S: Yes, sometimes they just take them to a place where they can rest. But something that you would think of as a traumatic death would not always be considered traumatic on this side. You would perhaps consider many soldiers to have died traumatic deaths. Yet sometimes they are some of the most accepting of what has happened, more so than perhaps someone who died in childbirth.

D: *I suppose it just depends on the circumstances and the individual soul.*

S: Yes, to a great extent.

THE APPEARED TO BE an established cycle of constantly returning to Earth again after being on the other side. It seemed to me that if someone were in a place where they *could* not die, that they would naturally want to they remain there forever. I was thinking of the way people on Earth are always searching for immortality.

S: No, you would be bored very quickly. If your lesson of the third grade is over, why would you want to stay in the third grade for the rest of your life? It could be comfortable but there would be no learning.

D: *There would be no challenges.*

S: That's true.   Death is necessary in order to progress. Stagnation would occur if there were no death in order to move one to the spirit side. This is an ongoing process which is best suited for the learning of much information. All is as it should be in this respect. If the lessons you were learning were finished then there would be a casting-off of the experiences which taught those lessons, and an assuming of *new* experiences to learn the more advanced lessons. It is simply climbing ladders, if you will, where each level of experience is growing in awareness from the one below it. So the surroundings which will be the catalyst for these experiences will be discarded as the new experiences are needed. Would you like to stay in your third-grade classroom and take fourth or sixth-grade classes? Or would it be better to be in a new environment and start with a new frame of mind? If you were left in the same classroom, you would tend to think the same. The frame of mind is very important also.

D: *I think that's true of many people on Earth. Sometimes if they stay in the same environment, they don't grow. Is that what you mean?*

S: That is exactly correct.

D: *They need the challenge of something new, a new place, new surroundings.*

S: New surroundings are very important to progression. Reminders of the past inhibit looking to the future.

S: Some people think that there is *no* life after death. (She gave a short laugh.) But once something exists, the energy which is that existence cannot be destroyed. Why is it so hard to believe that there is existence after the death of a physical body? You cannot destroy something like electricity because the energy is always there although in a different form. Why do they think that a human spirit and soul can be destroyed when energy cannot? That is what the human soul is - nothing but energy. For the soul is not merely a *thing* which is residing within the physical body. It is an energy. And as an energy, it can propagate as energies are wont to do. The correct perception of your personality would be as energy, for that is the essence of the truth of creation-that all is energy. Some forms are on lower levels such as the physical world around you; but they are energy and can be demonstrated as such by simple conversion processes such as fire. All matter is in reality, energy. It is simply manifested in a lower, baser form. And so you can see yourselves as pure beings of energy, nothing more, nothing less. There is no such thing as *matter*. This is simply a connotation which has been given to describe that which is apparent around the "physical" world.

S: Death holds many fears. However, death is the great denier, the great untruth. It is that which is most unspoken about, but yet most thought about. There is no need to fear death, for with its release there is again life which far exceeds that which is here on this planet. However, to those who would deny this life we would caution that by improper use, that is, by suicide or of that nature, one generates that energy which follows to the other side. And it is then necessary to be dealt with on the other side. It is, and never will be, appropriate to cast off a living body before its time. That is a waste which is not to be tolerated.

D: *I'm trying to make all this clear so people won't be so afraid of these things.*

S: Yes. The main problem you will have is not fear but philosophical dogma in the way.

D: *Do you mean in the way of explaining it?*

S: Philosophical dogma is the way people have of closing off their minds to what is. For example, people who follow different creeds of belief will find it difficult to comprehend some of the things that I have explained.

D: *You mean those who are brought up in the belief of things like Heaven and Hell?*

S: For example, yes. And the ones that are brought up in the belief that each soul has only one incarnation. That is foolish but that is what they believe.

D: *Yes, they think life is one time around and that's it. There are those who cannot accept the idea that they have lived more than once.*

S: Is it any harder to believe that you can be born once into a body than to believe you can be born twice or more?

D: *Some people have a hard time with the concept.*

S: Only those on *your* side. That is one reason why so many of them have problems with depression and such. Because they feel they're screwing up their only chance. If they realize that they have a multitude of chances, they could do their best each time and not feel bad for the mistakes they make. They can work it out the next time.

D: *They should just try to do the best they can this time around. It makes sense to me, but there are many people who don't understand it.*

S: There are many who do not want to. Many have fear of thinking of another existence after the one they are living, because perhaps the one they are living is so painful that they think it would be continuous torture to have one life after another. Many of the churches do not want people to believe in prior or successive existences because of the fact that it loosens their grip of fear and *they* no longer have control. The leaders of all of the great schools of thought knew of previous existence and

29

successive existence, but it was closed off to the general knowledge because of control. Even the Hindu school of thought uses this control in a different manner because they say that, "This man has done something in his previous existence to make him suffer now. Therefore, why should I help him? He has done something to deserve this." In this way they are using the same tactics as Christianity or any of the others. You have to remember that not all of those who say they are on the side of religion are. They perhaps are being warped by the darker side of things without themselves knowing it. Men have removed many things from the Bible and added what they wished. They have no cares, they think that, "This is what I wish it to say, and therefore that is what it says."

D: *People seem to have fear when something like this is brought up. When you try to tell them that the Bible has been changed many times throughout history.*

S: These things cause them to think and many people are afraid of free thinking. When you take away what people have believed in all of their life and say that it is different, or that perhaps their parents unknowingly lied to them, you are taking away their foundations of what they believe in. And man cannot survive without *something* to believe in, even if it is the belief that there is nothing. He must believe in something.

D: *In other words, they are frightened by a different school of thought.*

S: People said the same things of Jesus when He said that He came to fulfill the prophesies. They said that He was wrong, that He was crazy, that He didn't know what He was talking about. Every time someone comes up with something that's a little bit different or a little unusual, it's going to frighten people and they're going to say bad things about it. This knowledge is something that *needs* to be taught because man has to learn to be without fear in order to be what he *can* be. There are people who *need* to know these things. And it will strike a spark in them and they will recognize it as being the truth. It will perhaps help them find their way to become what they want to and need to become. They are the ones that are important, because they will eventually bring enough people on to their side. Remember, there were only a few, a handful of people, who believed in the message of Jesus. And now look at the world. Much of the world professes, at least outwardly, Christianity. The truth has been suppressed for many centuries and it is time for it to come out.

Chapter 3
A Near Death Experience

NOT ALL OF MY INFORMATION about the death experience has come from hypnosis. Occasionally people tell me about Near Death Experiences (NDEs) which they have had. This term was made popular by the work of Dr. Raymond Moody and Dr. Elizabeth Kubler-Ross. It refers to events people remember when they have literally died and crossed the threshold to the other side and have been brought back to our world of the living by the advances of science. The stories that people have recounted to me traditionally follow the pattern that other researchers have discovered. They also parallel the information I have found in my work, with the exception that those people have come back to report their experience whereas mine remained on the spirit plane until they were reincarnated into their present life. My subjects carry the memory, but it is buried deep within their subconscious and can only be released by the use of regressive hypnosis.

The case I will report carries many of the classical portions. A friend introduced me to Meg by saying that she had a remarkable story to tell me. Meg had not confided this experience to very many people because she was afraid of ridicule. It was too personal and private, and she felt there were many who would never understand the importance she placed upon it. She felt it had changed her life forever. Meg was not the same after it, nor would she ever be the same. She believed this was the reason she was allowed to retain the memory. It was a gift she could draw upon in times of indecision and stress. She explained that hypnosis would not be necessary to recover the memory from her subconscious because it had been forever emblazoned in her mind. Meg may have been hazy about some of the details, but she knew she would never forget it and no one would ever be able to convince her it had not occurred. It was a turning point in her life. Meg was a mature woman in her late 40s, married with several children. She had not read anything about NDEs, and she definitely had not been exposed to my material. She led an active life with many interests, but everything that had happened since the event had hinged upon its importance. It continued to color everything in her life.

We met at a friend's house where we could have privacy, and Meg settled into a comfortable chair to relate her story for the tape recorder. I was impressed by her need for accuracy and the careful way she avoided embellishment of any kind. She felt the need to recite it correctly, and she remembered it in remarkable detail. Meg agreed to allow me to print the story on the condition that I keep her anonymous.

This is what occurred, in her own words:

IT HAPPENED when I had surgery about 10 years ago, in 1978. I was due to open a bookstore in June, *but* accidentally in a routine examination they found a lesion on my lung. They couldn't decide whether it was cancerous or benign, so I had to have lung surgery. I must say that before going in I intuitively did not feel like I had a cancer, and I didn't feel too good about this surgery. I didn't have good vibrations about it. That's the only way I can describe it.

I had gone through a rather conventional childhood. I went to several different churches and then no churches at all. They were every type: Congregational, Lutheran, *etc.* When we moved out to the country I went with my next-door neighbor to the Baptist Church. But I was not raised with a fundamentalist background. In fact it was a very loose Christian background-loose in that I wasn't accustomed to going to church an awful lot. When I married my husband I joined his church which was an Episcopal Church. Again it was a very loose relationship and remains that today. Somewhere along the line I'd come to the conclusion that I certainly was at the point of being an agnostic, perhaps even an atheist. But I think because of my childhood habits I didn't dare quite become a total atheist. *Just in case.* (She laughed.)

I want you to know where I was coming from as I lay in the hospital the night before the surgery. I really was convinced I might not come out of this. I said what I thought might possibly be my last prayer. I whispered into what I would call the darkness, "I don't know if you're there, but if you are, this is the best I can do." And I tried to review everything, and to see if spiritually I had left anything undone. Then I said, "I *don't* really think you're there, but if you are, I really need some help." I went right to the wall. "I'm sorry I can't have more faith, but in all honesty this is the best, in the final analysis, that I can do."

So anyhow, I came through the surgery fine, but I felt like hell because I hurt. I was hurting so bad all I could think of was; when was the next shot? I'm putting this all in because I think I have to be honest. I was drifting in and out, and I was being given Demerol. So for the skeptics, they can say, "Well, she was on pain killers." It doesn't matter. The skeptics are going to say what they're going to say anyway. About the third day in intensive care, I fell asleep. And suddenly I was going down a very long, dark canyon. I felt very, very warm and very, very secure, but it was the blackest canyon I've ever seen. They were like mountain walls that seemed quite far away, and then suddenly they seemed close. At one point I looked on these mountain walls and instead of being all black they almost appeared orange with dark, flickering lights against them. It had something to do with souls, but I don't remember what it was. But it was a very warm, secure feeling.

As I was going down the canyon I saw a very misty place just ahead of me. And as I came upon it, I could see that there was some kind of a rock barrier blocking the entire entrance to this canyon. You couldn't go on, but there was just enough room to squeeze around it. There was mist everywhere.

And then I saw the people standing there. There were two men, and another shadowy figure. All of a sudden, I recognized who that person was, and then he was no longer a shadowy figure. This is funny, but he looked like Gene Wilder used to look in Willy Wonka. He had that wonderful curly, curly hair and was wearing a suit with white piping. My first thought was, "What is this?" And then all of a sudden I realized I was dying. I did experience a moment of fear there.

Then this man in this suit said, "You are at death." Those were the words: "You are *at* death." Then I realized that he was the "angel of death." He didn't say it, but I knew it. And I thought to myself he was a little intimidating. But when he said, "You are at death," it was so *kind* that I was not afraid. I was just not afraid at all. He was so kind. And he was so efficient. It was incredible.

And I remember pondering it; then nodding my head and saying, "I know." Now I'm going to say all of the rest of this in a jumble because I was getting information simultaneously. It was just coming in from impressions. Where someone said something I will quote exactly what they said. My first thought was, "There really is something after death! There really is!" I was absolutely *astounded.* I kept saying, "But death is so easy. It's so *easy.* It's like getting up out of *this* chair and sitting down in *that* chair."

These men were nodding their heads. And one of them said, "Yes, but it is *hard* to get there." I didn't understand it, but that's what he said. Then the man in the suit said, "And you are being given a choice." Now I thought of several things. One thought was, "Death is a *dancer.*" That's a strange thought, but I'm trying to relate what I got at the time in its purest form. I got the impression at that point that I was not *always* going to be given a choice. I also got the impression that not everyone was given a choice. That this was just at this particular time, at this point. Then I also got the impression that this "angel of death" was not this being's permanent position. I felt that he was just on assignment, and that he wouldn't always be having *this* assignment.

There were some other shadowy figures there, and I perceived that they were there to help me. Because he said, "Do you wish to stay or do you wish to go?" Now *stay* meant stay with them; go meant go back. It's not what you would normally think. It was the reverse. "Do you wish to stay or do you wish to go?" And I knew it was *wonderful* there, and I wanted to *stay*. (Excited) And so I said, "I want to *stay*."

I can't remember his exact words, but he said, "There are some things you have to know before you make up your mind." Then I was shown my mother and she was crying and sobbing. And he said, "Now your mother will be destroyed. And she, in her destruction will destroy those around her." And I'm sure he was talking about my father. I perceived that her life would just be *over* at that point. And in his love for her, his life would be over. But I said, "Oh, I want to stay." Because I perceived that time was so fast *there,* that it was nothing. They would be there so quickly, and they would understand when they got there. I also perceived another thing that whatever way I chose was just *right*. There was absolutely *no* judgment or censure, but what I chose to do was the right thing to do. Then I was shown my husband. He was crying and he was saying; "I never knew I loved her," which fits in with the way the marriage was at that time. I saw it would be very hard on him, but I said, "I want to *stay*." Because I knew that in just a little while everybody would be there, and they'd all understand.

Then he said, "Now, your children will be all right, but they will not go as far as they could." But I still said, "I *want* to stay." I knew my children would be all right. Maybe not do as well as if I was there; but they'd still not go under. To stay there was still the most attractive choice. And *then* Death said, "Now, you will have to stay close to your children." In other words, stay close to the edge. And I was told I would have to guide my children. I was just *astonished,* because that's not what I wanted. I wanted to go on over to this happy place and learn. I don't know how I knew I could learn there. It just came into my mind, and I knew. I hadn't seen it, but I knew the minute these people opened their mouths, that this was a place that I wanted to be. I just knew that there were answers there. The *answers,* I suppose. There were studies; answers; growth. This was just instinctive, but I *knew* it was a place I wanted to stay. I sure didn't want to leave it and go back to *these* problems. *I* wanted to be *there.* But I reluctantly said at that point, "Well, if I have to stay close to the edge, I might as well go back. I've got these responsibilities. And I can handle it better from *that* side than I can by just trying to stay close to my children and influencing." So I said, "Okay, I'll go." And they all seemed quite pleased that I had decided that, even though there would have been no censure or judgment.

I felt as if I was beginning to pull back. And I saw those other minor figures whispering, "She's going to go. She's going to go." I can't remember if they disappeared or if they went around the barrier. I think they went around the barrier. And I perceived that they had been there to help me cross over. But they weren't needed so they disappeared. Then I started to pull back, as if I was leaving. And one of these men spoke up and said, "Before you go, there are some things we want you to know."

Instantly I was in another place. I wasn't in the tunnel anymore. It was kind of like a backyard, and there was a circle of people. I've tried since then to guess how many were in that circle of people sitting around in chairs. I would guess maybe eight, ten men and women. I perceived that they were my council. And I knew that every single person has a council that has a responsibility for each soul down here. They sort of reminded me of a country Sunday school group meeting out at the church yard, maybe in the afternoon or something. I really couldn't see faces but this one person sort of guided me. I remembered his bare arms and his rolled-up white shirt sleeves, very much like men would do at a warm Sunday, summer, Bible-class type of thing. He took me over to a girl sitting under a tree and she had black skin, colored skin. And he kind of plucked at her skin. (She made the motions of pinching the skin of her forearm between her thumb and forefinger.) And he said, "This is so unimportant; this skin. This is so *unimportant.* It's just a little covering. It is so unimportant, it's laughable," and then they both kind of laughed. And I was thinking, "Why is he telling me this? *I know that.*"

Then the next picture was ... we were standing on a road, and there was at least one of my counselors with me. These two young men of East Indian visage were walking up the road. And they were there to show me myself. Now I was standing there and all of a sudden next to me was myself. I saw a beautiful, very large, brilliant, opaque shimmering sphere that I knew was myself. And I walked around, and I entered myself, this sphere of light. (She illustrated with hand motions the act of entering the top of this sphere and proceeding downward through it to come out of the bottom.) And I knew that when I came out I would have all my answers. I would know myself. And I *did*. But when I went into the sphere I descended. It was like being bathed in milky white, very comfortable. And I thought, "Any minute now I will reach the center." And soon I reached on through and emerged out the other side, sort of at a downward angle. I knew when I was in the center, *but* the center was exactly like the periphery. In other words, the center was exactly like the edges. Yet I perceived when I was in the edges and going through and in the center and coming out again. *But* the center was exactly like the periphery. They were just the same composition. When I came out I *knew* myself. And I stood there, and I felt embarrassed. I felt naked because I knew myself and I perceived my good and my bad, and I made no judgment upon myself. And I said, "I've got to work on that." And they knew me, too. They knew me totally. And they smiled and nodded. And the nice thing was that there was no censure. Absolutely none. No judgment.

This is where I get hazy. I cannot recall which came next. I looked up and the sky was suddenly darkened, and it was filled with stars. Some were huge and some were medium and some were tiny, and they were of varying brilliancies but not one outshone the other. Even if there was a very tiny one next to a huge, brilliant one, you could still see each with equal clarity. And I knew the stars were souls. I said, "Well, where's mine?" And someone said, "There it is." I looked behind me and there was my star. It had just risen off the horizon. And suddenly I was *there,* in the place where my star was. And I *felt* like I was interwoven into fabric. In that instant *I* knew that we were all totally connected and that no matter what happened we could not be destroyed. Even if something came and ripped the fabric, the fabric would hold. I knew that I could not be destroyed, nor could anyone else. That I was as I was as I am.

Then I was next back in the meadow, standing at that roadside. And I looked out across this beautiful sunlit meadow and there was a grove of trees. It was symbolic to me that there was a grove, but I perceived that within it was the tree of life. And suddenly, out of this grove of trees, came this enormous ball of lightning. I just watched it as it flew across the meadow. And it struck me right here. (She put her hand on her chest over her heart area.) It was as though I had the breath knocked out of me. It was as if every ounce of everything was sucked out of me and I was *consumed.* And what came into me was total, pure, unconditional love. It was so incredible. It went into every cell, and I could hardly get my breath. There wasn't anything I could give except love because that was all I was composed of. It had taken over every atom. And then I started coming back. And someone shouted to me, and it may have been my counselor: "Stay married. You're meant to be married." (Resignedly) Which I have done.

I came back. And I woke up and I saw the nurse in the Intensive Care Unit leaning over me with the most *concerned* look on her face. She was watching me. And I thought, "Don't worry, I'm all right. I'm not going to die. And I won't go away again." I also thought, "Oh, you don't know where I've been." I didn't tell anybody for quite a few days.

Later we discussed the possibility that Meg was dying and maybe the nurse had either seen something on the machines or in the way she was acting. When Meg was zapped by the ball of lightning that might have been an actual jolt to the body to restore lifc. She returned to her body immediately after being jolted. It could have affected her rather like the electric shocks administered to a patient after their heart stops.

There will undoubtedly be debate about whether this incident really occurred or whether it was a drug-related fantasy. But Meg has no such argument going on within her. She *knows* it was real. There is no doubt in her voice as she relates the incident. She knows because it changed her life forever.

As Meg said, "Maybe someone has to almost lose their life in order to find it."

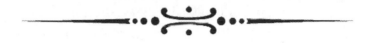

The rest of Meg's story:

Meg became a good friend and we remained in touch for more than twenty-five years after she told me this story. The NDE had such a profound effect on her lifc that she always told her husband that if she was dying, to allow her to go. She didn't want to be brought back. This happens with many people who have experienced this phenomenon. They are no longer afraid of death. They have seen the other side and are anxious to go there again when the time comes.

So years later she developcd cancer and was lying dying in the hospital. When her vital signs stopped her husband became frantic and asked the medical personnel to resuscitate Meg. It brought her back but she was very angry. She had once again crossed to the other side and did not want to return. She insisted that it not happen again.

As she lay in the hospital her pain increased and there were no more access to her veins to administer pain medication. Then one night a young male nurse entered her room and gently inserted an IV with pain medication in a small vein between her ring finger and the little finger. My daughter Julia, who was a nurse for twenty years, said that this is a very unlikely place to insert an IV.

Meg was more comfortable for a few days until the IV had to be changed. She insisted that they bring the young male nurse in to replace it because he had done it so beautifully. The doctors insisted that there were no male nurses employed at that hospital. So who was the young man who had so gently relieved her pain? A spirit from the other side? Her guardian angel? Whoever he was, he was definitely not from this physical Earth. He had helped to make her passing more comfortable, because she died a few days later in her sleep before anyone could bring her back to this world again.

I don't grieve for Meg because I know she is happy. She was one of the few who was able to see a glimpse of the other side. Even if it was only for a few moments, what she saw was so beautiful she knew she would not fear returning.

Chapter 4
The Schools

I WAS TO ENTER the fascinating spirit realm many times. This is the area that holds the most fear for humans, and the one that raises the eternal question, "Where will I go when I die?" Everyone wonders what will happen to them, whether there will be total oblivion or continuation of the personality. Even the most religious still harbor their uncertainties. I do not have all the answers, but I believe I can help through the information I have received in my regression research. Even the regressed somnambulist cannot tell you what they do not know. But when you obtain the same descriptions from many different people, you have to assume it has validity. Maybe it rings true because the majority would truly like to believe the afterlife is a place of peace and contentment.

I personally find the idea of staying in the ground until Resurrection Day or Judgment Day totally repulsive. Also the idea of floating around on a cloud playing a harp for eternity is not my vision of Heaven. I think it would get boring quickly. Maybe I find this concept of the schools attractive because of my insatiable curiosity and my constant quest for knowledge.

Whatever the case, I think this gives us the best description and maybe, just maybe, the answers to some of the haunting questions that plague us all.

Many times when I regressed different subjects they would not be involved with a life. Their answers would reveal that they were in-between, on various spirit levels or planes and in different places. The most common of these was the school. I asked for a description.

S: It is the school of knowledge. I see the hall. It has tall pillars and it's all in white. Real light-how do I explain it? The light comes from within and without, from everything and just shines.

D: *Do you mean like sunlight?*

S: Not that bright, but more ... lasting. It's very peaceful, very restful, very calm. It is a very nice place to be.

D: *Where is this school of knowledge?*

S: It's just here. It is on a different vibration from the existence known as Earth. It is on a separate plane of existence.

D: *It has no connection with Earth?*

S: We learn of what we have done, and in this way it has a connection with Earth, but none other than that.

D: *You said this is like a big hall; are all the classes held in the hall?*

S: No, they have classrooms off of it. This is kind of a main walkway, I guess. You can see anything that you want to see here. Just by visualizing it, it occurs. You can make it as nice or as bad you wish. If you're dealing with a guilty conscience and want to make yourself suffer, you can make yourself do that also. You can make the surroundings look like you want them, or the way you have visualized it. On some planes, including the plane that I am on now, it's like being on a higher plane of Earth, so the topography here is similar, but it has a finer energy level. I mean, there are hills and mountains and valleys, but they may not be positioned exactly like the hills there on Earth. There's greenery and such, but the colors are more intense and purer. One can also have buildings and such here, but usually their constructs of energy are influenced in such a way as to give off a certain image.

D: *Would the other people there see the same things you are seeing?*

44

S: Yes, the mountains and greenery are general features of this plane that everyone sees. It's Earth, but it's at a different energy level. And with it being a different energy level, the laws governing energy are different. The ground is solid and the hills are solid, and the trees and the animals really exist; they're really there. It's like the plane of incarnation that I will be going to again. But since the laws of energy are different, other things can be done with artificial constructs.

D: *Does everybody have to manifest it or is it just there all the time?*

S: It's there all the time. It's just a matter of personal perception as to whether or not you perceive it.

D: *Do you mean there are people who might come there and not see the same things you see?*

S: No, I'm speaking of people on the plane of incarnation. They would not perceive it because they're perceiving things at a lower level or a lower plane.

D: *Would this place be equivalent to what some people call "Heaven"?*

S: No. It is probably what they would refer to as "paradise." I'm making a distinction between heaven and paradise because paradise means a perfected Earth. Sometimes Earthly, but without the destruction and decay that exists on the plane of incarnation. And heaven refers to the higher planes of existence that the spirit knows of instinctively, although it cannot convey a clear picture of it with the inadequate vocabulary and concepts available on the plane of incarnation. Heaven refers to the higher planes where everything is energy. And paradise refers to these so-called "lower" planes where it's still similar to Earth because you're on a higher plane of Earth.

D: *Then whenever somebody talks about going to Heaven, they're going to a higher plane where there are no ... pictures, so to speak, It's all energy or are there*

45

scenes around them?

S: Well, it's mostly energy and energy manipulation. But when people speak of dying and going to heaven, what they actually do is go to paradise because everything must be taken in order, and things must be perceived and comprehended in order. You have to be prepared for higher levels so that you can assimilate them more fairly.

D: *But in the area known as heaven, would it just be all blank or would there be scenes, buildings or whatever?*

S: No, not buildings. Your perception is different and you can see the energies. It would be like fantastic displays of aurora borealis. You would be energy yourself and you could manipulate the energies to achieve different things and cause different things to happen. When you're in the higher planes referred to as heaven, you can look into the lower planes very easily and see the physical planes and see what's going on. It's no problem seeing things; it's just a matter of what level you're looking at as to what you sec. But there would be no surroundings because there are no horizons.

D: *But you said people wouldn't go there right away.*

S: That is true. Usually when one dies there is a period of transition where one can adjust to the fact that one is no longer on the plane of incarnation. When one adjusts to that fact then one has the freedom to move between the planes that one has access to, according to how advanced your spirit is.

D: *Is there anyone else there with you at the school?*

S: There are about 50 people just in my... class. There are others here, but we don't have much to do with them. They are working out other problems. They have different lessons that they have to learn, and they, must come to terms with it within their own selves. I just consider that I'm waiting. *I know* I'm going back. I learn here and I can look at and evaluate the things that happened while on Earth because I'm not hampered with worldly influences.

D: *When you learn, do you do it all by yourself or does someone help you?*

S: No. I get help if I need it. If I search or if I ask or I question, all things come and it's there.

D: *Who is teaching you?*

S: The masters. Each class has several. They teach you to study one's self.

D: *How do the people look? I mean, do they have clothes?*

S: Here they wear robes, but not always. Basically the way we look over here is ectoplasm in its various forms. Sometimes you will see someone with the shape of a body and they'll appear to have clothing on, but they'll be rather white and transparent looking. Or sometimes if they wish to look more solid, they do. And whatever type of clothing they want to project as wearing, they'll do it as being part of the type of image they want to project at that particular time.

D: *Then all of them don't look alike.*

S: No. And even one particular one will not necessarily look alike from one time to the next. It depends on what they want to achieve. But at this time in this place they have robes.

D: *What are you learning at the school?*

S: I'm studying life experiences and effects. I study long and hard in order to learn and to know. I put the pieces of my experiences together and compile them to make sense of my existence. I ask myself: How did these things affect me? How did I handle them? It is very peaceful and quiet here so I have much time to myself-solitude. I think and I work through these things. Sometimes I go back through experiences and try to understand. You see, in life I tilted my judgment to fit, for whatever reason usually to make me feel justified in my actions. And here I can analyze, so I go through the situation again to get a truer perspective of what really happened. I try to understand why I acted and reacted in such a way so as not to repeat previous

47

errors. We amass great knowledge here of lessons to be learned, karma to be dealt with. We learn many things about dealing with human nature and about the problems that I had to face. Also the problems I will be facing and the decisions to be made about that. And through this I will learn to grow and expand.

D: *Will you face these problems while you're there?*

S: No, the next time I'm born. I'm preparing to descend again.

D: *Did they tell you what kind of problems you will have to face?*

S: Some, but not a lot. We're just going over what I should decide and talking about work that I want to handle and what problems I want to deal with.

D: *You mean you're trying to figure out which ones you want to handle, or are there some you'll have to?*

S: Some that you'll have to. But right now it's really a learning situation.

D: *Do you think you will have many problems to face next time?*

S: Depending on what you call "problems." Many of them are just decisions and how I will handle myself and relationships with other people. When you go through something on Earth, be it good, be it bad, the important thing is your attitude, the way you accept it. How do you handle the defeats? How do you handle your victories? How do you deal with situations and problems? How do you accept failures? Are you gracious? You know, your life situations. All these are the sum total of who and what you are. And self-deception, that's a big one. People can't be honest and can't look at things. They make excuses for why they do things and justify it and twist it until they've lost all truth.

D: *Are there any particular lessons that you're having trouble with?*

S: I have to learn to speak up for myself. I have to learn to be more demanding and not let people manipulate me so much. Part of my problem is that I've been around so long and I'm always so aware that it's not that big a thing, that I sort of float through the situations. I've let people manipulate me because it really didn't make that much difference to me. So I have to be more decisive and learn to make decisions. I don't really like doing that.

D: *Do you draw these situations to you so you can work them out? Or do you plan that far in advance?*

S: I think you make many of the situations. Whatever is in your mind sometimes comes about. Your spirit knows what things you need to learn and then it creates situations without you really being aware of what's going on. But it all happens for reasons. When I'm there on Earth I won't really know, I won't really decide. I'll just think they're happening by chance. But they've all been thought about and planned out for purposes.

D: *Does anybody help you make these plans?*

S: Yes, sometimes I let other people here help me. There's a woman who's helped me a lot. She looks after me. Sometimes even in a life I seem to become more aware of her existence, for instance, when I'm growing out of being a child. Sometimes when I'm very involved in everything I'm not as aware of her presence. Here she sometimes shows me how certain actions will affect me in a life. She'll flash them like on a movie screen on a wall. And she will say things like, "This is what will happen if you do this; and this is the problem you will face." You know, she'll explain it where I wasn't aware of it. In life, there were difficulties when I knew something was wrong but couldn't see it. Sometimes she's made things that I needed to know knowledgeable to me.

D: *Do you know how long you're going to stay here?*

S: Not long. I know I need to get on with it. I want to learn all I can. I try to continue all of my learning as much as I possibly can. At times I think that I have pretty well got it and then there are always things that come up, something that I never quite thought of. (Thoughtfully) You *never* completely get it, I guess. But you can perfect it and try it. It's like putting something in a furnace and refining it.

D: *Do you like experiencing Earth?*

S: Well, even though I think there's nothing more I can learn, each time I learn something else. I have a tendency to be a touch rebellious. I know that I've not overcome it yet, even though I like to think I have.

D: *Is it mandatory that you return to Earth and inhabit a body again or do you have a choice?*

S: No, for there is no *have* to. If it is most appropriate, yes; then that might be the best thing to do. However, there is no rule that says one *has* to incarnate, for who is to say that one might choose *not* to reincarnate forever? It is up to the life force involved. I can stay here and learn or I can go back. I will probably go back. I look at the peace and I think I'm ready for the challenges.

D: *Do you make any decision as to when you come back?*

S: When I find someone who I feel will fit my need, then I have a choice. You get involved with other people. You build ties and emotions. You are open, you feel, you sense, and their lives affect you.

D: *Is it all planned in advance?*

S: It has to be because there are so many who wish to return and so few bodies to return into.

D: *Do you make all these decisions yourself?*

S: No, ours are the lesser decisions to make. The teachers and the masters help us decide the major decisions and the major happenings.

D: *It sounds like it would be complicated.*

S: Yes, but it works. It would be too complicated for you to figure out by yourself. Plus the fact that everyone would want to make things extremely easy for themselves and not have any problems. You wouldn't grow that way.

D: *Can you choose the type of person you will be?*

S: You have certain characteristics. You are the sum total of everything you have ever been or done. You are a person. You may be slightly imprinted through your childhood by the people you're around but that is more of an added element. It doesn't really change you. You are what you are, what you've done, what you've said, what you've thought, how you've lived and handled every situation. You are a sum total of all these things.

D: *What about free will?*

S: Part of that is ... each soul has a personality. Because of that there is free will in the fact that we know how that person will decide in any given situation because they are that person. Based on what they have done in their other past lives, the personality is very predictable. They can prevent certain things from happening just by changing or going against the character, but it's unusual for a person to change that drastically.

D: *I thought you meant that these things were set up and that was the way they had to be. That you didn't have anything to say about it.*

S: You wouldn't learn unless you made your own decisions. You have to handle your own mistakes.

D: *Then is our theory of predestination correct?*

S: To the extent that the predestiny you see is your own, and not determined by some God in the sky who says, "You shall do this and you shall do that. And you and you and you shall do some other." The predestination you perhaps see in your future is entirely your own because you, yourself, choose which path you will take. It might be relevant to say that the "you" I speak of here has a far greater scope than what you yourself are accessible to.

There is in each of us a far greater part than we are aware of. Each of us are tips of our own iceberg and it is this iceberg which chooses our destiny. That is why it is so easy to ascribe those experiences which you might call "unpleasant" to some god, some unseen deity in the clouds. Someone who says, "You shall grovel and wail and gnash your teeth, while the one next to you shall ride in splendor and enjoy a life of luxury." This is not the case at all. It is that each of us is simply speaking from our own very limited perspective.

D: *So things are not all "predestined"?*

S: Only to a certain degree. They are predestined in the fact that, like I said, you know the personality and that that person will ultimately come up to that decision. The personality basically stays the same. It only changes as you grow.

D: *Then you have an idea of what kind of situation they will function in. Some people say you don't have any choice about things.*

S: That's just people's way of saying, "Since we don't have any choice about the matter, why should I worry about what's going on, because it will happen to me anyway." And that's just a person's way of being very lazy about it and not wanting to grow.

D: *Then apparently they do have a great deal to say about it. Do you think it's already planned out who you are to meet and the people you will have association with?*

S: To some extent, because you have some type of a previous bond with most of the people that you meet throughout your life. You will have things to work out between two or maybe more individuals. Sometimes you come together in a trio; sometimes you come together in a whole group, with the things you have to work out with these people. Sometimes you're born among them, which makes it easier. This also explains why some parents and children cannot stand each other, because they hated each other previously. They decided they wanted to try to at least work something out, but they just aren't handling it very well.

D: *But once you go back into the physical body, you don't remember these things.*

S: To a great extent that's true. But there are always ways of tapping into their consciousness. It just takes time and study.

D: *Many people ask me why we don't remember our past lives. They think it would help a lot if we consciously knew about these karmic connections.*

S: It wouldn't; it would make things too complicated. Can you imagine how difficult it would be to function in the everyday world if you had the memories of countless past lives constantly bombarding you? You would never be able to concentrate on the lessons you have to work out during this lifetime. Sometimes when you're a young child you remember your past connections because you're still close to it. But then the memories you get in future years bury these memories and you forget, although they're still there in your subconscious. As a consequence, when you have a feeling you should do one thing instead of another and you follow that feeling, it's generally because your subconscious is subtly reminding you of a certain aspect of karma.

D: *Something you didn't do right before.*

S: Yes. That is the reason why, in general karma, you have been allowed to develop this technique of hypnosis and other medical techniques as a way of finding out about some of this past karma so that the people involved with this can progress even more swiftly. That has to do partly with entering the Age of Aquarius.

D: *It's some little shortcuts. But that's what many people think, that they should be able to remember these things on their own. They think it would help them work their problems out.*

S: They're expecting too much of themselves. It doesn't normally happen that way.

D: *It seems like it would be easier if you remembered the problems you had with these people.*

S: But then again it would be harder because you would bring the prejudices of the past forward with the remembrance. That's what we're trying to avoid. In some cases it does help. Some people can handle it a little better than others. But in most cases it doesn't work. If you're still angry because of the past feelings all that it is bringing forward is the anger, with not very much logic with it. And so it doesn't always help.

D: *But people say, "If I remembered what happened with them before, I could understand it and handle it better."*

S: That's not always true.   Because if they were mature enough to handle their grievances now, I would say they were probably mature enough to handle them in that prior commitment. But if they're having problems dealing with it now, on trust, as it were - just accepting them - they can't accept the problem of before to go with it.

D: *Then you think it's better that some people don't remember?*

S: Yes, on a whole. There are exceptions to every rule.

D: *Some people, their personalities are not advanced enough to understand these things anyway.*

S: This is true.

D: *Do you know what karma is?*

(A general definition of karma is: the universal law of balance, of cause and effect, where everything both good and bad must be repaid or balanced out.)

S: I think the word in itself... different people have added their own meaning. It's hard to really say, but as a very general word it means loving. As an example, you know that if you kill, that you have to face it again. For instance, let's say you killed for money. Then you must come around to the same thing again till you can overcome it. Situations are oftentimes turned around and you might be killed for money.

D: *Oh, a complete reversal.*

S: Yes, or you may have to leave a very delightful life where things are all pleasant and good. You cut it short. Therefore you have to experience the loss of something. It all comes around.

D: *I've also heard there are other ways of paying it back. It wouldn't have to be a life for a life.*

S: No, say you do a person a great injustice. You do something wrong to them. Then you may have to come back in another life and serve them. Maybe you'd have to take care of them and serve them and be their protector to make up for a wrong you may have done them before. So sometimes it's the dedication of a life. The giving up of yourself for that other person. What you do is always justified some way.

D: *What about you? Are you a young soul or an old soul? In other words, have you been around a long time or a short time?*

S: All souls have been around for the same degree. Some of us have chosen, for our own personal reasons, to incarnate into the body more often than others. That is where they get the term "old or young soul." Some are young in terms of Earthly experience. I have found that I like to do what I can in a tangible way to help not only myself but others. Thus I have had a tendency to keep coming back over and over.

D: *Then a young soul would be one that has not had much Earth experience?*

S: Yes, or just experience in the other realms because Earth is not the only realm of consciousness.

D: *You said you were going to the schools; that you were learning lessons there. Well, if you're able to learn lessons while you're* in *the spirit world, why is it necessary to incarnate in the physical form at all?*

S: There is great need for this due to the fact that-it is like reading a book. When you have read a book, the knowledge is within you, but you have not utilized it. And if you do not use this knowledge it has no worth. *You* cannot change yourself without experiencing a reason to change. It is stronger, more personal if you are experiencing or living the problems. It is not felt this greatly when you have just read about something. You can learn all about how to do something by reading the book, but unless you have the "hands-on" experience it doesn't do you a bit of good.

D: *They say it's difficult to experience on Earth in the body. That this is a hard way to learn lessons. Do you think that's true?*

S: It is a hard way to learn lessons, but they are more lasting. If you can learn a lesson through all of the struggles that you go through, it will remain with you.

I think we could use an analogy and compare this to a college course in chemistry. You can learn how to perform many experiments from reading the book, but until you have actually mixed the chemicals and followed the directions yourself and see the results, the experiments remain only words in a book. Through practice you understand the procedure and results more fully. Many people with college degrees have only book knowledge that they cannot apply to their own lives. This is where the "hands-on" experience comes in. This example can also be applied to mechanics and other similar occupations where there is book learning versus the actual handling of materials.

D: *Do you know how many lives you have lived?*

S: I have no idea. A hundred maybe, maybe more. I have lost count.

D: *It's hard to keep track?*
S: After the first fifty or so, yes.

I could see how this could happen because as I worked with one woman for a year on merely 26 lives, they began to blur together and I started to have difficulty distinguishing them from each other. I could see how they each influenced the other and how they were components of the whole integrated personality, like pieces of a puzzle.

D: *Do they keep a record anywhere?*
S: They do, but it's not important. It's just the experience that is important.
D: *Have you ever heard of something called the Akashic records?*
S: Yes, the records of life. There are those entities who are the guardians of the records and they are allowed to read them. Some, who have studied and have practiced for years have small access to them. But there are very few, and none that I know who are incarnate, who have full access to those records.

Another spirit saw these records as much more accessible.

D: *Have you ever heard of the Akashic records?* (She hesitated.) *Maybe you call it something else. Do you think there's a record anywhere of all the times you've ever lived?*
S: Oh, yes. I guess if I had to call it anything I would call it the Book of Life - a record of what you have done. It's on the stand over there. It's very big.
D: *Is that just your record or everybody's?*
S: Well, everybody can go to it and refer through it. You turn the pages, and if I'm looking in it then it reflects what I look for. If another looks in it, then it reflects

what they look for. It's a magical-type book.

D: *I was wondering how everybody's records could be in one book. It would have to be a big book.*

S: What you think you want to find, what you are looking for, is just *there.*

Another entity tried to explain the Akashic records on a more personal level.

S: True to your belief system, there are the Akashic records which may be accessed in order to withdraw personal information which you may seek. This concept of Akashic records is perhaps not totally understood. We would wish to define this now. Perhaps you could use an analogy of the safe deposit boxes in your bank. The individual boxes themselves store your personal belongings. The concept of the bank itself is a storehouse; however, each individual box contains only that which is relevant to yourself. And so you can see that you yourself store or, in fact, *are* the safe deposit box of your own energy. It is simply that we may go to your particular vault or box and withdraw that information which you seek. You, yourself, however, are the receptacle for this information.

D: *Do these safety deposit boxes contain all the records of our future as well as our past lives?*

S: They contain only that which is appropriate for you at this time. There are, of course, those areas of questioning which would not be appropriate for you to receive information from, and therefore you would find nothing of that sort in your particular box.

D: *How is the information deposited in the box? Is it by the life we live, our thoughts that we think or what?*

S: All that you experience, every singular piece of experience that you relate to in your life, is automatically fed into this as you experience it. It is simply as if a tape is being made of your life, and is then available to be referenced to any time.

D: *Is it possible for other people to have access to that tape?*

S: Of course it can be, as you already know through your work.

D: *Is that what happens in what we call a parallel life situation?*

S: It is indeed possible to cross reference others' Akashic records simultaneously and receive impressions of the experiences lived by another individual. This is not as uncommon as it may seem. An emphatic reaction is precisely this mechanism in effect.

D: *In other words, when we are exploring what appears to be a past life experience, we could be investigating somebody else's Akashic records?*

S: Or perhaps, your own.

D: *Is there any way we can determine the difference?*

S: Is it relevant to know? The fact that it is being replayed is, by virtue of the fact that it is being given to you, proof that it is relevant. Therefore, no distinction should be necessary as to who the record belongs to. The fact that it is being replayed is an indication that it is the appropriate replay for you at that particular time.

I have also been told that there are some things that are not appropriate for us to know about, and those questions would not be answered. That some information is as poison instead of medicine, and it's better not to let us know about some things a form of censorship for our own protection.

D: *There is the theory that all of a person's life is recorded as an energy. You use the analogy of a tape recorder. But there is the idea that all things, even thoughts and actions and everything produce energy, and that this energy remains intact. Is this a good analogy of a safe deposit box?*

S: That is accurate. It is also possible to erase this were it necessary. To remove perhaps a particular segment of an experience from the records that would serve no useful purpose, for example, the ovens of Auschwitz, the experience of burning Jews.

D: *Can we consciously do this if we are determined to?*

S: It is not for you to say, for you are merely a *very* small part of your entire self. It is your whole self which, in conjunction with the keepers of the information, would make that determination. It is not done on a conscious level. For you do not have access to the information which would make the determination as to whether any particular segment of your experience is suitable for erasure. This decision involves the keepers of the records in conjunction with the higher forms or levels of your awareness.

D: *You mentioned the erasure of events such as the ovens of Auschwitz. Are they erased because of their negativity?*

S: We would say that for those individuals who experienced the ovens, for the most part this was not an intended experience. So for their karmic protection, that is, in order for this not to cause problems in their subsequent lives, this experience could be erased. Such that their subconscious could not access the tragedy of such an occurrence, which would indeed cause problems in subsequent lifetimes.

D: *Is this part of the process that occurs when they go into the resting place?*

S: That is accurate. It is a healing process where these traumatic experiences are nullified by the healing energies.

D: *Could you explain then how that process works involving those who were perpetrators of those crimes?*

S: Their karmic records would reflect the punishment that would be appropriate for whatever atrocities were undertaken. For in so storing these atrocities there is also given that which is appropriate penance, to use the religious terminology. The paybacks would be evident on playback. And so during the readying for the next incarnation, by assessing that which needs to be healed, there would be given that which is the healing experience.

D: *I was wondering about the playback. Is the whole thing played back before you're reborn?*

S: Perhaps this is entirely an individual type of statement. In that, for some perhaps the entire incident would be reviewed. However, for others perhaps only a brief synopsis would be given. It is entirely up to the particular individual and the particular goals which are being planned for the upcoming lifetime. It is not possible to make one blanket statement which would cover all possibilities.

D: *Would you ever have to look over all the lives you have led, or do you just deal with the immediate ones?*

S: You deal with the ones that are not necessarily immediate, but the ones that you feel you are far enough removed from now to work with that particular karma. When a person dies, their next thoughts may not particularly deal exclusively with any of the karma incurred in the last life but may deal with the lives successive and previous to that, if you feel you are capable of coming face-to-face with what has been incurred.

D: *You mean you don't keep a score card, so to speak, on all the lives you have lived and go back over it?*

S: Not at one time, no. The records are there. It would be too much karma to deal with at one time.

D: *Then you don't go over the whole thing and say, "Now I need to do this and this to correct karma from the lives way back."*

S: If they are that far back in existence usually the problems have been dealt with.

D: *Do you remember what your first life was?*

S: If the lessons have been learned I have a tendency to forget about them.

D: *I always think the first time you do something you remember it more than others.*

S: This is not always necessarily true.

D: *Are there any rules or regulations about how many lives you have to live altogether?*

S: Some may be able to complete their karma in one life if they live a very exemplary life, and that is the end of it. Others must go on and on for many, many lifetimes to work out things that they have brought upon themselves and to learn what they need to learn. There are some who are very new in experience because they have perhaps just recently decided to try out Earthly incarnations. Others have been around since the beginning working on what they need to work on. Others who, perhaps, started at the beginning with the others but through long periods of rest in between lives or learning through other means, perhaps have only had a few lifetimes.

D: *Did you begin incarnating right away?*

S: Within a very short amount of time, which is a very long time from there to now. I have heard there is much information to be learned and gathered. If my telling any of this will help others then it will also help with karma that I have incurred in doing things against others.

I had been working with this woman for a year going over almost 30 lives and I felt I had only scratched the surface.

S: It will not be necessary to relate all of my lives because perhaps some were resting lives and mean nothing to anyone else except this entity. However, there are many lives that many lessons could be learned from.

D: *I am studying each one to see a pattern, a reason for karma being worked out in different ways.*

S: Yes. But do not always expect to find answers in what you receive. Even on our level we are just looking at it from one viewpoint, and our viewpoint is still very small in comparison to the whole.

D: *I have noticed that some of them are what I call simple lives, resting lives.*

S: Yes, where there is no more incurring of karma, whether good or bad.

D: *Many of these lives were not mental, intelligent lives. They were more or less physical.*

S: But they are important to the entity and to the rounding of the follow-end result.

A resting life can be defined as an insignificant life, although I do not think any life is truly insignificant. Each life is the unique story of a human being and, as such, all have merit. A resting life can be long or short. It is one where the entity appears to coast through a dull, seemingly meaningless life where nothing really extraordinary happens.

We all know people like this, who seem to skate through life with nothing bothering them. They do not make waves. Karma may be repaid and worked out in such a life; apparently without creating new karma. I imagine everyone needs a life like this once in a while as we could not continuously go from one traumatic life to another without slowing down and relaxing.

The resting life is perfect for this and thus it has merit even though the personality might seem dull and unimportant. This may also help us to understand people in our own experiences who are living this type of life now. We should realize that we cannot judge. We cannot know what type of life the person is resting from or preparing for; what their accomplishments may have been in other times and what they may accomplish the next time around.

D: *Is this school the only place you can learn?*

S: No, there are other types of schools in other planes of existence. Everything must be experienced to a certain extent, at least once.

D: *Do you go to the school every time you finish a life?*

S: Not always. Sometimes you choose to rest.

I had encountered people many times in the resting place. When they are there they do not wish to talk. They sound very sleepy and will volunteer no information, the same as a human would do if awakened in the middle of the night. They also can give no description, as though there is none to give. It seems to be a quiet, peaceful place to get away from everything and for a while (maybe a year or maybe hundreds) to have nothing to think about and no problems until they are once again ready to join the never-ending wheel of life.

D: *Is the resting place in a different place than where you are?*

S: No, there isn't a difference. Some people come to the school and then spend a certain amount of time resting before they go upon any avenues of learning at all. Others go to a place which is just for resting, where there is total silence and the essence of nothingness.

D: *That's the place I was asking about. Do they usually go there after a very traumatic life?*

S: Or when they have no wish to forget and want to carry it over, yes.

I was thinking about the story of Gretchen in my book *Five Lives Remembered.* She kept trying to return to her lifetime in Germany even though it was impossible. She was continually sent to the resting place until all memory of the persistent life was erased. Then she was able to reincarnate and function normally.

D: *Yes, I encountered a person who wanted to carry it over. She wouldn't let go and she was sent to a place that sounds like what you're talking about. Many spirits tell me different things but they describe similar places.*

S: All have an essence of the truth. We must gather things that we hear and learn from everything, instead of closing our ears to some things that we may not want to hear.

D: *Maybe you can help clarify some of these things. It can be very confusing.*

S: Confusion leads to ignorance.

D: *Does a resting life serve the same purpose as going to the resting place?*

S: To a smaller extent. The resting place is to completely erase everything up to that point. And the resting lives are perhaps they have just come from a stressful life and they need the rest but not necessarily to forget the personality because that is easily done. The resting place is for those who have problems forgetting the personality that they were or the problems that they had, and keep identifying with that facet of that entity. That personality would be too strong of an influence on the following lives. This is the type that you go to the resting place to forget.

D: *Then a resting life would serve a different purpose?*

S: Not totally different. Maybe just a different angle of that same purpose.

While living a resting life, there is not a lot of stress put on the personality. After a simple life, you could then go into one that would be more meaningful and again work out difficult karma. I think that it would be hard to continually go from one stressful life to another. You might need to slow down and coast for a while, and a resting life would serve that purpose perfectly.

D: *I guess they all have a reason, don't they?*

S: All things have reasons.

D: *You are the one who is going to school but it seems as though you are teaching me, too. We all have room to grow, don't we?*

S: And I still have a long path to follow.

I asked her to continue describing the various places of learning.

S: There are an ultimate number of schools and resting places, depending upon the need. Sometimes you need to go back and think over the lessons you needed to learn in that life, and explore them to see what you did accomplish. Sometimes it is what you want to accomplish that causes you to go to school. Sometimes you just go directly into another life.

D: *Are there any rules or regulations about these things?*

S: Not if the choice is the self. Umm, unless in special cases. If it is felt there will be too much carry over, then you would either come here to school and try to work it out or you would go to the place of rest.

D: *But you can go right back into another life?*

S: Yes, if the soul wishes.

D: *I thought maybe you had to wait so many years or something.*

S: Not always, no. It depends upon that particular soul's capacity to handle things that will be thrown at them-the problems that they will face. Some need more time in between existences to be able to cope with going from one to the other, or to just forget.

D: *Is it better to forget before you come back again?*

S: In many cases, yes. If there is no need for lessons carrying over that you need for the next existence, then there are many good reasons to forget. Otherwise the person would be continually trying to get back into the life that they led

66

before, which is not possible.

This was what happened with Gretchen in the German life in Five *Lives Remembered*. It took her 200 years in the resting place to finally reconcile herself to not being able to return to the life she had left. It was such a strong, violent life that when she was finally able to return to Earth it had to be as a complete reversal in personality. It was the only way she could cope and continue with her Earthly lessons.

D: *Are there cases where it would be better if they didn't forget?*

S: In those cases there is something to be learned from the previous existence that has direct bearing on what they are to go through and experience in this life.

D: *In those cases is it better to come back right away?*

S: Sometimes. But sometimes you must prepare yourself longer to deal with the knowledge of a previous existence.

D: *Would karma enter into the decision to come back quickly?*

S: Yes. It depends also if you are trying to work certain things out. Sometimes you must wait for others who have not passed into the different realms. Not always is the time that you will be born of your own choosing. Some of the masters would help you come to this ultimate decision. Also the person the karma is needed to be worked out with.

D: *Does the other person have to agree?*

S: It depends on certain circumstances. Not always is their agreement necessary.

D: *Then they can be working out karma without knowing about it?*

S: Without their approval, yes.

D: *In that case, it would be your own karma you had to work out, is that correct?*

S: Yours mostly, yes. There are certain guidelines that one must follow.

D: *The teachers and masters that help you figure all this out, is their decision more important than yours?*

S: It's not that it is more important. Many times they are viewing it from a different angle of perspective. They view it from their experience and they will share their wisdom. Most times their judgment is sound and you will pay to see it from that perspective also, and in this way you learn.

D: *In other words, they see things you don't.*

S: Yes, because they are standing back from the situation, so to speak.

D: *That makes sense; you are often too close to it to be a good impartial judge yourself. Are there ever times when a soul is made to come back when it doesn't want to?*

S: In some cases, yes, but maybe not because it doesn't want to. Suppose that the last life they enjoyed so much was as a man, and they are made to come back as a female. If they had the choice they would choose to be male again. There are times like this that happen, yes. It depends on any given situation. It is a much easier existence on this side, but then the soul does not learn as much because day-to-day experience teaches you more wisdom. The wisdom of dealing with people who have vices and problems. It makes you grow a lot more than those who have access to great wisdom. A soul might have to go back if they are not looking at something from the right perspective. They would be shown what perspective they need to look at it from, by living through it. Before anyone comes into a life they observe the balance of karma and they observe how it is. And they see what aspects of their karma would be worked out best in this particular situation and this particular balance of karma. Their spiritual masters might give some suggestions to help them figure out what they want to accomplish in this life. But no one is ever made to go into a situation they absolutely abhor. It's generally done by a consensus of opinion between the person and their spiritual masters. They won't like many aspects of the life in particular, but the majority of the life will be something they can handle. And these extra things they're not too fond of are looked upon as spiritual challenges, something for them to accomplish and to work for. How well they handle these things that they don't care for is one of the things that helps them work off some of their karma. On the spiritual plane when they come back and it is seen that they handled it well, that reflects good upon their karma.

D: *I was thinking of one individual case. This girl had committed suicide in another life and was* made *to come back into this life. The situations and everything appeared to be right but she didn't really want to come back.*

S: Sometimes this happens when, for instance, the soul has been in the spiritual hospital, and the masters are saying, "Well, it's time for you to go back because you can't stay here forever." And the soul indicates outward resistance to do that because they are basically afraid. But inside they know that they must do it if they ever want to get out of that situation and improve. Although they will give the impression of being unwilling, they know that they must. So in that respect they want to get past this aspect of their karma and go on to bigger and better things.

D: *But in that case they are* made *to go back?*

S: Strongly encouraged, shall we say, because they cannot stay in the spiritual hospital forever, and so they have to come back. The souls that are sick and damaged need stronger guidance than those that are healthy. To an extent they have lost their responsibility to decide these things. Now on the other end of the scale, souls such as this vehicle (the subject) and yourself had to be held back and told, "Wait a minute. You can't go back yet; you have some more learning to do." You were impatient to go back and get involved again.

D: *You mean we were too eager.* (Laugh) *But this girl I was thinking about is very unhappy here in this life. She is definitely not working it out very well.*

S: Well, it takes a few lifetimes to figure out how to work it out and be happy in the process. As long as she doesn't end this lifetime in suicide that would be progress right there.

D: *She had to come back into a situation with the same people again.*

S: Well, undoubtedly the main challenge she has for this life is to not end it in suicide since she's in that situation again with the same people involved. The main challenge is to be able to deal with those people for a normal lifetime and not cut it short. If she is successful in that then it'll work out better with the next life and succeeding lifetimes. Eventually in succeeding lifetimes it might be altered to where she just has to deal with one or two of the people at a time instead of the whole group. And she'll also learn to be happy again.

D: *I've heard that you are the one that makes the final decisions, and this was a case where somebody else rather forced her to come back. I was wondering if that was a contradiction.*

S: No. The people who are seemingly forced to come back know it's for their own good. After they are given time to think about it they realize that they really do need to come back or they'll be stuck in that one position forever, and they would never progress. Never progressing is the closest thing there is to the Christian concept of Hell.

D: *Just staying in the same situation and making the same mistakes?*

S: Yes.

D: *Are you allowed to go other places or do you have to stay at the school?*

S: Sometimes we get to visit other planes of existence to show us how the spirit must deal with these. Each of the levels in their own way have lessons to teach us.

D: *When I speak to other spirits they sometimes describe their surroundings differently.*

S: Much of that is what that individual visualizes, because most of the schools arc anything you visualize them to be. From your set of experiences you may see it one way, whereas someone else may see it as something totally different and it will still be in basically the same place.

D: *I thought maybe it was such a large place it could be many things.*

S: There is also that, too. There is an infinite number of planes.

D: *One spirit told me about a golden boat that would go back and forth between the Earth plane carrying the souls. Have you ever seen anything like that?*

S: Possibly that is her own visualization of what she thought was going on. There are some who say they see golden stairs or a bridge that they walk across. Others just see a large hall of light and they come toward the light. Much of that is individual experience coloring what they think they see and so that is what occurs. Anything that you can visualize can be real. For you are the master of your own destiny, of your own house, of your own vessel or receptacle or any other way you wish to perceive the concept of a spirit being in physical body. You are the master of your body and you are the master of your destiny. You create that which is manifest in front of you. You are co-creator here. That which you find in front of you is of your own making and creation, whether on the physical or spiritual planes. All must attune to this responsibility for all are co-creators of their manifest destiny.

71

D: *What about a life where someone is handicapped? Does that serve a purpose?*

S: Oh, yes! It's a humbling experience. You are forced to really come to terms within yourself with who and what you are, and to look into yourself and not at what the people in the world think of you. It's so easy for people to have the tendency to think of themselves as other people see them, which is not so. You are different things. You are what you really are, then you are what you think you are, then you are what other people see you as ... and then you change. But when you're handicapped you are given something that you must overcome. And one of the things you must learn is not to be affected by the ridicule. You can't take other people's cruelties personally. That is something *they* have to deal with themselves. They don't understand or maybe they're frightened. What people don't understand oftentimes frightens them.

D: *But the people they are hurting don't realize that.*

S: No, they just cry for the moment.

D: *Did you ever have a life where you were handicapped?*

S: (Pause as though thinking.) I think that I was totally; no, I wasn't born that way; but I lost my sight.

D: *Do you think you learned anything from that life?*

S: I learned persistence. I learned not to take the things we see for granted. To have a greater appreciation. I learned a type of feeling and I learned...(surprised) to trust.

D: *Then it was worth it. I think anything is worth it if you learn something from it, don't you agree?*

S: Yes.

D: *If other people try to help heal you and it's something karmic that you have to deal with, will the healing work?*

S: No. If it's something that is planned for a purpose to bring a person to a certain point then the healing won't work.

D: *But is there any harm in trying?*

72

S: Oh, no. There's a certain love, and a certain blessing that God gives to those who draw upon their inner resources to help others. There is a giving process when they give of themselves and it is its own reward.

The following is from a regression where a young girl had a lifetime in which she could not hear or speak. I was talking to her immediately after her death.

D: *It was not a bad life, was it?*
S: There was no further karma incurred, no.
D: *Well, you couldn't incur any karma in a life like that, could you?*
S: Yes. If one fought against it and just, more or less, gave up. The fact is that if you were handicapped and didn't struggle to accomplish anything, then you would incur more karma.
D: *You mean if somebody is handicapped and they just "give in" or they want everybody else to take care of them and do things for them, for instance? This would be the wrong way to handle a handicap?*
S: Yes, and they never try anything. In order to gain benefits from lives of that type, you must always strive for greater heights, and not let it pull you down.
D: *In spite of being handicapped, you must always try to do better. This way you are paying back karma or debt? But if someone just gives in and doesn't try to do anything, then they are making more karma for the next time. Is that right?*
S: Yes.
D: *But what about those who are retarded? That would be a different kind of handicap, wouldn't it?* (She frowned.) *Do you know what retarded means?*
S: I'm not sure I understand your viewpoint.
D: *Some children are born and they never really grow up in their mind. Their body grows up but the mind stays like*

a child. It is a handicap of a different kind. Do you know what I mean?

S: Yes. But again there is always the ability to try to make oneself just a little bit better each time. Striving so that they try to overcome any deficiencies in the self.

D: *Do you think anytime a person is born with a handicap or develops a handicap, they are doing it for a reason?*

S: Yes, whether it is to atone for something that they have done in the past or just to try to further themselves along the pathway.

D: *Then some people will have a handicap even though it is not for paying back a debt?*

S: Yes, because much good can be gained from this. They can learn understanding. They will not be as quick to judge as others.

D: *So it's not always a bad thing that they're trying to pay back.*

There are more souls in line for the handicapped bodies than the normal ones. The karma they pay back in one of these lifetimes would normally take at least ten lifetimes to repay. Because look at what they are learning. And what are they teaching their caregivers: the parents or others with whom they have made contracts to experience this with them. We must also not forget the influence that handicapped people have on others. What lessons are being learned by those who have daily contact with them? What lessons are being learned by others? What emotions, positive or negative, are being aroused? And also what kind of lessons are being rejected? It emphasizes again that no matter whether we wish to or not, everyone is constantly influencing or affecting others every day in many ways. The lessons are gained in how we accept and handle these things, or in how we reject and deny them.

Chapter 5
The Grand Tour

WE DISCOVERED THE TEMPLE OF WISDOM
Complex on the spirit plane quite by accident. I
was working with a young man named John who
had been having some physical problems. He wondered if
there might be a place in the spirit realm where he could obtain
some healing. I was unaware of any place of that nature but
I am always willing to try an experiment to find out. The other
information in this book was obtained by subjects in trance
who found themselves in the spirit form when they were in the
so-called "dead" state between lives. This time would be
different. After John had entered the deep somnambulistic level,
I purposely directed him to go to the spirit realm and see if he
could find a place that dealt with healing, if indeed such a
place existed.

When I finished counting, John found himself in beautiful
ethereal surroundings. He was informed that this was a portion
of the Temple of Wisdom which was a large complex
containing several different departments: The Temple of
Healing, the Tapestry Room and the Library. I am often
disappointed because I cannot also enjoy the visual wonder of
what my subjects see. Like a blind person I must rely on the
verbal descriptions of others, and often mere words are
inadequate to truly portray the marvels they find in these other
dimensions.

J: I am in the Temple of Healing now. It's a *beautiful* place.
It's a round rotunda, and all these brilliant lights are coming
through gem windows that are located up high on the

ceiling. There are blues, reds, greens, yellows, oranges, turquoises, every color that you can think of except black and white. They are not represented here but every other color is, and they cast these beautiful rays of light down onto the rotunda floor. Here comes the guardian of the Temple of Healing. He walks up to me and smiles, and he's taking my hand now. He says, "You have come for some treatment, haven't you? Your soul has gone through a great deal, hasn't it? Stand here in the center of all this light and let this light energy be with you."

D: *Is that what this place is used for?*

There was no answer. He was obviously experiencing something very profound as indicated by his bodily movements and facial sensations. I was not alarmed because it seemed to be a pleasant experience.

D: *Can you tell me what's happening at this time?*

Still no answer. He apparently was very involved with the experience. His whole body jerked convulsively several times. This went on for a few seconds.

D: *What does it feel like?*
J: The different lights are swirling all around me and feeling and cleansing me. This is why I'm not able to talk at the present time.
D: *I just wanted to make sure that everything is all right. Is it a good feeling?*
J: It's ecstatic. (Several more seconds of silence followed as his body continued to occasionally jerk.) Oh, it's a wonderful feeling. I feel so rejuvenated. (A pause of several more seconds.) Ahh! It's just *wonderful*. Ohh! It's just waves of color and energy all around me taking out all my pain and soreness. And now he takes my hand and leads me away from this. He says, "Your soul is cleansed

of much negative energy that has been around you. Feel the sense of peace that comes. You must concentrate on learning to heal yourself." (A big deep breath.) Ohh! That was a *wonderful* feeling. This is a beautiful place for people who have been very ill in the physical body. When they pass over they are taken here so that their astral and spiritual bodies may be rejuvenated and healed in this rotunda. Afterwards these souls that are no longer tied to bodies are met by their spirit guides and conducted into the different areas where they need to go to learn more about their soul's evolution. There's a long line of them. But because I asked to be healed and I'm still in the human form they said it was okay for me to come first and be allowed to go through the chamber. They call it the "Chamber of Colors and Light."

D: *Is this unusual for someone who is still in the physical body to come to this place?*

J: Yes. The guardian says not many people afford themselves of this opportunity while in the astral traveling state. "But they should," he says. "We are here to also be of service to the souls that are still incarnated as well. If they would like to come, we would be happy to welcome them. For always there is a loving energy that goes with all this healing. "This is a wondrous, loving place. It's nothing like a hospital or anything like that. It's like a beautiful temple, and above this round rotunda are these gem windows. I'd say they're about five, six feet tall, and they're made up of different colored gems. The light pours through them and bounces into the center of the rotunda and it swirls you with energy. That's where I was. Oh, it's just a wonderful, wonderful feeling. Now the guardian says, "We will talk to you about your health. It's very important to keep a positive sense. And to be aware that your spiritual mission is to help and serve other people, John. Don't worry about your health problems. They will be manifested out of your body by your positive energy. If you desire to lose the weight that you have on this body, concentrate on the form you would like to manifest, and you will be that manifestation. But it's important for you to concentrate. The use of alcohol and tobacco are not helpful for your spiritual growth so these things must eventually be cut out of your life. You will not grow with these energies inflicting your body for they are painful for your body, and your spiritual bodies. In time you will, if you desire it, manifest all the natural and beautiful things that your soul has. You will attract the right energies, so do not worry about your health because we are healing and you will be healed. If you need to go to this temple ever again, just wish to be here and you will be here. He's really loving. He's just given me a big hug and he says, "Now it's time for you to depart this area."

D: *Before we go I wanted to ask him about these people that are in line. Are they people who died from illnesses?*

J: He says, "Yes, these are people that have died from very long-term illnesses, as well as people that have suffered immensely before crossing over. They are people that have died of different diseases like cancer, from automobile accidents and such." They're not really lined up in a line. I mean, there's a sense of order, yes, but it's not like they're one behind the other. Each one is in turn to go through this chamber of light energy.

D: *Do their guides take them through this?*

J: Well, there are guardians walking among them. In fact, some of them have come with their family members.

D: *Are these the ones that came to meet them when they died?*

J: Yes, their family have ushered them to this place.

D: *Will they be cleansed, so to speak, or healed by this before they're allowed to go on anywhere else?*

J: Yes. They need this healing process because what they went through has been very painful.

D: *And this would be the first order of business after they pass over?*

J: Yes, this healing energy is one of first things that people experience if they have suffered immensely in the physical body through a disease or an accident. This has caused illness or negativity within their etheric bodies. So these etheric bodies *have* to be healed before they can progress into the astral and work in this level. This is a very important place for these people. They're led to the middle of this center space. And this is where all the rays of light come down and surround them and swirl around them and take away any of the negativity that their etheric body might have. Then they are reunited with their family and guides who usher them into different areas throughout the astral world.

D: *I've never heard of this healing temple before. I thank him for the information.*

J: He smiles and says, "I'm here always to be of service. This is my mission, my life, my being; not *life, being."* He's just a warm, radiant, loving energy. His touch is magical. It's like a mother's love, you know, the way a mother cuddles her child. It's that type of love that you feel. He says this is an opportune place for all souls to gather whether they be incarnated or discarnated. He says this service and this area of healing is welcome to all. Many people who use the psychic healing powers should project this image, for they can be healed in this area. He says, "Now that you have witnessed it and taken part in it, John, it is important for you to describe this place to other people that could use it. This would be a wonderful tool for Dolores to use to help heal other people. She could guide them through hypnosis into this healing temple where we'll take over and help. So this would be a wonderful service that Dolores could use. And by giving and sharing in this area she'll also grow." This is the message that he has for you, Dolores.

D: *I am very grateful for it. Are there any regulations about who can or cannot come?*

J: He says, "All souls are welcome to come here if they're willing to take the transit and the journey. Not *all* are willing, or evolved enough to make it. But if they are willing and would long to be healed, we are here to be of service." In time they might have to come back, depending on their negativity. But, once they have a treatment he says most souls will go on. They do not linger here. They do not usually want to come back here unless it's important for them to come back. This is the law. That's all he said, "That's the law. The soul knows best. We're dealing with one's soul bodies, not so much with one's conscious vehicle. When the soul is the master or it understands what is going on, it knows the law. No one becomes dependent on this energy. (Laugh) They do not become healing 'junkies.' It does not work that way."

D: *Then if I led someone to this place in the trance state they would receive healing through this process if they were willing.*

J: He says, "Yes, if they're willing we are here to be of help. If you tune into us through a meditative or hypnotic state we are here to be of service because that is what our energy is. It would be very easy for you to channel this." He says for Dolores to use it to be of service. He says, "Once we are of service all things are made manifest for us. Each one of us has a spiritual talent. And for you, Dolores, this is a wonderful way to express part of your spiritual talents."

D: *It sounds like a very good idea because many times people ask me for advice on their health.*

J: He says this would be a wonderful way. To put them into trance and let them travel to this temple of light. This would be a wonderful service for it doesn't heal the physical body as much as it heals the etheric bodies. Those are the bodies that lie within man as they incarnate.

D: *But I would think any healing would be mirrored in the physical body also.*

J: It does. But the person has to use a positive sense, too. That's important. There's a gold place here that's really marvelous. It's radiant with beautiful gold designs all over the walls.

D: *Is this a separate place from the healing temple?*

J: We're still in the healing temple. I'm walking around it and talking with the guide. He is showing me the different ray energies and how they come through. It's like being inside a jewel box. It's that wonderful. Most of the whole temple structure itself radiates an electric gold color. I mean, it's like a gold-brown but it's a real healing color, and it looks like it has filigree carved into it. There are opals and all different types of semi and precious stones set into the walls. But the most important ones are the jewels that are in the windows where the light comes through.

D: *Well, I thank him for allowing us to enter there and for giving you that treatment. Do you want to leave that place now?*

J: Yes. He hugged me and said good-bye.

D: *We should leave because other people are waiting for the same treatment.*

J: There are people, yes. Each one is stepping up into the light.

D: *That is a very important place for us to know about. There must be many places over there that we don't know exist. You said that all these buildings are part of a complex? I wonder if you might take me on a tour - so to speak, and we could find out what else is there.*

J: Okay. The guardian says the tapestry room is important, so I'm walking down this beautiful corridor with walls that look like lapis lazuli and marble. At the end is this big door-way. I'm opening the door, and there is a *dazzling* bright light.

D: *What is causing the bright light?*

J: It is a man, or a spirit form. He says he's the guardian of the Tapestry Room and is allowing me to enter. (This same Tapestry Room was featured in *Conversations with Nostradamus,* Volume II [revised edition].) This is a very honored place. There is a wonderful aroma in the air. It smells like a combination of a fresh breeze tinged with salt and perfumes from a garden. It's almost like incense. It's a beautiful room and it's very, very tall. It goes up for maybe two or three hundred feet. No, maybe a hundred feet would be more accurate. The ceiling has a rounded point like a church nave. There are windows at the top of it and on either side of the walls. They're up high and they light up the room. And there are chandeliers that hang down from the ceiling that look like Aladdin lamps. But there are a lot of them, maybe about 15 or 20. The walls and the floor seem to be made of marble. And there is some heavy furniture at different intervals, like groups of chairs and tables opposite the tapestry. They're not contemporary and they're not antique, but they're very functional, comfortable and inviting. The guardian says sometimes teachers bring their students here to explain the wonders and the intricacies of the tapestry to them. It feels like I'm in a special museum where people can come to examine and study this. I'm going now to look at the tapestry. It's so beautiful. It's metallic; made of metal threads and they're just gorgeous. They glimmer and shine. (A sudden intake of breath.) And it looks like it *breathes.* It's like ... it is alive. I mean it just undulates and sparkles. Some of the strands glisten, and others are kind of dull. It's really hard to describe. It actually is like a living thing, but it's not frightening; it's beautiful. There are all different types of threads. And, oh! It's just *glorious.* Nothing on Earth could ever be compared to it. There is just no way to describe how glorious this is because it's so vibrant it's almost electric. And the guardian says that each thread represents a life.

D: *It sounds very complicated.*

J: Oh, some of it is complicated, but it makes a beautiful design. An eternal design. And... I can see the world beyond that. By looking at this tapestry, I can see any event that has taken place.

D: *What do you mean?*

J: It's like looking through the tapestry, and I can see people's daily lives, and they're connected as a thread into this tapestry. Now the guardian is explaining that every life that has ever been lived is represented as a thread in this tapestry. This is where all the threads of human life, the souls that incarnate are connected. It illustrates perfectly how each life is interwoven, crossing and touching all these other lives until eventually all of humanity is affected. The absolute oneness of humanity is represented by the tapestry. It is one but composed of all these many parts. Each cannot exist without the other and they all intertwine and influence each other.

D: *Well, if it's composed of everyone's life, then it would be alive. Does the guard care if we look at it?*

J: Oh, he doesn't care; he knows that we have a purpose. He says, "Go ahead, please look at it, but don't look any deeper. I *don't* want you looking at other people's lives because spreading that knowledge can be detrimental to their development." (John went back to the description.) The tapestry is huge. It seems to be about, oh, I would say at least 20 to 25 feet tall. And it seems to go on *forever*. It would take me hours just to walk the length of it. It must go on for a mile or more. It runs along the left-hand wall, and the light coming in from the windows shines on it. But there's a point that I cannot go beyond.

D: *Do you know why?*

J: The guardian of the tapestry says that is part of the spiritual evolvement of all souls. Only spiritually evolved people have access to that part of the tapestry. It's like a little sign that says, "Do not go beyond this point." (Laugh) But it's not so much a sign as a feeling that this is as far as I can walk. It's like looking at the most beautiful creation of art. It's made up of strands that range from a tiny piece of string all the way up to cable size, as thick as your wrist.

D: *I had pictured them as threads.*

J: No, they're not as small as threads. I called them that because they're inter-woven, but it goes from a tiny string in some places to larger sizes. Most of them are kind of rope size and then they get thicker and thicker as they go along. There are greens, blues, reds, yellows, oranges and blacks. Yeah, there are even a few black ones in there. The black ones stand out because they don't seem to go as far as the other colors do. Hmmm. That's strange.

D: *Do these colors have any significance?*

J: I'll ask the guardian. He says, "Yes, they represent the spiritual energy of all souls."

D: *Well, what would be the significance of the darker colors as opposed to the brighter ones?*

J: "The darker colors," he says, "really have no significance. The black are special for they have chosen a very unusual path."

D: *I thought the darker colors might mean they were more ...well, I'm thinking of negative lives.*

J: No. He says there is no negativity in this tapestry. The black ones have just chosen an unusual way of manifesting. But he says, "Do not question that. That's not for you to know at this moment. You have come here for another purpose."

D: *Yes, I wanted to ask a few questions. You said there are teachers teaching their pupils about this tapestry. Is there a way they can look at the pattern of their past lives?*

J: Yes. I'm looking at one group right now. The teacher is dressed in nice robes, and he has a very benevolent look on his face. He is pointing out to different souls what is happening and what has happened. He's teaching them about this tapestry and what the different intricacies of the patterns mean. He has something like a shimmery pointer. It's golden-colored with something at the tip of it that looks like a crystal, but it's actually a diamond that lights up with its own light. He points to a thread in the tapestry and that thread, cable, rope or whatever you want to call it, will seem to light up on its own. He points out different characteristics about lifetimes, about how people have evolved and where they have to grow. They're all taking notes, not so much with pen and paper but with their own heads.

D: *Is he explaining to these pupils about their own lives so they can make decisions in future lives?*

J: Yeah, I get the impression they're there to study their past lifetimes and how their thread has woven itself into this tapestry of life. This is what the ancients call the "Akashic Records." (I was surprised.) These are the Akashic records that advanced souls understand. He says some of the records are kept in book form, but those are for souls who are not as highly advanced.

D: (I didn't understand.) *Then everyone wouldn't have a thread in this tapestry?*

J: No, all life has a thread in this tapestry, but only advanced souls are able to understand the concept of the tapestry, and to have access to it. Lesser developed souls have Akashic record books they can look through. It would be like a child going into a college library. They should go to the children's section of a local library instead.

D: *Then they wouldn't understand what they were seeing even if they came here?*

J: Right. They wouldn't understand this because the tapestry has a purpose. It goes into the higher dimensions, even above here, and this is a very complex

85

place. This tapestry eventually ends in Godhood where it's all brightness. It all leads to this beautiful light.

D: *Can you ask the guardian if many people who are alive ever come to see this tapestry? Or is it unusual for us to be here?*

J: He says you'd be surprised at how many people have come to this room who are still in the body. Many come to view it as a work of art. He says this has sometimes been an inspiration for artists who are skilled in painting, sculpture and the textile arts. They sometimes come here because this is one of the most glorious works of art in all creation. It has many different designs, such as wild contemporary patterns, Oriental designs or Native American arrangements.

D: *How do they get there?*

J: He says some come in the astral state when they dream. Others come while they are traveling within the soul worlds when they use meditation, astral projection or hypnosis like you are using now.

D: *I wondered if it was unusual to come while you are still in the body.*

J: He says, "No, not as unusual as you might think. You'd be surprised at the numbers that *do* come here, but not all of humanity is ready to come to this place just yet."

D: *Can he tell we aren't dead?*

J: Yes, he's walking along with me and he says he knows I am still in the body. He sees the silver thread that lies behind me.

D: *Oh, he knows you're still connected to a body. And that we are doing this as a kind of experiment.*

J: Yes, he understands that. Most of the other people don't have silver threads coming out of their bodies.

D: *Well, has anyone who came here while still in the body ever been refused entry into that room?*

J: He said, "You'd be surprised. We have had to ask people to leave this area. One soul came and tried to tear his thread out of the tapestry. He thought this would be the best way to end his existence. The man was suffering from some type of dementia in the earth plane, and he didn't realize he was really in the spiritual plane. He was very confused. We had to guide him back. He is now in an institution and being heavily sedated so he doesn't go into these trance states that he was able to do so easily. But he came to try to destroy the tapestry, or to destroy what he thought was his thread. In actuality, it wasn't even his thread."

D: *But there aren't many people who try to do things like that are there?*

J: No, that was a very rare case. That man was given great spiritual strength in his physical incarnation, but he thought it was delusion and that has left him unbalanced in the mental body. As a result he is being physically restrained as well as being given chemicals to keep him from astral traveling. He would have been a great world server if he had allowed himself to find his pattern. But he allowed his intellectual side of his nature to gain too much on him.

D: *I suppose that's one reason why they have a guardian there.*

J: Well, you have to have a guardian. Sometimes strange things happen here because this is a portrait of time, and things have to be kept in balance. There are checks and balances along this tapestry.

D: *You said sometimes there are other people that are asked to leave? Do they try to see things they shouldn't or what?*

J: He says, "You *can* see things, because behind the tapestry is your sense of time and you can find a cord and go through time. Most people do not need to know about their future while they are still in the body, unless they are going to use the knowledge for a spiritual course."

D: *Are these the type of people who are asked to leave?*

87

J: He says, "No, this is the place of love and no one is ever asked to leave here unless he tries to deface the tapestry or is abusive. We just have to watch the tapestry because sometimes in rare cases things do happen. In the past, great forces have come *through* the tapestry itself. One time you had nuclear explosions and there were many people leaving the planet so quickly, they came *through* the tapestry. So we have to be here to be of service to them."

D: *I guess all kinds of strange things happen there, I appreciate you telling me these things. We were curious.*

J: Yes, he says, "That's understandable. Do not worry. We are well aware of your mission and your soul's growth. I am here to be of service to all of you."

D: *We're trying to use this information in a very positive way if we can. Would I be allowed to come if I was going to use it in a negative way?*

J: No. Nothing can be disguised or hidden here. We know your motives better than you know them yourself.

D: *I try very hard to be positive. Is there anything else you would like to see in that tapestry before we leave it?*

J: I see my own thread now. It's silver and copper in color, as it weaves through the tapestry. The guardian of the tapestry is saying it's time for me to leave. He says, "You don't need this knowledge. In time you can look, but not at this present time." (Pause) He's discussing my soul's growth. And he's sort of calling me for task on it. (John laughed.) He says I was such a ray of light, and I had allowed myself to grow dim. That's why I had to go back to the earth school.

D: *So you can make amends?*

J: Well, by understanding universal laws and love, I could gain my light back. It's easier to go through the earth school than to incarnate on other dimensions. It's quicker.

D: *How do you feel about him telling you that?*

J: Well, I don't like it. I'm embarrassed, actually. I feel very chastised. I mean, he's perfectly right that it's my fault. I've sidestepped my responsibility, so I had to incarnate. But it's not like he's pointing his finger and saying, "No, no, no, no, no." He's doing it lovingly. He's embraced me now, and he says, "Good luck on your mission."

I could not resist the temptation, so I asked, "I wonder if my thread's in there anywhere?"

J: Yes, your thread's there. Your thread is a bright shiny copper color that gets stronger. It starts out kind of small and then it gets bigger and bigger, influencing many other threads. This tapestry is very magical. (Abruptly) He's asking us to leave. "You were looking at your own life, and that's not good to do at this point."

D: *No, but that's just human curiosity.*

J: But now he is showing me the steps. (Laugh) And he's saying, "Why don't you take a walk down there and see what's there."

D: *Like we shouldn't get too nosy, I suppose.*

J: Yes. He's saying, "You've had enough to look at for now." I think the guardian of the tapestry was implying that we shouldn't look too much into our own future.

D: *That makes sense. Because if we knew what's going to happen to us, would we still do the things we were planning to do? Okay, then do you think we should leave there?*

J: Yes, I'm walking down the staircase from the Tapestry Room now. I'm inside the Temple of Wisdom, walking down the hall. It looks as if there are precious stones in the walls, like emeralds, rubies, peridot and crystal. It's so beautiful. It's very radiant and very hallowed. You feel ... it's a very hushed feeling. Ahead of me is the Library. I'm walking into it now. It looks as if precious stones are on all the mantels and doors, and they shine with their own light.

I'm in a huge study. There are books and scrolls on everything, and all types of manuscripts on the shelves. There is a beautiful light streaming in illuminating the whole place. It's made of gold, silver and precious stones, but they all reflect light so you can read. The whole building seems to be made of this wondrous material.

This library in the spirit realm was not a strange place for me. I have journeyed there many times with the aid of my subjects. Several have mentioned it and their descriptions vary only slightly. The guardian of the library has always been eager to help me in my quest for knowledge, and I have used our access to this place to gain information about many various topics.

D: *This is one of my favorite places. I like anyplace that has books and manuscripts. Are there other people there?*

J: Oh, there are people in the other part. It's a big area; almost cathedral size. There's a man there-he's a spirit, and he is just luminous. He's talking about preparing for the Earth school, and there are only a few people listening to him right now.   Other people are in groups or walking around silently carrying manuscripts and books to different places. It's the air of ... (he had difficulty finding the word) like scholars. They're studying. Everybody has a sense of purpose, and there's a sense of serenity. There's music that seems to fill the whole place. It's just barely audible but it tinkles. It's pretty music.

D: *It sounds like a very beautiful place.*

J: Yeah, it's really nice. Everything glimmers and everybody is in beautiful robes. The clothing looks as if it's transparent but electric colors shine through them. They're the people's auras.

D: *Is there anyone in charge? How do you find anything?*

J: Yes, there is a spirit guide who is the guardian of the library.   He is at a desk there and he is writing at the present time. And I am asked, "What is your request?

D: *Is he very busy at this moment?*

J: Oh, no. He says, "No, no, no, no. This is wonderful. To be of service is very important."

D: *All right. Can he look up information for us?*

J: He says there are some restrictions.

D: *Can he tell us what they are? I like to know when I'm breaking any rules.*

J: He says, "It's not good to delve too much into your personal futures. That is a 'no-no' ruling. That's not good, it causes disharmony."

D: *All right. We're not going to do that. Are there any other restrictions?*

J: He says that's the main restriction.

D: *Are people that are still in the physical allowed to come to the library?*

J: He says, "Yes, they come through their astral travels, their dreams. Actually dreaming is astral traveling. They come and not all the time are they aware of what they're doing because it's kind of like a little bit of a fog for them. It's rather rare that we have people who are incarnated that *seek* us. There are a few, but not many." He is showing me around. There's the library with the huge rotunda where people are gathered in groups and studying and discussing issues. They are able to go into viewing rooms around the perimeter of this room to view things if they wish. All knowledge is stored in these but it's not like a computer. People don't need computers here. Information is just relayed by intelligent thought. And he says we could go into the scriptorium. This is where things are read. This is where people that can relate to writing and reading like to go. It's part of the library complex.

D: *The scriptorium is a different part in the library?*

J: Yes. It's for people that are not very advanced souls. They're medium advanced souls that still need the written word to make sense to their consciousness.

D: *They wouldn't understand the viewing rooms?*

J: Well, they would understand them, but this is how they choose to learn, by reading from the book.

D: *In that case they can take the books and sit there and read them, and also write?*

J: Right. Write *in* them too. Some of them do.

D: *Is that allowed? Wouldn't that be changing them?*

J: He says, "Yes, it's allowed. Anything for the soul's growth is allowed. That's why sometimes you see children born with horribly disfiguring diseases. Everything's allowed. It's all for the same purpose of reaching spiritual perfection."

D: *But I thought they weren't allowed to write in these books because they were eternal records and shouldn't be defaced or changed.*

J: The tapestry is the eternal thing. That's the only thing that's not touchable. But, he says whatever is necessary for a soul's growth is allowed. For some people its books. But for most advanced souls it's just information.

D: *Then those are the ones that can absorb the knowledge better in the viewing room?*

J: Yes.

D: *I was wondering if there were any restrictions about who could come to the library.*

J: There are no restrictions, this is true, *but* low level energy souls find it very hard to step into this realm. They feel frightened or afraid of this area and thus he says they do not seek to come here.

D: *I wonder why it would frighten them.*

J: They still carry most of the negative qualities of their former existences. Greed, jealousy, lust, things that lower one's vibrations. So as a result they stay mostly down on what he calls the "lower astral world." They really have difficulty entering this area, they're kind of repelled.

D: *It doesn't sound like they would be looking for knowledge anyway.*

J: He says, "Well, we are here to be of service for them. In fact we have branch libraries down among the lower astral world. And it takes a really great spiritual entity to man these stations. But they hardly ever get used. These lower entities are still seeking out experiences in the physical form. This is why they hang out in places that are degenerative or degrading to man's soul.

D: *I was curious about why we were allowed to come into this place.*

J: Your sole sense of purpose is manifested.

D: *So they know the reasons why we are looking for information.*

J: Oh, they understand. "Just by allowing yourself to enter a circle of white light we know you are of the higher astral. And we can read your motives behind what you are seeking. Nothing can be hidden."

D: *Would we be allowed to look at some of this information?*

J: He said you can go into the viewer.

D: *Where is that?*

J: He's taking me into this other room.

D: *Okay. I am interested in these different planes of existence. I thought it might be easier if you could see these things in the viewing room, instead of actually going to the different planes. That might be uncomfortable for you to try that. But if the guardian could give you information about them or show them to you, it would be easier. Would he be able to do that?*

J: Yes. He says the astral world is divided into three parts: the lower, middle and upper astral planes.

D: *First of all, I am curious about the lower planes, so let's start there. Can he tell us what they are like and what type of people or spirits are there?*

J: Yes. We've walked into the viewing room and he's showing me. He says, "Just call attention to whatever you wish to see and all kinds of images will come in."

They're on the walls.

D: *Is it like a screen on one wall or what?*

J: Not really like a screen. It surrounds you. I'm in the middle of it watching it. And he says that the lower astral is just terrible. He says, "We pray for these lower entities, but it's as if they are tied to earth. They're not in human form but they're still on the earth." And they are like... Ohh! (A sound of disgust) This is gross!

D: *What do you see?*

J: Well, I just saw someone get shot. (Uncomfortably) And there's a whole group of spirits watching that and shouting, "Oh, isn't that great! Look at those blood and guts! "

D: *You mean they were watching a physical person get shot?*

J: They're watching two people. A black man and another black man had a shoot-out with each other over a drug deal. And there's like...oh! About a thousand spirits watching this. It's almost like, "Oh, there goes another one! Where are we going to go next? Oh, look at this girl! She's getting raped! Let's watch that!" They're witnessing all this brutality. And the guardian tells me, "They *have* to watch this to see how they've lived their own lives. They've lived like this, in a very degenerate way." And he says these spirits have to learn from this.

D: *Do you mean that after they died they just stayed around these areas or what?*

J: No, they were forced. They couldn't go any higher. You see, their vibrational rate, spiritually, is very low. They're a dense vibration and they can't go any higher up, so they have to watch the physical world. They interact with this world.

D: *I was thinking that sounds something like our version of Hell.*

J: It is a version. It is a Hell. Because until they learn how to reincarnate and become more spiritually advanced, sometimes they repeat similar situations over and over again. And he says some of them are almost beastly. That's the word he used, "beastly."

D: *I've always thought that there was no such actual place as Hell.*

J: It's a Hell for them, yes. Because if they used drugs or alcohol to excess, or let their lust drive rule them, it still controls them. They still have that desire after they pass over, but they cannot manifest it. That's why it's so important before you leave the planet to not have any of these...what are called "vices," because you carry them with you into the next realm. He says, "For instance, we've got people here that want a cigarette, but they can't smoke because we don't have cigarettes over here. So they'll spend time hanging around with physical people that want to smoke. Or we have spirits who have done drugs, who want to shoot up and have made that a pattern in their lives. They will be around people who are shooting up."

D: *You mean they try to get the same sensations by osmosis or something like that?*

J: Yes, they try to. That's why they hang around them. People who have let their lust drive them in life will be around places where lots of lust is taking place in the human form, like the houses of prostitution and things of this type. He says these are the lower denizens of the astral.

D: *It sounds like a vicious circle, like they aren't going anywhere. How can they get out of that plane?*

J: He says this is why it is necessary for people to pray for their loved ones because that will help them to see the light. It is like their own personal Hell that they live in. *But,* he says when they sense that they've had enough of this, guardian spirits come to them. After they have learned to say, for instance, "I'm *tired* of looking at all these people doing this stuff that I can't do." Then the guardians come and conduct them and start showing them ways that they can make a transformation for themselves. But he says, "When it's time for them to reincarnate again, we *do* process them." He says they all go to the computer room which is an area where they can be re-evaluated. The computer room sets them up and matches the time when an incarnation is going to be taking place and what type of lessons that incarnation will teach. They are shown how they can use that lifetime quickly. But he says, "This is all going to be changing very shortly because the Earth is going to be too highly evolved for these spirits. So we're going to be shipping these souls out to a ..." (John laughed suddenly.) You know, its like, "Okay, you had your chance here. Next boat is going to Arturis." (Humorously) It's kind of funny actually. This spirit guide had a good sense of humor. (Laugh) He's jovial, he's a little rotund and he's saying, "Yup. You had your chances here. Now we have to ship you out to those other planets that are over near Arturis."

D: *Are those planets that will have negativity on them?*
J: Yes, he says those are still evolving planets. But these spirits won't come back here because this planet Earth is changing. These spirits we are watching are the low, dense vibrational souls. He says, "Now, the higher vibrational souls are different. When they cross over they usually head for the Temple of Wisdom and Knowledge because they've been there before."

This could be where the schools are located.

D: *They bypass all of that negativity.*
J: And he says, "Then there are the mid-level souls. They like to manifest themselves in happy situations with their families that have crossed over. There are houses and lake resorts and boats for them."

D: *Similar to their lifestyle on Earth, you mean?*

J: There are all different types of houses built up along one of the banks of the lake. On one of the steep hillsides there are all beautiful houses. This is where people live if they choose to, especially people that have a hard time adjusting to the astral world. They'll spend much time here.

D: *Do you mean they want to live in a house that's familiar to them?*

J: Right. They can live in a house that was like their house that they knew in the physical.

D: *Do these houses contain furniture and other people and things like that?*

J: It contains other people and they manifest whatever they want. So if they want furniture in the art deco period, they have furniture in the art deco period. If they want furniture that's rattan, they have rattan furniture. If they want King Louis xiv, they can have King Louis xiv. Whatever style they want, they can have it. (Laugh) You see, these people aren't highly advanced souls. They're just *there* waiting for their next lifetime. It seems as if only the highly advanced souls are in the libraries and the other different areas of the complex. These other souls are still Earth associated.

D: *Maybe that's all they can comprehend.*

J: That's very true. You've got a good point there.

D: *Maybe they think that's all that can exist on that side.*

J: They are usually among people that think the same way. The guardian of the library is saying, "As the old saying goes, 'Birds of a feather will flock together.' Remember that. That's the saying that your world uses. People that are high entities and high energy will be drawn together, just like people who are lower energies have lower entities drawn to them." The people of this level want to retain their familiar life-style. But they use this to clear up things with themselves. This is why much family karma takes place during later incarnations because they have had strong attachments over at this mid-level. There's a low-astral, mid-astral, and upper-astral. And the mid-astral are these types. It's kind of like suburban America. There are nice houses and people are basically talking with their friends and their relatives and they're having good old memories. Sometimes spirit guides come into a house and talk to them and tell them they should start preparing for their next lifetimes. And they say, "Well, we just want to enjoy our families a little bit longer. Do we have time? Is it really necessary for us in our spiritual growth?" And he says, "Well, yes, you do need to go up to the temple." And they're kind of fearful. It's the attitude of "I don't know about that."

D: *They want to stay with what is familiar to them.*

J: Yes, they don't like to go any further. But they're able to manifest good things and they're pretty happy. Then we go into the upper astral. He says it's just like you have different social classes. Mid-astral's nice; it's like going to a nice suburb. But the upper-astral's just gorgeous with such beautiful scenery. There are gardens and the prototypes of all the beautiful mountains, oceans, streams, lakes and waterfalls. They're all there and they're just wonderful. There's this beautiful jewel-like city where the Temple of Wisdom is located. There are mountains surrounding it where some of the people that are upper-astral entities live. But they come into the temple. They're souls that like that sense of comfort of home life and family life. He says many very evolved souls like this type of life. This is why they have their little villa houses on the slopes of the mountains. It's beautiful.

D: *It sounds like the spirits are going to whatever area they are familiar with. And they won't go on to the next level until they're ready. Is that correct?*

J: Right. He says that you have to advance to a certain level. But he says the upper-astral is where you want to go when you come over here. He says, "This is *the* place, it's just gorgeous. The mid-astral, it's important. That's where a majority of the souls come to. They're neither good nor bad, they're not degenerate, they just want to see their family and their friends. And they need time. But when it's time for them to go up to the computer room, it's time for them to go."

D: *They don't have anything to say about it.*

J: No, they can't really; and that's what is sad. He says, "That's why you have so much more choice when you're in the upper-astral. Knowledge is freedom."

D: *Does everyone go to the computer room eventually?*

J: Oh, yes. They all go. This is the processing room. But he says the lower entities have only a few more years to incarnate through all this negativity. He can't show me the computer room. It's a processing room where basically only the spirit guardians are allowed. It's a very important area, but he says even you in the astral state cannot go into it right now.

D: *That's all right. We don't have to see it. We just like to know about these things.*

J: This is the processing room where souls are lined up and matched with the appropriate bodies for them to incarnate in. But, he says it's different when a spirit from the upper-astral wants to incarnate. It's like he has good documentation so he's given priority. (Laugh) I mean, some of them are just *shipped out.* (Laugh) That's what I get the impression of. He says that's true, some of these souls are. He says much of the pain and suffering of the people that have died of famine in Ethiopia and such things as that has been caused by past lifetimes of complete indulgence. He said these lives are being processed into higher spiritual energy for them.

D: *Then they're put into a life where they wouldn't live very long. Just long enough to try to repay some of those indulgences.*

J: To suffer. To teach them that they have to grow spiritually.

D: *Well, is this computer room also where the final karmic connections with families and things like that are worked out?*

J: This is like a huge computer processing center. I see what it looks like somewhat but I can't go in it. There's a line of souls, all dog-eared, waiting to get in. But when a higher-level soul comes, it's like he's given priority service. They already know that he's gonna be processed through quickly. He's ushered in another direction.

D: *Then many of these lower-level souls are the ones that are sent to live such horrible lives and to die en masse in these countries in the catastrophes and the famines. They're the ones that come back to live in those places?*

J: No. He says not to look at it like that. They're paying for lifetimes where they've misused their bodies. He said you could do the same thing. You misuse your temple; you can suffer because of it.

D: *Would the version people have of Heaven fit with any of these astral planes?*

J: He said the upper astral would be very much like Heaven because it is very beautiful.

D: *That is their version of Heaven?*

J: He says, no; the people who believe in Heaven and Hell are still in that mid-level of intelligence. No, it's not a Heaven or a Hell that they are given. They're given a nice suburban tract house in a very suburban-looking area. This is what they expect and so this is what it's like. There are no angels with harps up here.

D: *I was wondering about that; if there was anybody floating around on a cloud with a harp.* (Laugh).

J: There are no clouds. The upper astral, though, is just so beautiful. It's full of gorgeous jewel-like flower colors. It could really be a Heaven.

D: *That would kind of go along with the version people expect of Heaven. Are there any other higher planes that he can tell you about, or is that the ultimate?*

J: He says this is the advanced grades when you reach the upper astral. Yet there are even more advanced grades above this. "But you are still tied to a body and so there are other things to be concerned about." He says, "Don't look further. At your level of awareness, John, that is enough."

D: *Whenever you go to those higher levels, do you ever come back and incarnate again?*

J: No. He says that you have much more important missions to work with in the universal plan. And that you don't usually take *physical* incarnation again unless it is a very important mission. He says great men in history, for instance, Jesus and Buddha, have been very high upper-astral entities that did come back.

D: *They came back for a purpose then.*

J: Right, a very important purpose.

D: *I was just wondering if our goal in our evolution was to go on beyond that plane.*

J: He says we go beyond the upper astral and we go into spiritual rejuvenation and learning to be a universal spirit. Then we're not just tied to the astral areas of the Earth. I can't understand that. But he says, "It's not for you to understand at this present point." (Laugh)

D: *What is our goal eventually?*

J: Perfection. We increase. As you know from your law of physics, energy is neither created nor destroyed. It just changes its form on its drive back to its source. And by the time it reaches its source it's of the same energy. He says this applies to spiritual physics as well. He says, "There's the clue. You think it for yourself."

D: *But eventually the goal is perfection. And in order to attain that you have to go through several lives on Earth and then evolve above that?*

J: He says each lifetime teaches you a different quality that you need to learn in your quest for perfection. You don't just have *several* lifetimes. Some people go for three, four, five, six *hundred.*

D: *Of course, many of them have to keep repeating lessons, don't they?*

J: Right. He says some advanced souls can do it in maybe ten lives. But the average number is about 120. (Abruptly) He is saying that we have seen enough and now it is time for us to leave this area. He's leading me out of the library and showing me the steps leading outside the Temple area and down into a wonderful, breath-taking garden. He said, "Why don't you go see what's out there." I get the feeling we may have been asking too many questions. I'm walking in this garden and it's just beautiful. There are fountains and conduits of water. The birds are singing. The smells of the flowers are just wonderful. There is a glowing spirit here and he says, "Let's talk about the garden. It's the prototype of all the flowers and trees and ponds and lakes and fountains that you have on Earth, so it's much finer." Everything is exquisite. The flowers are like hand-cut jewels. Their scents are just miraculous. Imagine the best, most expensive perfume in the world just sprayed all over the place. I mean, it's just that type of wonderful scent that's in the air. It feels like nature just reaches out to love you. And there are beautiful butterflies. Oh, it's just wonderful. It's so beautiful here. And this is a prototype of what gardens look like in the material world. This is *the* world, the *real* world. The astral world is the real world and this garden is prototype for our Earth gardens.

D: *I'm thinking of flowers on Earth. They will bloom and then they will fall off.*

J: No, these are eternal. They never change. That's why they have jewel-like perfection.

D: *Like the most perfect rose or something like that?*

J: Yes, each petal is exquisite. The flowers are like the most perfect jewels.

D: *Is it the same with the trees? Would it be like the most perfect examples of these trees? Is that what you mean?*

J: He says that the trees in your world, the material world, are just a reflection of these.

D: *I guess I was thinking the opposite, that maybe the astral world was a reflection of this world.*

J: Oh, no, no, no. He says, "This world is much better. All beautiful things that are created in your physical world have their counterpart here in this world. And the Earth is just a reflection of the spiritual world. Your world is so coarse and crude." That was the guardian of this wonderful garden that said that.

D: *Then each place has a guardian.*

J: Yes, each place in this complex has a different guardian. There's this beautiful lake.

D: *Where is that?*

J: In the gardens. There are all different types of houses built up along one of the banks of the lake. And everything, the fountains, the Temple, the mountains and landscape is perfect and eternal. The intensity of the colors is breathtaking. It is impossible to describe the incredible beauty of this place. Well, he's saying that maybe we should go back. He says, "You've had your tour. Now, go back. Go back, John!"

D: *All right. But isn't there any other place up there that I need to know about?*

J: No, not right now. He says some areas are off-center because it's like dragging a toddler or a preschooler into a college. He says this information is not necessary for you right at this present point.

D: *All right. But tell him I'm trying to find out about these things so that people who are afraid of dying will know what it's like over there. That's the main thing. Maybe they won't be afraid if they know.*

J: He understands what your service is. He says that's nice and that's wonderful. But he also says there are some things that we do keep hidden.

D: *Well, I can appreciate that.*

J: And he says, "Take care now. Feel happy and high in love and light. Bless you and let the white light surround you and make you feel safe and happy."

D: *Okay.   Then he thinks we should not ask any more questions today or try to find out any more information? Is that correct?*

J: (Surprised) He's gone!

D: *Well, where are you?* (Pause) *Do you see anything at this time?*

J: I'm in the gray. That's all. It's all gray. Some kind of clouds.

D: *Okay. Apparently they want us to stop asking questions. Is that all right with you? But I guess you don't have much choice, do you?* (Laugh)

J: (Perplexed) I'm not there anymore.

D: *That is all right. We did find out quite a bit.*

I then brought John back up to full consciousness. I was a little disappointed that we couldn't continue longer with our exploration, but when they stopped the flow of communication we had no choice. It was as if we were allowed entry up to a certain point. But when they decided it was time for us to go they simply pushed us out the door and closed it behind us. The scene had been completely cut off. This was a very unusual occurrence. It demonstrated that we certainly were not the ones controlling this session.

Chapter 6
Different Levels of Existence

INFORMATION ABOUT THE DIFFERENT LEVELS of existence began to emerge when I was speaking to a woman who was in-between lives and attending school on the spirit planes. But this time it sounded like a different school than the school of knowledge I had been told of earlier, although there were some similarities. She said it was located on the seventh level.

S: I am learning how to take on day-to-day experiences in life and make them worthwhile and enjoyable and make a lot count. We are learning about the different stages that are occurring on Earth. And we are trying to help different people become knowledgeable so that humans can take the necessary steps forward.

D: *Do you mean by being a guide of some kind?*

S: To a certain degree, yes. Maybe helping open people up to the realms of possibility.

D: *Are you able to do this from where you are?*

S: Mostly it is done from here. We make an effort to attract the attention of individuals that we feel are capable of handling the knowledge and the information that we can give them. There are only a certain amount of people who are open to those on the seventh level. There are more who are open to those on the sixth. But we are trying to open up the ones who are, for instance, the spiritual leaders or the inventors. And those who many people would not consider to be important, in the extent that they won't be remembered for the next 200 years. But they are doing something that is important. Maybe being a father to someone, who will be known, or maybe guiding or teaching such children.

D: *Do you try to work on the mental level?*
S: Yes. Through their dreams and different things like that.

It would seem that this seventh level is where the inventions, music and creative influences come from. I have always felt that these things are spread through the atmosphere whenever the world is ready, and that whoever is open and could pick up on these ideas would be the one credited with the invention. I think those on the other side do not really care who does the actual creating, as long as is done when the time is right. This would account for the cases of many people all over the world working on the same thing at the same time and rushing it toward completion. Many famous inventors and composers have claimed that their inspirations came to them during dreamlike states when they would naturally be more psychically open to these helpful influences.

D: *Could you explain about these spiritual planes or levels?*
S: If you would like to envision an inverted pyramid, God would be at the top or the longest edge, and humanity would be at the bottom or at the point. The planes are in-between and as they go higher in number, they become more spiritual. As one advances in the planes, one broadens one's awareness and becomes closer to God. However, this pyramid analogy lacks in several aspects, one being that the top or longest part would be infinite. To be God, it would have to be infinite.
D: *How do we advance through the planes?*
S: You're advancing through your planes right now. Incarnation is one manner.
D: *Is it a matter of simply spiritual development?*

S: Spiritual development, yes. Physical development is another.

D: *Do we have to live more than one life in order to advance?*

S: You need not live any lives at all if you so desire. It is not necessary to incarnate; it is simply more efficient.

D: *More efficient for what?*

S: For you. For your time. For your learning experiences. It is more complete learning to incarnate than to remain spiritual. These are short cuts, if you will, to the ultimate destination.

D: *And what is the ultimate goal?*

S: To be one with God. To join with God again and reach perfection, and then you don't have to come back any more.

D: *Have many spirits or souls reached the highest level of these planes?*

S: Many have already joined God and need never return to lower planes again.

D: *How many lives does it generally take?*

S: It varies with different individuals. If they can stay with the goal they have set and the pattern. And not forget why they are there, and stay in touch with their inner selves and stay strictly on the path, it doesn't take as many. But too many people get caught up with the ways of the world. Their egos and their vanities are built around them and they lose contact with the spiritual, deeper truths of the reasons behind their existence.

D: *If we didn't incarnate, how would we reach God?*

S: Through other methods. Through helping, assisting incarnated beings. Through being a guide, a teacher, a helper, a friend on the spirit planes. There are many different methods.

D: *What is the objective of physically working up through these planes if it can be done from the other side?*

S: We are ascendant beings. We are forming a ladder. There are others whose entire purpose is stationary. This is similar to people in a marathon. There are those at certain points who do nothing but hold the water and give it to the runners as they pass. These runners are ascendants, if you will, from the beginning to the end. Angels are the assistants who do not climb but merely serve. Our purpose is to start at the beginning and run until we get to the finish. However, there is no first or last place. All who cross the finish line are winners in that race.

I was curious about these levels. Some spirits have called them dimensions, but from their descriptions, you can tell that they are speaking of the same things. I have been told there are several, from ten to thirteen to a possible infinite number, according to whom you are speaking to. But they all agree that as you climb higher you come closer to being one with God.

D: *Can you tell me about the different levels?*
S: I could not explain it to make you understand each plane or dimension because you don't have the experience to understand it. But I will try to give you some information.
D: *Is the Earth considered the first level?*
S: The level of the Earth is considered a fifth level. There are several levels below that. There are the elementals, who are some of your lowest, on the first level. That basic plane is composed of pure emotions and energies. They are but a basic energy, and you progress upward from there. They are life forms which have no individual personalities but are merely collective life forms waiting for their time, as humans waited for theirs. Elementals have a future where they will become personalized. However, they are in their waiting period at this time. Don't underestimate their potential for they can be very powerful. Neither berate or underrate them, for they have a future quite remarkable, as the human

future was before the present.

D: *Do elementals have anything to do with what we term "possession"?*

S: Not in the typical understanding. Possession is a reality; however, elementals are drawn and not invaders as such. Elementals can be directed so they tend to be influenced quite easily and can be swayed one way or another. (See Chapter 10 for more information.)

D: *What about the other levels?*

S: There is the second level which are protectors of the trees and the hills. These are different from each other. Elementals usually deal with places. Whereas, with those that protect the trees, each has a tree or their own type of plant. It is like when the Greeks spoke of the sprites and driads and different things like that. That was much in this level of understanding.

D: *Do they have any intelligence?*

S: More mischief than intelligence, though they are basically very kindhearted. It is a matter of progression. Your physical level is just another energy level. It is simply a matter of perception where you are most comfortable. This determines which level of incarnation you go to. Some people come back as fairies and leprechauns because that's where they are comfortable perceiving.

D: *They can do that?*

S: Yes. Usually they incarnate as the ones referred to in your language as the "little people." They are more in tune with the spiritual level because they are aware of the energies involved and how to manipulate them.

D: *Then such beings do exist?*

S: Yes, they *do* exist, but they exist in the spirit realm. They do not exist in a physical manifestation. But they *can* appear as a physical manifestation. That's very important. They *can* appear. But they're very spiritual. Their souls, just as your soul, are growing towards perfection. And they have recourse over all plants and animals of the forest, and also of the sea and of the air. They're like the movers and shakers behind things in this area. But when they do manifest they manifest as a human-like creature in green areas. This is why we have stories of leprechauns, fairies, elves and such.

D: *In their normal state they're like a spirit, but they can manifest as little creatures? Why do they manifest in such an unusual form?*

S: It is part of the plan. They are tested to learn how to take care of nature. When they have learned to do that, then they can go on to take care of themselves.

D: *What do you mean by that?*

S: Exactly what I said.

D: *Does that mean they can evolve and eventually incarnate as humans?*

S: You've been fairies before in other lifetimes, yes.

D: *Oh? All of us?*

S: Yes. All of us. You really cannot talk too much about soul evolution at this present state of your development. It is difficult for you to comprehend. But they are moving up the ladder just as we are moving up the ladder.

D: *Is this why humans are so fascinated with these things?*

S: Probably because they've been there. They've been these fairies, especially those people that are very in tune with the Earth. They are still recalling reflections from their lifetimes as a spirit on the Earth as these type of creatures.

D: *Well, according to our folklore, they are supposed to have magical powers and things like that. Is this true? Do they have the powers that are attributed to them?*

S: That's just folklore. They do have surprising talents. But to uneducated people who weren't aware of the spiritual realm, when they manifested, they saw them as a spirit rather than a physical life form. They do have life though, in a spiritual sense.

D: *It's difficult for me to see them as a spirit and then changing into a manifestation.*

S: They're allowed to do this when it is necessary. That is why they don't appear very often to humans. If you are clairvoyant, you can see that all nature has its spirits taking care of its endless tasks.

D: *Do they experience death as we know it?*

S: No, they don't experience death. They just individualize more. They go away from the group soul into more striking individualism so that they can work out their karmic fate.

D: *There has been such long, on-going folklore; it would seem there has to be some kind of basis to it. Is there any reason why people see them in different ways, like elves, fairies, gnomes?*

S: Some take care of the creatures of the lakes and the waters. Others take care of the creatures of the forest. Others take care of the creatures of the Earth's carpet, the grass.

D: *This is why they look differently; have different shapes, different forms, different personalities and such?* (She nodded.) *Do these creatures ever create anything negative?*

S: No, because they're programmed not to.

D: *Well, I'm thinking of folklore.*

S: Yes. But there are demons out there that masquerade as these beings. These are often negative astral entities that have lived on the Earth and are upset because they cannot reincarnate there again. They can cause problems. This happened more often in the past. You see, humans have rather ignored these spirits because of their technological advancement. Demons used to torment people as fairies, as animals. But now that humans have moved away from an agricultural-type of lifestyle into a technological lifestyle, it doesn't happen as often.

D: *How would people know which was which?*

S: You shouldn't worry about it. Nature spirits really don't manifest that often to mortal people. It is not that common. But when they do, it is for an important reason. Usually it has something to do with land or with nature itself. For instance, maybe people are going to abuse the land that is sacred to these spirits, and they will cause trouble then. They will try to contact people in their sleep and their waking hours to say, "Please do not abuse this land."

D: *That sounds like some of the Indian lore that we have heard. But they don't manifest as often as they used to.*

S: No. But they do things that are beneficial for the plants and the animals in their care.

D: *One thing I was wondering about. Does each plant and animal have a separate protector?*

S: No, because plants and animals all have a group spirit. And these group spirits are tended to by these spirits that you would know as leprechauns and fairies. There are *individual* souls that take care of the group souls. And the individual souls are the elves, fairies, *etc.*

D: *This is so difficult to understand. I thought maybe it was a group soul that took care of all the plants, and then this individualized.*

S: They're separate beings because the group soul is not as evolved as a helping soul.

D: *Then the fairies and elves are helping souls, rather like our guides and guardians.*

S: They're like pixies, yes. They are like guides and channelers for the plant and animal kingdom. These kingdoms are aware of these spirits.

D: *It is rather like the way our guides and guardians help us.*

S: Yes. Except that they are for the animal kingdom and the plant kingdom. The leprechauns or elves or whatever you want to call them are a distinctive soul-type that is evolving spiritually into human incarnation. They will have that opportunity in the future. In fact, we have been that type of energy in our previous lifetimes, but now we have taken a human role. These spirits are of service to animals and birds that have the group souls. They are there to help them since animals do not have individual souls. The way that animals see life is through their reproductions. This is how they live on.

Much of this sounded very similar to folklore and mythology, which we have dismissed as superstitious "gibberish." Maybe because the ancients were living closer to nature, they understood more about these basic principles. It was very clear to them, but it also frightened them. Apparently out of their respect for nature, they invented stories and populated them with distinct types of creatures whose names have come down to us in folklore and myths. This appears to have evolved from their attempts to understand this spirit realm which we have chosen to ignore in our mechanized and complicated society.

D: *But then in their evolution these spirits eventually do become humans.*

S: Yes. I am really not supposed to talk much about this information. But, yes, they are learning to develop into humans. They're a young soul. They're full of love for all humanity and all of nature, but especially nature. They will move up the scale of evolution after the Earth shift, for then they will start incarnating in physical bodies. They are preparing the world for this Earth shift at this present time. That is why people are being guided to certain areas throughout the country to live. When these spirits incarnate in a human lifetime the world will have changed from a low planetary vibratory system to a high planetary vibratory system, and this will reflect their light and their lives. Many of them will come into operation and incarnate to help rebuild the world, and to produce food and have attunement with the animals that have been traumatized by the Earth shift.

D: *What will happen to our type of spirits?*

S: As the Earth shift occurs, different changes happen to groups of souls. We would evolve up to a higher sense of consciousness.

D: *We wouldn't want to incarnate on the Earth at that time?*

S: We will also reincarnate on the Earth just to fulfill our sense of karma. But most people who will be coming to Earth will be spiritually evolved. All lesser evolved beings are being sent to another universe to begin their cosmic journey again.

D: *It sounds like there's going to be many changes after the Earth shift.*

S: These nature spirits are preparing for it. I really shouldn't talk any more about it.

The subject of the coming axis shift of the Earth and the mechanics, are discussed in more detail in my book, *Conversations with Nostradamus (3* volumes).

D: *Well, what about the animals? You said they do not have individual souls?*

S: No. The spirits of animals are different from humans. It is just so different from the soul of a human that I cannot explain it very well. They have group spirits, and these are worked out with the other elementals. Some animals, such as cows and horses, have the herd tendency which is easily identifiable as a group spirit. But animal spirits do not have personality as humans do. They are life forces, however, and do inhabit bodies-animal bodies.

D: *Do they have incarnations the same as humans do?*

S: It is incarnation, yes. There is the filling of the physical body with a life force, yes, so it would be incarnation in that respect.

D: *Does an animal spirit ever incarnate as a human being?*

S: *(She frowned and seemed puzzled.)* Yes, it does-eventually. It is part of its spiritual growth. Just like you will go on to higher levels, so does an animal's spirit separate from the group spirit and become an individual soul and begin the process of growing spiritually. Many of the people on Earth have been animals in other lifetimes on other planets, eons of time ago.

D: *And this was part of the evolution? I am curious about where we began. What type of an energy were we when we first started?*

S: We must go through all the series of development: gas, matter, plant, animal, human, spirit, divine.

D: *Then an animal is part of a group spirit and it can become individualized and break off from the group?*

S: Yes, it happens because of love. Humans showing love to an animal gives it a personality. Love helps it to separate and makes it more individualistic. This raises their consciousness. This is why you should always be loving to all creatures. But I don't understand about those noxious creatures like *bugs* and *wasps* and mosquitoes. *(She made a disgusted face, and I laughed.)* They are part of the plan. Most of the bugs were put there for a reason, but I feel some just do not need to be there because they are not really productive. But after the Earth change, they are not going to be there anymore.

D: *Would the animal spirits be on a certain level?*

S: Some are in the second; some are in the third; and some of them are somewhere in between. For instance, an ant would be on a different level than a much-loved dog or horse. There are not always distinct levels saying this is on this one and that one is on that one. There are many facets to each character. There are also those who are in earthly human form who are on these lower levels. They are allowed to do this in hopes that they will raise themselves. Some people are on the third level even after they have incarnated. They are those humans who have no conscience. They just live an existence. They do not live a life. They live less than a life.

D: *How do you mean? Are they bad, or just have no interest?*

115

S: They do not have the intelligence to be either good or bad. There are very few of these. There are more fourth-level incarnates than there are third levels. What you would call a sociopath would be a fourth-level individual. Again, they have no conscience, but they have the intelligence to know how to use this against others.

D: *The ones on the third and fourth levels that are antisocial; would these be the murderers and criminals?*

S: Yes, for a great part. They are those who have either fallen down to that level, or have not reached up to the others yet. There is no conscience. And then there is the fifth level which is your day-to-day existence. There are also some who reach over from the sixth level and come from there to the   earthly plane.

D: *Is the sixth level above the Earth?*

I was trying to physically fix these levels in recognizable places with definite boundaries which I later found out was impossible.

S: The sixth is the one known as the spirit's realm.

D: *Would those be spirits that didn't want to leave the Earth?*

S: Sometimes they are those that are locked into the earthly plane by either their own motives or their family could keep them there through grief or whatever.

D: *The Earth is on the fifth. After that are the sixth, seventh and on higher? And these are where the schools are located?*

S: The schools and the masters and other things, yes. The eighth and ninth levels are reserved for the great masters. If you reach the tenth, you are one again with God.

D: *Well, do people ever go backwards? I was thinking about the theory that humans incarnate as animals.*

S: No. Unless you are extremely beastly. In other words, if you acted like an animal and you wanted to become an animal, you could, yes, but that is very rare. This is not usually allowed. It was at one time possible. However, it is no longer. It was done during the early days of the experimentation, but no longer. It is not that it is not possible, but that it is not allowed. If a person had dropped that low they would probably stay upon this side until they had raised, rather than going any farther down the scale. It is possible for a person to drop to an animalistic level mentally, but they would be unlikely to enter an animal's body. Once you have attained the human consciousness, it is very rare that you go back to an animal light existence because you have evolved out of that.

D: *Then the humans that are incarnate would be in the third, fourth and fifth levels.*

S: Sometimes the sixth.

I wondered how that would be possible if we are incarnate and the sixth level was the spirits' realm.

S: You have heard of the expression that a person has one foot in one world and the other in the next. These are the individuals who are very open to everything around them.

D: *Are they able to switch levels at will?*

S: For the most part, once they become aware of it and begin dealing with the two worlds, yes. And there is the seventh level which has many of the schools of knowledge and thought. It is from the sixth and seventh levels that much of the knowledge comes. Some humans operate on two levels without realizing this. An example is an inventor who has no idea where his knowledge comes from.

The thought occurred to me that we have often heard people talk about the seventh heaven. It is supposed to be a place of perfect happiness. I wonder if the original concept came from this theory of different levels?

D: *What level is the resting place on?*

S: It has no level. It is. It exists because of a need for being without stimulation of any kind. Therefore, it has no level. You go there to be without.

D: *Is it in a special place away from the other planes?*

S: Not necessarily *away*. It is in amongst the planes, but it is complete unto itself. It is hard to explain. To use an analogy, it would be like when you are going straight up from the surface of your planet and the air gets thinner. As you go up, you come up to the level of the clouds and you see a cloud that is very thick and solid-looking. It is separate unto itself, but it is still part of the air. The resting place is like that.

D: *Every time you go between lives, do you go to a different level or back to the same one you left?*

S: Sometimes it depends on what you accomplished in that life. If you, instead of being uplifted, were perhaps downgraded in a life, then you would not go back to the same level that you had left. Sometimes you would go straight into another life. Other times you would go into a resting period. Sometimes you would just go back to a school, but not necessarily the same one you left. Maybe you have other lessons to learn, or you're reviewing what you need to learn the next time around. Maybe you're trying to decide if you want to come back, or if you want to stay there and work for a long period of time.

D: *Is there a school on each level?*

S: Yes, there are many schools on each level: schools of light, schools of thought. They each are using a portion of what is the natural law and order of things. They are trying to open the individual up to that portion of the truth so they can find the way.

D: *You don't go to the next level until you are ready for it?*

S: That is true.

This sounded like moving from grade to grade at school. Maybe that's what it is like, with Earth being just one of the classrooms.

D: *Do you mean there are certain requirements before you can go to the next one? You may end up going backward or moving up to the next level according to what you have accomplished?*

S: Yes. And once you get past a certain level, like about the ninth, it is very, very rare to ever incarnate again because you have passed a great need for lessons like that. Unless, like I said, you are downgraded by a certain existence where you are so overcome by the temptations you face day-to-day that instead of uplifting them, they downgrade you.

D: *It would seem that when you get to those upper levels you would be beyond those temptations.*

S: If it has been many eons since you lived an earthly existence, it is like someone who has been denied something. If a child has not had candy for a long time and is offered candy, they will most likely gorge themselves on it. It is this type of thing that sometimes happens. It is not as common as in the lower levels, but it does happen. Even the greatest of avatars [demigods] can possibly be tempted, yes.

The avatar is a demigod who comes down to Earth in bodily form. There are many examples in the scriptures of the Hindus. The ninth level apparently would have been where the master teacher, Jesus, came from. This would also explain the story in the Bible of his temptation by the devil. This was his battling with his own inner self.

D: *There must be something about Earth that does that to people.*

119

S: On Earth the thing which you call evil, the darker side of things is more active than it is here. And the pull is greater, yes.

D: *It makes it very hard to resist that.*

S: But then again, in the resisting, it makes you stronger when you do. Here where existence is very easy and you don't have to resist, you are perhaps not growing as fast.

D: *So it appears that you go back into a life with all the best plans and intentions and you can't always stick to them, I guess.*

S: "The best laid plans of mice and men oft gang agley." [Robert Burns] You never know what will happen until you get there. It's sometimes useful to travel backwards to help those below. Often those in the higher dimensions return to the physical world to raise people's awareness.

They are called bodhisattvas in Buddhism and are described as people who have achieved enlightenment and yet chose to return to the physical plane out of compassion for their fellow creatures. In this form of Buddhism, Jesus was a bodhisattva or enlightened one.

S: There is a dispensation given to those who would do this. It is allowed, so to say, and it is done.

D: *Will a soul eventually go to all these different dimensions or planes?*

S: That is what we are all working for. That is the ultimate goal. The ultimate plan is the oneness, a reunion with God.

Others have given these same descriptions in different words. I do not think they are contradictory. Everything they tell me depends on the growth of the spirit that is doing the reporting and the accuracy of their perceptions and their ability to report what they perceive, given the limitations of our language. Every single entity has said that our language is totally inadequate to describe what they see. Often they try to compensate by using analogies, but even these are woefully ineffective to portray the whole picture. What lies beyond the veil is so overwhelming; it is difficult at best to communicate the information back to our mortal senses. We can only try our best to understand these entities within our human limitations. It is either that, or not seek the knowledge at all.

THIS IS THE REPORT of another entity about the various planes of existence.

S: The different planes occupy the same space. For example, you right now are existing on the physical plane, yet your spiritual aspects of yourself have reflections on the spiritual planes. This is because the spiritual planes are here too, but the vibrations involved are of a different frequency. With the spiritual eyes, many times it can come across as appearing almost like a physical place. It is here at the same location of the Earth; it is just a different frequency. It is like your radio. It is the same radio, and the vibrations that come through it occupy the same space at the same time, but it is on different frequencies. And you adjust the frequency receiver to receive a particular set of vibrations at any one time. So it is with these different planes. They exist at the same time but they are on different frequencies so they do not collide, so to speak. I am not sure I have made myself clear.

D: *I think I understand. That is what I've heard, that you can be on one level and not be aware of the other planes.*

S: Yes. Or if you become aware, like through meditation or what-have-you on this plane, you are only dimly aware because you are of a different frequency. You are able to alter part of your frequency enough to complimentary interact with another frequency to know that it exists. But there will be a barrier there. Hence the description of seeing through a glass darkly, or a veil. There are different planes, but there are also intermediate planes where you can interact with others from other planes if need be. For example, some of the ones that you've been interacting with on the physical plane in this process of working out your karma may be on a different plane. They may not have been born yet into the physical plane, and you would need to consult with them to see what they were deciding for their next incarnation. You may need to discuss how it would work out best for both of your karmas, as to where and when to incarnate. That's one of the purposes behind karma and reincarnation. You can go to these intermediary planes for these purposes while in a sleep state. When you are between incarnations, you can also have access to higher planes.

D: *Can you go to these other planes even though you are not that advanced? Or are there something like barriers that would only let you go to certain levels?*

S: You go as far as your understanding and comprehension allows you. Your mind is the only barrier. It is according to how far you've been able to open your mind and understand. And there are always people to help you if you desire or need it for opening your mind further.

D: *I've been trying to understand these levels. I keep trying to picture them as having distinct physical boundaries, which I am beginning to realize, is probably impossible.*

S: It's not like distinct physical boundaries. To use an analogy, on your plane standing on the ground would be like being at one level. As you go straight up away from the surface of your planet, you go through the atmosphere which the scientists have labeled into different layers, stratosphere or what-have-you, according to how thin the air is. But this doesn't happen at different levels. It is just gradual transitions from one level to the

122

other. As you go straight up from the ground, you don't see the different levels of atmosphere. You just notice that things are gradually changing and becoming different as you go further up. The spiritual planes are like this.

D: *Do you know how many planes there are?*

S: No. There are countless planes, I think. Some planes are for special purposes, and other planes are just general.

D: *What is the highest level that someone can go to if they are progressing, as you said, higher and higher?*

S: Well, I really don't know if 1 can tell you anything about it because I am not sure there's a limit to how high you can progress. I am not aware of any limits and my perception only extends upward so far. But those who are more advanced than I can perceive further because they are more advanced. At my present level, all I know is that one can continue to progress. And the more one progresses, the more positive your karma becomes.

D: *You don't want to stay on the same level and keep going around in a rut, I guess. After you leave the level of incarnation, do you go back to the same spiritual level that you left?*

S: No. Many times it depends on things that have happened to you while you are incarnated and the way you handled them. For example, if when you incarnated, you started making a regular practice of meditating and such, that will help you progress even while you are on the physical plane. Then, when you return, you are able to go back to a higher level. If one temporarily becomes stuck, so to speak, at a particular level, it is usually because there is something there that you need to learn, but you are having difficulty absorbing.

I tried to get more information from this entity about the levels on Earth that were below the physical (human). I said I had heard that the lowest level was the energies of things such as the rocks and plants and trees.

S: I think you are referring to elementals. All of the universe - including all of the planes of this universe and some of the other universes, for that matter, but I'm speaking only of this universe right now - all of it is energy of various intensity and different levels. You perceive the physical plane as being solid and physical simply because the energy of your body is compatible with it in that way. But it's all energy too, as your atomic scientists are aware. The energies embodied in the various levels of creation, such as the rocks, trees and such are not necessarily lower or higher levels of energy, or not necessarily lower or higher planes. They're just different vibrations of energy or spirits, if you wish to call them that. They are living forces with power and life behind them. They just operate according to different rules. I mentioned to you how, on the plane that I am on right now, the energy rules apply differently and operate differently. That's the way it is with these other energy levels as well. That's why things that happen which seem inexplicable on your Earth happen because they're often influenced or caused by entities on these other energy levels. They can interact with your energy level. Do you understand?

D: *I'm trying to think how they could influence us or cause things to happen that are inexplicable.*

S: Well, you have folklore about the little people and such as that to try to help you understand these different energy levels. The concept of the little people truly does exist. It's a set of entities on a different energy level. It's a different type of incarnation that one can go into. For example, one way these other energy levels can influence you is by interacting with whatever psychic abilities you may have. And another way, by helping you to be sensitive to changes of the weather or what-have-you or different things like that. Or perhaps if a strange series of what could be called "coincidences" had happened, it would be due to influences from these other energy levels. This is

124

going to get confusing, I fear-not confusing to me but confusing to you. For example, if one desired something very strongly, the strength of that desire and the thoughts about it put out a certain form of energy. The entities on these other energy levels will be aware of this. And they may influence things in a subtle way to help this to come about.

D: *Do these other entities ever influence anything in a negative way? Or would they be allowed to do that?*

S: Yes, there are some that do. It's like Yin and Yang, keeping things in balance. Usually the ones that influence things in a so-called "negative" way are either being mischievous, or the person who put out the energy concerning different desires was not clear in what they wanted. So they *perceive* what happens as being negative.

D: *I guess I was thinking about our ideas of bad spirits or demons.*

S: No, these are not like that.

This line of questioning will be followed up in Chapter 10 which deals with Satan, possession, and demons.

D: *What about the area the Catholic Church refers to as purgatory? Is there any such place in the levels?*

S: No. The nearest thing I can see that would possibly equate with purgatory would be the place of resting for the damaged souls. But it is not a place of punishment, not like the Catholics imply with their term of purgatory. There's really no such specific place as purgatory or Hell. Any experience like that is created by your own mind as a result of things that have happened in past incarnations.

D: *I was going to ask about Hell. Some people have described places that seemed "bad" to them when they've had near death experiences. Do you know anything about that?*

S: They were expecting this. It's the result of someone believing they have lived a life sufficient to make them "go to Hell." Due to the type of life they have lived they have attracted negative energies and influences unto themselves. When they cross over to the spiritual side of things, the negative influences are still clustered about them. But now they are conscious of these influences and they can perceive them because they are on the spiritual plane themselves. These things surround them totally and it affects their minds and makes them think that they are at a place that is very unpleasant, when in reality it's a state of mind due to the negative energies that have been attracted to them in their past incarnations.

D: *But it's not a place where they would have to stay?*

S: No. The condition of Hell is all a matter of what state your mind is in during the period of transition. The idea of Heaven and Hell has become somewhat of a fable or a legend from your perspective. Those who choose to believe this create their own reality to such an extent that when they do pass over they find that elemental reality which they themselves helped to create, and therefore it is indeed real. The descriptions of Heaven and Hell in your holy writings are a result of people who have had near death experiences. They come back and describe what they saw. And what they saw was how they perceived the spiritual energies around them during the period of transition. But they did not cross over far enough to be able to realize what was actually going on. If they reported something that was good and very pleasant, that was reported as being Heaven. Those who reported something that was very horrible and terrible, that was reported as being Hell.

D: *They always talk about fire and things like that.*

S: The negative energies can torture the mind in a way that would make you feel like you are burning. This is not a physical burning because the mortal body has been left behind.

D: *Then how can I help people to understand these things when I write about this? They've been taught for so long by the church that this is the way it is.*

S: That's a good question. Write these things that you find out from this unit and others and correlate the information. Encourage people to read books on near death experiences so that they can overcome this mental attitude they have that death is something to be feared. Death is no more to be feared than breathing.

D: *I've heard that if some people die and they're afraid they're going to Hell, then that is what they will see. They figure they've lived a bad life and this is the only thing they can expect, so this sets them up for a bad experience.*

S: Yes, it does, because that's one of the attitudes that helps attract negative energies. If they're expecting a pleasant experience then that's what they will have and it will make the period of transition easier. They'll be less likely to need to go to the resting place to work on their attitudes and such to dissipate negative energies. If they can develop positive attitudes in life, this in itself will help dissipate the negative energies. People who cross over in this negative condition are often sent to the resting place because they need to work through these problems. And to work on their attitude or whatever it was in their particular case that attracted these negative vibrations. They need to figure out what they did to attract these and what they can do to help themselves grow and improve so that these negative influences are no longer attracted. When they work on the different aspects of themselves, and as they correct or heal a certain attitude or what-have-you, the energy of attraction is no longer there. The negative influences dissipate or drop away since there is no longer the energy there to hold them. It's like a combination of magnetism, electricity and gravity or something like that.

D: *What would happen if somebody reincarnated before these influences had dropped away?*

S: Usually they try to give them time in the resting place to start making positive progress towards having these negative influences dissipate. If one were to incarnate before they are worked away ... I'm not sure what happens. I think it's just added to their karma. I could be mistaken. I think when you are born, when you are young and innocent, you're protected from these for a period of time-until you reach what is called the condition of accountability when you start to realize right and wrong. At that point when the mind reaches enough maturity to know right from wrong, since the state of mind was already there, it would generally choose the state of mind that will keep those forces attracted to them. And usually they will end up attracting more forces or negative energies. It's just a matter of going to the resting place when they die and working on these attitudes so they may dissipate.

D: *I was wondering if they came back with these forces still with them, if that would mean they were starting off on the wrong foot, so to speak.*

S: They're given a grace period, so to speak, when they're still innocent. But when they reach the age of accountability, when they start making their decisions on whether or not to do something, on whether or not it was right or wrong, or whether or not they wanted to do it, regardless of whether or not it was right or wrong. At that point these attitudes will expose themselves again and the energies will return.

D: *When does the age of accountability start?*

S: It's different ages for different people according to how they have developed. For some people it may be as young as five years old. For others it may be as old as twelve or thereabouts. It depends on the individual.

D: *It depends upon their perception of right and wrong?*

S: Yes. Some individuals never lose their innocence. Those who are mentally retarded or what-have-you, keep their innocence their entire lives. When they die, it's lucky in a way, because they don't have to try to dissipate the negative energies because they did not have the perception to have these attitudes to attract these energies. Plus the difficulty of living that type of life will help them to work off much karma, too. It would change much bad karma into good karma.

D: *I wonder why somebody would want to come into a life being retarded or severely handicapped.*

S: It's a way of not having to continually go through the cycle of the resting place. Some people are able to go ahead and work their problems out in the resting place before they are reincarnated. But others are not always so successful.

D: *It seems that the more knowledgeable people are of what actually occurs; the better it will be for everyone, although the church won't agree with me on my ideas of what is better for people. (Laugh)*

S: No, but then it never has. It's a matter of power for them. Religion was corrupted into a political or power play, such that what was spiritual became a tool for the sublimation of the masses in order to control their behavior. There are in their embellishments some aspects which would perhaps be true in a very elementary sense. However, the overall picture is grossly misunderstood at this time by most on the physical plane.

D: *The church makes people afraid that if they don't do what they say then they will go to Hell. I think it sets up a whole attitude of fear. If people can get a rough idea of what it's like, they will be better prepared.*

S: It's hard to project precisely what it's like due to the limitations of the spoken language. But perhaps this will give them a clue as to how the actual concepts are.

Chapter 7
So-Called "Bad" Lives

S: The one absolute true and loving God, who is the master of all universes, is not a vengeful and hateful God. There is no such God in any universe. He has no use for retribution. There is no need in His scheme of life for punishment. There is already enough punishment on your Earth at this time without adding to it. We would say that the concept of karma is an effect, it is not a cause. The concept has been given through careful consideration as an explanation of why things happen.

D: *To us it's difficult to understand why some people seem to be more depraved than others. An easy answer is simply to accept it as karma from another life. Do you have an explanation as to why some people's lives seem to run quite smoothly their entire life, and others have so much turmoil and conflict?*

S: Perhaps it's because you're looking at one life at a time. Were you to look at that soul's progression with an extended view; that is, perhaps 100 lifetimes instead of just one, perhaps you would see that not all lifetimes are easy for everyone nor are all lifetimes difficult for everyone. There is given in each progression the experiences which are appropriate for *that* particular lifetime, be they easy or difficult. The experience that is the lifetime is not the truth of the experience. It is the lesson that is learned from that lifetime. And therein lies the truth. The *lesson is* the fruit of the lifetime and not how easy or how difficult it is. Again, were you to see an extended view of many lifetimes you would see that in all cases there are those which are easier and those which are more difficult. By saying that one is in a very difficult lifetime for this time period would only mean that their lessons require a lifetime which is comparatively more difficult than someone else's.

D: *So what is the purpose of reincarnation? To correct what you did in the past?*

S: The purpose is to learn more. To always learn more. For never can you learn all there is to know in one simple lifetime. The purpose of living again is not to correct, but to add to. Your knowledge cannot be complete with one simple lifetime. Many lifetimes must be lived to enable you to completely understand those lessons which you yourself assigned to yourself. There is no stern taskmaster with whip and shovel in hand ready to bury your body and punish you on the other side, and then return you to this land of displeasure. The experiences of life and rebirth should be viewed with a more positive outlook. That is, one of learning and loving and not of punishment and sorrow. It is all in attitude. For that which you create, you live, and that which you live, you create.

D: *Are there only good spirits where you are now?*

S: Evolving spirits. There is no good or bad.

D: *But people do have bad lives. How do you view that?*

S: People have bad lives because they're not dealing with the problems that are thrust out, problems that they themselves help to choose. They think that because they have no control over what happens to them, why should they have to work at it. Life has to be worked at; it can't be just skated through from day to day.

D: *There are people who do very bad things during their lifetime. What purpose would that serve?*

S: Sometimes that's not all the person that is doing it. Sometimes it is other forces getting in on that. And it doesn't serve a purpose except showing others that this is how low a person can fall to. In that manner it serves its purpose. But no matter how far that person, or that soul goes down, there is always room to bring themself out of it - by work and preparation and by facing the problems they'll have. This is what needs to be worked on.

D: *It says in the Bible that we must learn to be perfect.*

S: It is not expected of humans to become perfect, although some have. This is, of course, the exception rather than the rule. To *strive* to be perfect is the lesson.

D: *I was thinking that the only way to become perfect is to learn all these lessons, which is very difficult on the Earth plane.*

S: One learns what is perfect by experiencing that which is not. So it is as important to learn what is not perfect as it is to learn what is. There cannot be the understanding of that which is given until there is experienced that which is taken.

D: *Does that mean that everyone has to experience so-called "bad" lives in their progression so they can under stand these things?*

S: We would not say that one *has* to. However, many choose this as a method of accelerating their learning process. None wish to remain any longer than they must in physical form, for that is not a true state of being. So, those lessons which most rapidly accelerate one's learning to the point where one need not incarnate further are the lessons which are most cherished or sought.

D: *I thought I understood you to say that we had to have the bad in order to understand the good.*

S: There is no rule which says that the bad must be experienced. There is however the reality of the insight which comes from experiencing the one in order to fully understand the other. This is not a rule; this is a fact.

D: *Yes, I've heard it said that you cannot appreciate happiness unless you've known sadness. You know the opposites of everything.*

S: That is accurate. And so it would be appropriate to look with compassion on those who seem to be in their most negative state, as they are learning those lessons which will allow them to become most positive.

D: *Do you think they chose these negative experiences for their growth?*

S: Many do. Many find themselves in these situations and so it could be said that they are given a gift in order to experience those lessons more fully.

D: *It would seem that no one would want to have negative experiences if they had a choice.*

S: That is accurate. One should look beyond the experience itself at the lessons gained in order to understand why one would choose such an experience. There would not be a wholesome personality involved were one to derive pleasure from this or that "bad" experience. The disharmony is a lesson in and of itself in order to more fully appreciate and to comprehend that which is of the harmonious nature. The lessons are learned, however, in this manner.

D: *I was thinking that the person who is coming into a life may decide to have some negative experiences to pay back for something he has done in the past?*

S: We would not say "pay back," for that is not an accurate concept of universal law. One might necessarily *need* to understand the reasoning behind the commission of an act, in order to enlighten the individual so that this act need not recur and hinder their progress. In order to establish this awareness then it would be necessary for that entity to experience the complimentary reality, or to be on the other end of the stick, so to say.

D: *That's what I meant; they would choose these experiences on purpose. But the warning would be given that they might overdo it once they get into the physical.*

S: These warnings would be more appropriately given concerning other physical energies, not necessarily about any one particular lesson involved. Many of a physical nature are pleasant but are harmful when indulged excessively. And one could then possibly lose sight of one's path due to an overindulgence of any particular energy.

D: *That's right; you can overdo the good things, too. I suppose it would be very boring if you just had a good life with nothing happening and no problems to solve. Do you think the main thing is that a person learns something from the experience?*

S: That would be the whole reason and justification for the experience in the beginning.

D: *But some people don't seem to learn anything. They just seem to go on and on making the same mistakes.*

S: Until they eventually learn. And then it would not be necessary to repeat these mistakes.

D: *I have been told there is no punishment no matter what they do.*

S: There most certainly is punishment. And the worst punishment of all is that punishment which we deal ourselves. *We are* our own judge and jury. *We* decide which is appropriate behavior and which is not. And so we must decide our own penance when we find we have transgressed those laws, universal or personal, which dictate what is acceptable and what is not.

D: *Then we do it ourselves. There is no God or higher judge that dictates the punishment to us. Is that correct?*

S: That would be a fairly accurate statement. However, there are situations where the entity's awareness has become so clouded from overindulgence that insight has been lost, and an awareness of the scope of the problem cannot be appreciated. Then it is necessary for a higher order to assist the individual in appropriating those experiences necessary for the clearing of the entity's awareness.

D: *That makes more sense. Some people say you do it all yourself. But I had one girl who had made many mistakes in past lives, and she had a guide instructing her in what to do next. It seemed like a contradiction because she had no choice in the matter.*

S: There always are contradictions when one sets up an absolute law. For absolutely there will be contradiction.

D: *Someone else said that this proved she could not manage her own affairs, so to speak.*

S: That would then be an accurate statement.

D: *Do you think sometimes the personality gets caught up in these negative experiences and situations and doesn't try to change?*

S: This is accurate. Many find they have lost the path of their intended goals and so seem to maintain these negative experiences. This is a true possibility when incarnating and is one of the risks involved. This awareness of the possibility of losing sight of one's path by overindulgence in the physical energies is explained prior to each incarnation.

D: *The masters offer them the choices by saying, "You can do it this way but you might get carried away."*

S: This is given as a warning, and not so much as a choice. The entity themself must choose their path with information given from Akaskic records and universal truths. With this information these entities then determine what would be most appropriate for that incarnation, and the circumstances of how to manifest that reality.

D: *What about sin? Is there any such thing?*

S: Sin is basically doing what you *know* is wrong. Doing it knowingly. You can't sin if you don't know that it is wrong. You have to have morals to be able to sin. This is where man differs from the animal, the fact that man has conscience. When he kills someone and he knows that it is wrong, that is sin. When an animal does it, he does it unknowingly; therefore, the animal is without sin. He does it mostly for survival or for food-never senselessly.

D: *Then if someone does something without meaning to or if they don't realize they are doing something wrong, is that a sin?*

S: It's a lesser sin. They have the sin of being unaware which is something that has to be learned. You have to learn to be aware of your fellow beings; to the point that you don't *want* to hurt them, that their pain is yours.

D: *I always wondered if they considered anything a sin on your side.*

S: They consider it great injustices.

D: *Well, on Earth we have the Bible and it says that many things are sins.*

S: Many of those that you have been told are sins-like you hear of the "Seven Deadly Sins" that the Catholics thought up-were later additions that they added at their own wish. It was a control.

D: *Then the people on the other side do not consider these to be bad?*

S: Some of them are, but each person has to work out their own. There's no such punishment as saying this person is going to be thrown into the pit of fire for everlasting. There's no such thing as that, unless that person is punishing themself in that manner. *"They"* don't do it.

D: *People say everything is black and white and goes by the Bible.*

S: But the Bible itself has been changed throughout the centuries to what they feel is right or what they feel the truth to be. For centuries that was the control they had over the people, the masses. By saying, if you don't do what we say is there, then you will burn in-as they called it-Hell.

D: *But they say it is the Word of God.*

S: It started out that way. And to a large extent it still is. But everyone can warp it to his or her own viewpoint, to say what they think that it should say. It is a very noble book.

The intention was faultless but the transcription was somewhat faulted. There are in-accuracies. However the intent is as true today as it was during Christ's reign.

D: *Did these inaccuracies come from the translations?*

S: Not so much intentional, but merely mistakes which are bound to happen in a human endeavor. But there are other great books that have been written that are just as valid and also teach enlightenment. Things like the *Bhagavad Gita,* the *Koran,* different things like that.

Later when this subject awakened, I asked her to pronounce the name of the book, *Bhagavad Gita,* and she could not. Neither of us had ever heard of it. I found a definition of the *Gita* in *The Dictionary of Mysticism* by Frank Gaynor. "*Bhagavad Gita:* Sanskrit for *Song of the Divine One.* The title of a celebrated philosophic epic poem inserted in the *Mahabharata* [Hindu sacred scripture] containing a dialogue between Krishna and Arjuna which clearly indicates the relationship between morality and absolute ethical values in the Hindu philosophy of action (karma yoga). It is considered to be one of the most influential philosophical poems of Sanskrit literature. The exact date of origin is unknown." Sanskrit is one of the oldest languages on our Earth and is considered the "mother" of the modern Indo-European languages. There are many translations of the *Gita* available in English. The *Koran is* the sacred book of the Moslems and is considered by many Moslems to be too sacred to translate into *any* language although there are English translations available.

S: All paths lead in one direction. Some have a few more sidetracks along the way but everyone can learn from all these things and would be a more well-rounded person for doing so. By being close minded you lose much of the experience of life. You should never rely on one path as being *the* way, *the* ultimate. For in all paths there lies truth and in all paths there lies falsehood.

You must spend your life sifting through them to find what *is your* truth to discover; what you know to be truth for yourself. It does not have to necessarily be truth for others and you must accept this. It is not an easy path to be different.

D: *Society usually discourages things like this. Is it wise to encourage people to question?*

S: Yes. For in that questioning they will find truth and it will sustain them.

MURDERERS

D: *What happens to make a person become a criminal?*

S: There are many reasons why this would happen. This could be a taught function. That is, many are taught through parental neglect or abuse to become criminal. Criminal is a definition which speaks of stepping out of social boundaries; that is, overstepping those boundaries which are socially acceptable. Of course, with varying social customs it could be seen that some activities at one point, even in one culture, could be criminal and yet in that very same culture in another time frame would not be. From a spiritual standpoint there is no such thing as criminal as this is a social phenomenon which speaks of overstepping social boundaries. We would ascribe to the philosophy of doing harm by retarding one's forward progress. However, from a spiritual point of view there is not what you would call criminal activity. This could be a manifestation of a spiritual imbalance. However it would not be spiritually criminal, it would be socially criminal. Actions manifested on a physical plane would overstep or step out of those social boundaries which would then color or decree that the activity is, as you would call it, "criminal."

D: *You said that no higher deity punishes you, that people do these things to themselves. Suppose someone had been a murderer. How would they punish themselves?*

S: They can choose to go back and, for instance, have to leave that existence at the prime of their life when they are the happiest. In that way they are punishing themself because they are putting themself in the place of the person whose life they cut down, at whatever time. They have to know what it feels like. They have to see it from the other side.

I think we all know of cases like this. It is one of the most difficult to understand. Why seemingly good people who have never harmed anyone are cut down in the prime of their life, and why others are killed suddenly just when they are finally realizing a life-long dream. It has always seemed so unfair, but apparently on the ever-balancing scales of karma it makes perfect sense.

D: *Then this is a punishment they have chosen for themself?*

S: That is their own choice. No one is ever forced to go back into the body.

D: *I have always thought that a murderer would be repaid by being murdered by someone else. A sword for a sword, so to speak.*

S: There are other alternatives. Because if it were true that the only way he could work it out was to be murdered himself, then that would shift the negative karma to someone else. This would simply be shifting the load around rather than working it out and getting humanity in general past that.

D: *What if they were killed by their former victim?*

S: Then the former victim would have the murder on their karma. Although they were murdered in a former incarnation, the working out of that karma does not involve turning around and murdering somebody else. That is a rather drastic means of working it out. There are other alternatives which are the soft way, as some people

140

would call it. And it works out better in the long run, working it out the gentle way.

In my work with regressions I have had cases of people being born into a family with the same victims they had killed in a former lifetime. In these cases they are trying to work out their karma with each other through love. Maybe this is one of the soft or gentle ways. This would seem to be a much better way than, "I will kill you because you killed me."

Also, as was mentioned in an earlier chapter, it may be worked out by having to return and be a servant or a protector of the one they had killed, thus dedicating their life to that person in that manner.

ANOTHER VERSION:

S: Something violent like a murder committed in the heat of passion will take several lifetimes to pay back. And those ways of repaying are as numerous as the times it has been done. It depends on the individual karmas of the people involved. Generally what happens is that in their future lifetimes they will continually be involved in a close relationship of some sort with the person they murdered. And that is usually, in the first few lifetimes, an antagonistic type relationship. Because the person who was murdered finds that for some reason they fear or hate this person and doesn't understand why. And meanwhile this person, the murderer, feels compelled to know them and be around them because he wants to make up for what he did in the past lifetime. It takes several lifetimes to work it out. One who does something as violent as murder has almost indefinitely lengthened the amount of time he must stay in the physical portion of the karmic cycles before he can go into the spiritual plane to remain and continue through his karmic cycles there.

D: *Then murder is one thing that can't be worked out as easily on the spiritual. It has to be dealt with on the physical?*

S: It is best to work out things that have violent karma like that on a physical level because the physical level is base enough to handle the violent vibrations involved. To work it out on the spiritual level, there's a risk of disrupting other people's karma because it's a delicate balance.

D: *Isn't there always the chance that the person might kill again if this is very strong in their karma?*

S: This is the purpose of the schools in-between lives. To help them work it out, to where they would not be as apt to kill again in future lives. We try to prevent them getting locked into a vicious cycle.

D: *If they continue to do these things, it would seem that apparently they weren't over there long enough to get rid of these feelings.*

S: They'd go to the resting place. How can I explain this? If the spirit is in the resting place not because it's been damaged but simply because it's not advanced, and if they decide that they want to reenter the physical plane, there's really nothing you can do. You allow them to enter the physical plane because they're a healthy spirit, they're just not advanced. But the spirit that has been damaged by something that they have done in their past incarnations, even though they may want to enter the physical plane, they would not be able to because the damage they have sustained prevents them from doing so without help from someone who is higher up. Sometimes the damaged spirit will be assisted to reincarnate for a specific purpose in working out a specific part of their karma. But at other times, even if a spirit wants to go and it's not time yet, then they say, "No, you have some more healing to do first."

142

D: *I was wondering if there was any way you could stop them if they wanted to come back.*

S: If they're a healthy spirit, no, they can go ahead and reincarnate. And the forces that govern the universe keep everything in order and make sure that they don't try to reincarnate in a body that already has a spirit.

D: *I run into cases where someone dies and they want to come back immediately. They don't have any time over there at all.*

S: Yes, that often happens when they're in the period of transition. As I mentioned, after they have completed the period of transition if they decide to come back immediately; if they are healthy they are able to do so. They just work on more karma. But most spirits choose to stay on this plane for a while to learn more and to advance more. Because the learning and preparation you do here carries over in your subconscious and in your attitudes about whatever wisdom you are able to gain. In this way you're more successful in your karma.

D: *Then it's not really good for a spirit to turn right around and come back immediately?*

S: Not really. It could be counterproductive. But some spirits are impatient.

D: *I think some of them are so wrapped up in the physical they think that is all there is. In those cases where they come back immediately they wouldn't have had any chance to work on karmic relations or see their patterns, would they?*

S: No, that's true. They are usually the people who think their lives seem all messed up and confused and complain, "Why doesn't anything ever go right?" It is because they came back disorganized.

D: *They didn't have any plan of action, so to speak.*

S: Right. So everything falls apart at the seams, so to say. They came back too soon and were ill prepared. If they could have waited just a little bit and organized themselves, then things would have gone much better. Now sometimes if a spirit just doesn't seem to want to change, they are kept in a special place between lifetimes to help them grow and develop for the next incarnation. But it's kept on a very delicate balance and it is done very carefully.

D: *What kind of a place would that be?*

S: It's hard to describe. There's a different plane for working out special problems like that. It's not used for a long-term working out like the higher spiritual planes are. It's mainly used in-between lifetimes to help somebody work out a specific problem, so they'll be better prepared for the next lifetime and can make progress on their karma. If this were not so, some would get locked into a vicious cycle and would never progress and that is not good. So they are helped to progress in-between lifetimes because everything in the universe must continue to progress.

D: *Would this special place be like a school? Or what kind of an atmosphere would it be?*

S: It's like a retreat.

D: *Keeping them in isolation away from the others?*

S: No, it's like going to a monastery to meditate and contemplate. There they meet with others that have similar problems and with a spiritual guide. They must work out these problems and figure out why they did what they did and where they need to develop to overcome these things.

D: *I was thinking of the version people have of Hell. It wouldn't be like that?*

S: No, that is a notion developed by the Christians. It really doesn't apply. It was mainly developed as a political device to help build the power of the Orthodox Church and to help overcome the influence of the Gnostics. This is a plane where you go to learn and to contemplate your mistakes and what you have done. There are always advanced souls who are there voluntarily to help you develop and to help you prepare for the next life. Because it's a growing process. It's like bringing up a child. When a child does something wrong, you wouldn't throw him into the oven.

Which would be figuratively similar to our belief of Hell. Throwing the sinner into the fire.

S: You set the child down and talk with them about what they did wrong, and help them to realize why it was wrong and try to find a better action to use in a similar situation in the future.

D: *But what if the person refuses to listen and wants to go back into the physical anyway?*

S: If they're not ready to go back into the physical they cannot because everything must be balanced just right for them to be able to go. If they have not learned anything from seeing a major mistake, then things are not in balance yet and they are given some more time. Sometimes if someone still hasn't learned anything from a particular mistake and refuses to listen, they are sent back into a similar situation and they'll have a further chance to realize alternative actions. The masters try to do this in a way that will not have a serious consequence on the spirit's karma so it will not be as difficult for them to progress.

D: *But you hear about people that don't seem to have any morals at all.*

S: That is true. It doesn't work all the time. There are a few who are incorrigible. But most souls want to grow and want to become better and more advanced. It's just a matter of telling them and getting them to open up to the knowledge that is there for them.

D: *What happens to someone who just seems to be animalistic? They seem to have no morals or conscience and keep repeating the same mistakes?*

145

S: Sometimes these are spirits who are not very highly developed. They have much karma but they really don't care. They just want to enjoy the physical sensation of being on the physical plane. They really don't care about the karma that they rack up, so to speak. There is another special place on the planes. Your physical equivalent would be like a hospital. It is for these souls that are very damaged, and we try to help them become better. It's much like psychotherapy and sometimes it takes a long time. What gains you make are so minuscule that it's hard to keep track of them, and it's a very slow process. Mostly advanced spirits work with these because it takes an inordinate amount of patience and knowledge.

D: *To me that seems like the humane way to do it. But I keep thinking of our concept of places like Hell. There is never a time when a soul is so damaged, as you said, that they would just wash their hands of them and throw them out?*

S: No. There's no place to throw them out to. All of us are *here*. We all interact with each other and we must work with each other. And the ones that are particularly difficult to work with are helped by the spirits that have the greatest amount of patience and knowledge.

D: *Of course this is always benefitting that person's karma too; to be able to work with someone like that.*

S: Oh, yes, these are usually spirits that are close to or have reached their ultimate.

D: *They would have infinite patience. So there's no way they would just say, "Oh, forget about it. There's no hope for him."*

S: No. They keep working with them. Sometimes after a few incarnations some so-called "human" feelings start to work their way into their hearts, in spite of themselves. And they start to realize that there are higher planes of life and existence. That's when they finally start working on actively doing something about changing their karma.

To give an example of how damaged these souls are that come to the "hospital," in your plane there was one called Adolph Hitler. He was *not* sent to the hospital because his soul was not that damaged. He was sent to the learning portion of the plane, the retreat. He needed a quiet time of reflection because he had become-well, another metaphor-his nerves had become jangled. The problem in that lifetime was that he was an extremely creative person. He would have been a creative genius but he had no outlets for it because the Depression culture he was raised in did not allow for creative outlets. There was an inordinate amount of energy behind this creativeness, as there always is in these geniuses. It had to have another outlet somewhere and it warped his outlook on life and hence his thoughts and it developed into the final outcome. That which happened reflected mainly on his father's karma rather than his.

D: *(This was a surprise.) I wouldn't think of it that way.*

S: Because the root of the problem started when his father refused to let him study creative things.

D: *But still, Hitler was the one who did those horrible things.*

S: It's hard to explain. (She paused, trying to think how to word it.) He started out with good intentions, wanting to be an artist or an architect or what have you. But he was not allowed to develop in that direction, and the energy there was warped. His main mistake was not being able to handle that energy in a constructive form, in another form besides creativeness. So he turned it to destructiveness. That is the main thing that he's had to work out.

D: *It seems as if he could have found an outlet for it in a more creative form, even though his father wouldn't allow him to do that.*

S: Yes, he could have become an engineer, for example.

D: *Isn't that kind of passing the buck, to blame his father?*

S: No. Hitler has to share his part of the blame, too. But it cannot be set solely upon him because the problem started with the narrow attitudes his father had developed. His father could have developed broader attitudes.

D: *But still it seems as if he didn't have to become so fanatical in his actions. You know what happened there.*

S: That was caused by the intensity of the creative energies. Had he been able to develop into an artist instead, he would have been a crazy artist and fanatical about that. But it would have been accepted as being Bohemian.

D: *At least he wouldn't have harmed anyone.*

S: True, except maybe himself.

D: *But as it was, it snowballed to where he affected millions and millions of people. I would have thought he would have ended up in the "hospital."*

S: He wasn't that damaged. Twisted, yes; damaged, no. Mainly what he needed was quiet and time to straighten things out. Those souls who are in the hospital have been so damaged by having gone through the same portion of karma over and over and over that they feel as if they're stuck in that karma. Whereas, in the case of Adolph Hitler, this was the first time this had happened to him. In his former lifetimes he also had a strong creative impulse and he was in situations where he could let it develop. But in this lifetime it was blocked. The lesson he had to learn was how to handle that energy when he could not have things the way he wanted it-to handle it in any way that would fit in with the pattern that he had to live in. And he did not handle that aspect well. That was the main part of his karma that he is going to have to rework in a future lifetime-being able to handle undesirable situations.

D: *Well, didn't he create more karma for himself by what he did and all the people's lives he affected?*

S: He created more karma for himself, true. At this point it's difficult to say how much since this happened so recently.

D: *You mean it's not all analyzed yet?*

S: Yes. It will take several lifetimes, several incarnations to be able to see just how it affected the balance of things and how much more he has to work out.

D: *I was thinking of all the millions of people that were killed as a direct result of his life.*

S: That is true, he sent the orders for them to be killed but he was partially influenced by people around him. And he did not derive the same amount of direct physical pleasure from it that the actual executioners did. What I am saying is that he gave the orders for these people to be killed and that does reflect on his karma, but the men who received these orders to build the gas chambers and use them, the guards and others took direct physical pleasure in seeing these people die.

D: *Yes, he didn't really do the actual killing, but he did nothing to stop it.*

S: He merely made it allowable for these people to be killed. That's why it reflects on his karma, that he allowed it to happen. He encouraged them to do it but he kept his own hands clean, so to speak, by not doing it directly himself. It reflects badly on his karma that he created a political system that would allow this. Many of the men in the system were doing this because they wanted to. They were misfits in normal societies and they took direct physical pleasure in committing these atrocities.

D: *But he also had the fanatical obsession with obliterating a race. He began the extermination of the Jews, a whole race of people with his fanaticism and persecution.*

S: Yes. He was against any race that was not pure German; "Aryan" as he called it. He wanted his beloved Deutschland to be in the same sort of situation that the United States had been in 100 or 150 years earlier, with space to grow and become a major power, and have space for the people to multiply. He wanted to have a huge nation with many Germans and be able to use their culture to influence the whole world, the way the

Americans had. And he wanted to obliterate any race of people that stood in the way of this goal. This was part of the twisting process of that creative impulse, because clearly it was impossible to do this without harming many people. Had he been able to become a creative genius he could have contributed to that mighty culture of Deutschland that he loved so well.

D: *I was thinking that he had such a prejudice that that would have a karmic reaction too.*

S: That was just part of his soul being twisted. He was able to work out that prejudice through contemplation and meeting with the spiritual masters.

D: *He is definitely one example that is very difficult to understand.*

S: Yes, it is a very complex situation.

D: *What about somebody like a "Jack the Ripper"? Would that not affect him at all in his next life?*

S: Certainly it would. And please, we tread very carefully here, for we wish not to offend your sense of proprieties nor your moral standards. For we feel that your sense of morals is very delicate and we wish not to disturb these. However, we would please ask that you bear with us while we give you an insight which you might not have. Perhaps there were lessons learned from that experience of, as you say, Jack the Ripper, which were positive for this person. Of course, there was much harm done to the victims, and by your social standards the crimes were heinous. These acts were not acceptable social behavior. However, again it could be said that this individual learned through participation in those acts. Maybe a lesson of what indulgence is, of what it is to be self-involved and without regard for human life. This was perhaps an important lesson for that individual. We would also say that perhaps there were those lessons learned, difficult though they were, by those you would call "the victims." And could we also perhaps inject another possibility here. That the participants in this episode, unseemly as it is, were voluntary from the inner planes. That they had contracted from their planning stages before their incarnations to participate in this event. And to so give to your society a yardstick by which the standards of your morals could be measured. An example of what is or is not acceptable social behavior. Do you see that in all actions, whether good or bad, there are lessons learned? Not only for those who are direct participants, but those who are bystanders or observers. So were it to be said that this was a horrible crime, then that could be accepted. Yet it could also be accepted, without denying the horror of such crimes, that many lessons were learned by all involved. And let me speak of the life force. That consciousness which was in the body was not killed. It was simply transferred to another plane of existence. The life force, which is even in every cell of your body, was transferred and was not lost. The simple physical makeup of the body changed from one of an organized state to one of a disorganized state. Technically speaking, death is nothing more than rearranging molecules on a physical level, and displacing consciousness from a vehicular enclosure to one of a free nature. Life has always been and life always is. There is no such thing as taking life, for life simply changes to another form. We speak here strictly from a technical point of view with all moral standards and emotional values removed.

D: *What about the victim? The person who is killed violently by another person? Is this traumatic to them?*

S: To a great extent it also depends upon the preparation for souls. There have been a great many souls who came to this side through wars who were not traumatized at all. They knew that this death would occur to them and accepted self-same. Others were exceedingly traumatized, so much so that they had to go to the resting place. It is not always an equal situation. Two people can

151

die side-by-side at the same instant with what you would look at as the same amount of trauma. And one may be traumatized by it and the other not.

D: *Does this have anything to do with the age of the souls and their previous experience?*

S: Not so much the age of the souls as their understanding of the Christ in all-self. At times a young soul can comprehend this with greater understanding than one termed an old soul.

D: *You told me once that the way someone dies has meaning as well as the way they live.*

S: This is also true. In many cases certain types of death will erase great karma. Long, slow deaths are meant to bring learning to that individual. And if they learn through that they will amass great good karma.

SUICIDE

D: *What about suicides?*

S: Yes, those are very tragic cases, for this is truly one of the saddest truths which exist. There are simply no words to describe this situation in all its entirety. The suicide must come to the realization of the gravity of what he has done. For there is not simply the breaking of the contract, the individual's soul energy is thrown into complete disharmony. The suicides, depending on what shape they're in, sometimes go to the hospital and sometimes to the contemplation area. More times than not, one or two other entities are assigned to this person to explain why it is extremely wrong to take life. To take the life of self is the only thing that can truly be considered upon this side to be sin, because life is so precious. These people are confused and mixed up about what life is really all about and what they need to accomplish. They are not able to see the solutions they can work out with the karma they have on hand. And in between lifetimes they learn to broaden their outlook and to look at greater aspects of things, so they can work out problems without giving up on them. Suicides normally do not go back into the body quickly. Usually it is too traumatic. They can't solve the problem that caused them to commit suicide quickly enough to go back into the body that soon. They are talked to and helped. They have to learn why they did it and what brought them to that point. It usually takes a long time before they are ready to face it. If it is extremely bad they are taken to the resting place so they will forget the trauma of why they got to this stage in life, to the point where they would contemplate the taking of one's own life. Suicide brings upon that soul much bad karma that will have to be erased by much good in preceding and succeeding lives.

D: *If this is the worst thing anyone can do, do they punish themselves when they come back?*

S: Sometimes it's not in the life they directly go into. They don't always go into a life that would be working on the problems that they had in the one directly previous. Sometimes it takes several existences to come to the point where they feel they can face those problems. But all problems are eventually dealt with. You can't avoid it. The best way to handle it is to come back into a life that will have its fair share of problems like the last life did. And the suicide is paid back by working out these problems and hanging in there and being viable and living to a ripe old age and having a good well rounded life. It may take several lives like this to pay back the suicide and to help balance the karma. You get on the right track by working out the problems that you gave up on before. A suicide *must* face the same situation and problem again until they learn an acceptable way of solving it. They can never run away from it. They only prolong their progress and create disruption.

153

D: *I know you have difficulty with our concept of time. But how much time is involved before a suicide finds release?*

S: This varies from individual case to case. Each soul does not learn at the same rate as the other. It depends upon that soul's confusion and feelings of worthlessness and loss, more than any other thing. Suicide is not forgiven lightly but it can be worked out. It is not impossible to be worked out, like some would have you think. Nothing is impossible to work out; it's just that some things take longer than others because some things are more complicated. Yes, the killing of self is the ultimate wrong because that throws the karma out of balance. Killing yourself, murdering yourself, that's not working out any karma. That's creating more karma.

D: *Some people commit suicide to escape a problem.*

S: To commit suicide to escape a problem just amplifies that problem that they will have to live through again. They are not escaping anything; they are just making it worse upon themselves. They are really not solving anything; they are simply creating more problems. Suicide is no solution.

D: *Would suicide ever have anything to do with other people's lives?*

S: Yes. Many times when a suicide happens it is an opportunity for the other souls in the family to learn from the experience. For example, say a boy kills himself and from that experience the mother realizes that she was too overbearing and she learns to be more understanding. Then she has learned from it, although it has been a hard lesson.

D: *In some cases wouldn't this be karma on the family or the friends that were left behind?*

S: (Emphatically) *Never* is suicide part of karma! Suicide is one aspect of free will.

D: *I see. Then it can never be viewed as being good for*

anything.

S: That is correct. There are no winners.

D: *But does it ever happen to directly influence somebody else's karma?*

S: No. Because the person who suicides would be cutting their karma short and it would not be fair to them.

D: *I've heard that people more or less have a contract when they come into a life. And suicide would be reneging on that contract-not fulfilling their commitment.*

S: Before someone comes into a life they meet with their spiritual masters and they figure out, in general, how much karma they can work out in this life if they make their decisions well. It's almost like a classroom assignment. The person says, "Well, this is what I will try to get accomplished in this lifetime." Now, if they don't get it all accomplished it does not reflect badly on them. The fact that they are working on it and trying, this is what matters. And if midway through, just as they were barely getting started, they cut it short by killing themselves... well, not only have they not accomplished anything they said they would try to, that they earnestly promised they would try to accomplish, but they have created more karma that they need to work on. So it's a negative experience all around.

D: *They still must work out their problems and their karma. It would defeat the purpose to leave before they accomplished this.*

S: That is accurate. But if there is an "X" amount of work to be done in a lifetime, and should this "X" amount of work be done or accomplished before they have lived a full lifetime, then should they wish to pass over, there is no need for them to continue in the physical should they wish or desire not to. Then departure can be arranged through proper channels. It is the casting off of the body prematurely or before the job is done that can never be tolerated.

Chapter 8
Guides

ALMOST EVERY CULTURE in the world has beliefs in guardian angels or protector spirits. Do they really exist?

S: There are guardian spirits. Usually it is someone that you have had a close bond with before and they are attending school or whatever on the spirit plane. They are helping you go through your learning period and helping protect you. These are serving their purpose on the spirit level.

D: *Are they assigned to a certain person?*

S: They can choose their own affinities. They are with you from the day you are born.

D: *Then you're not alone when you enter the physical body.*

S: No one is ever alone. The aloneness is a walling of one's self away from others. There are always others there to share the experience if you will just break down the walls and allow them to help you.

D: *If they are not incarnate, how do they help?*

S: This is somewhat difficult to explain because of a lack of understanding of the spirit level. But there is work to be done on a spirit level as well as on the physical level. There are those who, after an incarnation, must go to schools on the spirit level, and some of these will be teachers in schools. There are many other ways that they can help, including guiding those on the physical plane.

D: *Do they always have your best interest at heart?*

S: Most of the time the ones that surround you do, yes. You must learn to protect yourself from those who perhaps do not.

D: *Is your own personal guide powerful enough to keep the other influences away?*

S: Yes. As long as you also learn to surround yourself with what is good. This will keep away anything that is negative. There is no good or bad; there is only positive and negative. Any experience that is learned from is never negative.

D: *But it is sometimes difficult to know whether something is good for you or not. How would you know if other influences are trying to sway you the other direction?*

S: By opening yourself up to perceive what the final outcome of what they are recommending will be. All, every one of you are able to see. And if you see that things will go wrong, then you know that this entity does not wish you well.

D: *But you know humans-they can be fooled.*

S: We are not perfect. Otherwise we would no longer enter the body.

D: *How can we know if it is our guide that is trying to influence us and not be fooled?*

S: If you think of yourselves in your daily lives, often you are in conflict with yourselves as to whether to do this or that. As an example, in dieting, when one may be giving in to the temptation of having a chocolate sundae. That part of you which craves the sundae is asking for gratification. And yet the higher part of you, which recognizes the need for diet, is saying, "No, we shall not." So you can see there is a division within yourself. Your guides feel as if they are a part of yourself and an extension. In this manner you know that this is your other soul that is speaking. If someone is just giving you advice and you feel hesitant about it, you must perhaps watch that source from which it comes. If it is from your guide, it will feel very right. He will never *make you* do anything, he would only suggest. If force is involved it is definitely not a positive entity because then your free will is overridden. You make conscious decisions and are not being told to do this or that, for this is a human endeavor as well. The guides do not run the show from the sidelines as some seem to think. They have their part to play and you have yours. It is a mutual, consensus agreement, a partnership between spiritual and physical. They do their work and you do yours.

D: *There are many people who do think that those on your side run the show.*

S: Yes, and they must be led to understand that there is simply a shared responsibility in these matters. Many decisions are purely human and are based on human thought, human experience and human concept. Guides try to assist you with their wisdom and their experience. If you are torn between your decision and your guide's guidance, this is not wrong; this is simply a choosing process. They are merely there to offer help and assistance. It is not demanded that one strictly follow one's guides. They are merely assistants. You are the master of your destiny.

D: *Then our guides and spirit helpers try to influence us to do the right thing?*

S: This needs to be clarified. Influence is not an accurate word. The guides and helpers do not try to influence. Assist or enlighten would be more accurate. The difference may seem very subtle but it is very important. Earth is the plane of choice. You have complete freedom to choose that which you may. If you need assistance in your choice, that is their purpose. They merely help and try to show or clarify. It is not as if you were puppets being manipulated from the other side. You have your destinies firmly in your own hands. They are bystanders who are able to assist at a moment's notice and are waiting for whenever you ask for their assistance. They do not prod you into some imaginary destiny; you create your own destiny. The same thing can be said for you while you live in the physical. You should help each other unselfishly. Some people feel that they must help people whether they like it or not. You should not feel like *you must* help, regardless of your emotional state at that time. You should give help when you want to; then you can give the best quality help. What we are saying to you is this: Please don't feel you must help everyone all the time. Feel only that you should help when you feel you want to help. Forced help is worse than no help at all.

D: *Is this where free will comes in?*

S: That is exactly what it is.

D: *Then you are saying that because we have free will we are free to follow or disregard any advice we receive? And this goes for the spiritual as well as the physical?*

S: That is correct, but please visualize something before we leave that statement. If you saw a child playing with a bottle of poison, you would naturally run and grab this bottle from the child, would you not? Suppose the child slapped you and pushed you back and continued trying to open the bottle. What would you do then?

D: *I would persist.*

S: Suppose the child prevailed as strongly as you?

D: *Then I would say he deserved what he got.*

S: And so say we.

D: *Then is it possible for a guide to keep us from injuring our self?*

S: Yes, it is. They will inform you of an imminent occurrence. This is merely assistance. I can give you an example of what you might think would be a guide taking over for you. While driving, if a car were coming down the street at you unbeknown to you and was on a collision path, your steering wheel might suddenly veer to the left and out of harm's way. Of course, this doesn't happen, but if your guides were allowed to do this, that would be what would occur. You do the steering; they merely inform you.

D: *Would they ever do anything like that in the case of an emergency?*

S: If it was necessary. It has been done before but only under extreme situations. I'm not allowed to discuss this in detail as it would pre-influence you as to the workings at hand. But for the most part you need to know that your destiny is what you make it. Again, I say, forced help is worse than no help at all.

D: *But it's nice to know that we have help if we need it.*

S: That is correct. We on this side are often amused by the impetuousness and impatience of humans. This is because of the difference in the spiritual and physical worlds. In the spiritual world, a thought is as good as done. Merely thinking the thought produces the desired effect. In the physical, things are not quite that easy; thus the human must learn patience.

Since a thought on the spiritual plane makes things occur instantaneously, it is significant that on Earth we are given much more time between the thinking and the materialization of the thought, so that we have a chance to change our mind. If things occurred instantaneously here in our physical world, there could be many problems. Because of our human nature with its many flaws (selfishness, envy, jealousy, *etc.*), we would probably create chaos. We are not as pure minded in our intentions, and they have said before that the intent is the most important thing about what we wish to materialize.

S: The relationship between guide and guided is fluid and mercurial and changes from incarnation to incarnation and even within a single incarnation, as needed. There is no rigid set rule. The means are dictated by the need.

D: *How are guides selected for people?*

S: They are selected by the need at that period in a person's life. Some may be a guide throughout the incarnation. Others may be temporary or may come and go as needed. Through the course of a lifetime we may have several different guides. Their functions change as our lives change.

D: *Is there a difference between a guide, a counselor and a spirit? I have heard these terms used at different times.*

S: The guides *are* spirits. A counselor is of a higher order than a guide. A counselor has much more knowledge and experience from which to draw. A tank of experience, if you will. A guide is much more intimate and close to an actual incarnation. Such as one who possibly has recently left an incarnation and thus is still familiar with the intricacies of physical life. A counselor has usually been removed from an incarnation for some time and is drawn in for information. While the guides are more recently from an incarnation, the counselors have progressed above the incarnational need. Thus each in their own right is quite capable of doing the job each is assigned. A guide may know more of the physical. A counselor may know more detail.

This sounds rather like a schoolteacher going to a professor or the principal of the school for more advanced advice regarding a student. The teacher would naturally know the pupil on a more intimate basis because he is with him every day. The professor or principal might not be familiar with the student at all, but can offer advice because they have much more knowledge and experience. The principal also has not related to the pupils in the classroom on such an intimate level for quite a while. They are more removed from the situation, but as such they can give a much more unbiased opinion. I then asked if we could find out the name of our guides.

S: They will speak to you when it is necessary or relevant. There are really no names used here on the spirit plane; there are only sounds, vibrations and colors. Naming is a habit peculiar to the human race. It allows for easy identification. But these names which you like to give to guides are somewhat derogatory or misleading, for names have a vibration and attaching or assigning a name to a guide can give it the wrong vibration. So it is best to know a guide more by vibrations than by name.

D: *You said it was possible for anyone to become a guide. Does it take quite a while to get to the position of being a guide to someone else?*

S: It depends solely on how you develop your karma. Some people who are able to really develop their karma in a positive way become a guide within one or two cycles of lifetimes. But others have to work on it longer. It just depends on the individual development. It's really a matter of attaining a particular spiritual plane. Once you've attained this plane you can be either a guide or sit on the general council (see Chapter 13) depending on which way you need to develop at that particular point. When you're in spiritual levels below this plane, then you're still growing in other ways and you're doing other things to help, but not as direct as being a guide.

D: *I've heard it said that some people ask when they cross over, "Will I now be allowed to guide other people?" And the answer is, "How can you be a guide when you still need a guide yourself?"*

S: Well, there are always those that are more advanced than you to help you out. It's like an adult guiding an adolescent who in turn turns around and helps a child, who in turn turns around and helps a toddler to stay out of trouble.

D: *I thought you have to go through a certain number of experiences or requirements before you could be a guide.*

S: That's so. When you get to the level where you can guide an individual person on the physical plane, then you've reached that stage of spiritual development where you can handle that responsibility in a spiritually mature manner without flubbing up. But that doesn't mean that you've stopped all your growing because someone more advanced than you is still helping you with *your* growing, while you in turn are helping someone else who's not as advanced with *their* grow*ing*. And that's the way the whole system works.

D: *But you could still make mistakes if you weren't ready for the job, so to speak, of guiding someone.*

S: But you're ready for the job when you're given the job. That would be a mistake on the ... there are no mistakes like that made. When you cross over, the energy patterns are perfectly clear and you can tell right away where someone is compatible and where they fit in and what level they're at and what they can do. And that's what you give them to do. You give it to them in such a way that it helps them to grow and develop so they can attain new abilities.

D: *Then there are no slip-ups.*

S: Right. Because that would be a slip-up in positioning, not a slip-up in what they can or can't do. If you give a person something that's beyond their capability, it's not their mistake; it's your mistake.

D: *Well, they always say you can learn a lot from teaching other people. Who are the ones who make these choices? You said it would be a slip-up on the part of whoever was telling them to do these things.*

S: I was using it as a metaphor.

D: *I was wondering if there was anybody up there who was saying, "All right now, it's your turn to go back and be a guide," or something like that.*

S: No. Since everything is energy here, everything is done according to how you fit in with the energy. As you work on helping other people, you're building up energy on your own. And when you get a certain amount of energy built up then it's time for you to re-enter the physical plane, because it takes energy to go back through the barrier and continue working on your karma once again from that level.

D: *Then you know it yourself. There's no one that says, "Well, it's time now for you to do these things."*

In our society we are used to having someone in charge of things. So I was trying to fit all this within those boundaries.

S: Correct. Everything's perfectly clear to everybody, so it's not a matter of telling anyone what to do because it's apparent to you and everyone else what needs you have and what you can and will do. Everything is seen in the form of energy here. Every thought and intention has energy that is apparent. And when it's time for you to go back and re-enter the physical plane, that's when the general council comes in and determines where you fit in the pattern. And that determines when and where and to whom you are born on the physical plane.

D: *Then the council has a lot to say over it.*

S: It's not necessarily having "say" over it; it's just a matter of helping, of making sure that the energy continues to flow the way it should. When someone needs to return to the physical plane then they re-enter that level of energy where they should in a way that's compatible with their energy and the surrounding energy, to make sure it ends up putting them back into contact with people that they have been in contact with before in other lifetimes. And hence you come up with linked karmas.

D: *What would happen if somebody is all set up and it's all planned out where they're supposed to come back, and at the last minute they change their mind?*

S: They don't, though.

D: *What if they decide they want to wait or they don't want to go in right at that time?*

S: The time for procrastinating is already past when you have set up the process for re-entering the physical plane. Before you decide to enter the physical plane you can spend as much time on the spiritual plane as you wish. When the point comes when you decide it's time for you to re-enter the physical plane, once you make that decision, it's set into motion. Then you're stuck with your decision because your energy starts flowing in that direction, to be redirected back into the physical plane. It's just a force of the universe that once you start the process, you have to follow it through.

D: *I was thinking in particular of babies that were stillborn; that maybe the spirit had decided to change its mind at the last minute and not come in.*

S: No, what happens with babies that are stillborn is that the parents bearing the baby need that experience in their lives at that point for their own development of their karma, for some reason or another, depending upon the individual circumstances.

D: *Well, I thought it would make sense, that maybe the spirit was not quite ready and wanted to wait or was trying to get out of the contract, so to speak. Or also in cases when they die when they're very young-just a few months old.*

S: The ones that die when they're very young, in those cases they are usually spirits that are advanced enough to occasionally go to the physical plane, not necessarily because they need to work out an aspect of their karma, but to help out someone else's karma. They do it to help them when for some reason the other person's karma will be benefited by just having a particular spirit within the realm of their lives for a short duration.

D: *Just a few months?*

S: Or even a few days. Then the spirit re-enters the spiritual plane and continues with what they were doing.

Later on if they need to go back to the physical plane to work out another lifetime of karma, they go ahead and do so. But sometimes more advanced spirits will volunteer to go to the physical plane for a short period of time to help give another spirits' karma a nudge.

D: *I keep thinking that they had something like a contract that they had to fulfill and they were hesitating or were wanting to renege on that contract.*

S: Contract is a bad word. It does not apply at all. Because when a spirit makes the decision, "I want to re-enter the physical plane," they don't make the decision until they're ready to follow through on it. If they feel like they're not ready to follow through on the decision, why make the decision? Once they decide, their energy starts flowing in that direction. And it's fitted into the overall pattern in such a way that it continues to develop their karma and fit into the overall pattern of the universe.

D: *The other spirits have given me these words. I guess we're trying to put this into terms we can understand from our physical viewpoint. That's why these words seem to apply. They were also looking at it from different viewpoints, I suppose. And I may have been talking to spirits that were not as highly developed.*

S: That's a possibility. Sometimes when it is time for the spirits on lower spiritual levels to re-enter the physical plane they don't perceive how the energy affects the whole system. They don't realize that their making the decision is a type of commitment. I will use an analogy. On your world you have a type of entertainment called a water slide. It's like pouring some water at the top of the slide. You can't recollect the water until it reaches the bottom of the slide and runs off the edge. This is like entering the physical plane again. Making the decision to enter the physical plane starts the energy flowing, and that's the equivalent of pouring the water out of the container at the top of the slide. To be able to recollect the water in its former state, that is, recollect your energy on the spiritual plane, you have to go down the slide. In other words, you have to follow through.

D: *You can't stop half way.*

S: Right. It's not because someone is holding a gun to your head, so to speak, and making you do it. It's just simply one of the laws of the universe on how energy flows. Once energy starts going through this pattern, the energy has to complete this pattern before it can be turned to other things. The spirits on lower levels of development have not been able to get a grasp of this overview yet, and so if they make the decision that they're ready to go back and they start having second thoughts they may feel like they're being compelled to go back. It's not because anyone's making them go back; it's just simply because they're already into the process of being poured onto the slide. They have to go down the slide before they can be collected at the bottom edge, so to speak.

D: *Things are already in motion.*

S: Exactly.

D: *Then these answers could be from people that are on lower levels of development.*

S: Yes, or perhaps they felt that you might not be able to understand answers from higher levels.

It is obvious that I would naturally be speaking to spirits at many levels of development. So their answers may not be contradictory. It is merely the truth from their viewpoint.

D: *But there are people in the physical who seem like they don't want to be here. They're very angry.*

S: Yes, these are spirits who are having trouble with negative karma and they're being somewhat recalcitrant. And the spirits who are attracted to negative karma are usually somewhat angry about being on the physical plane again because they're convinced they're going to screw up some more.

D: *That's why I get the feeling they were made to come back and they don't want to be here in the body.*

S: And so it's as if they're in the process of running around in that vicious cycle that I mentioned earlier.

Chapter 9
God and Jesus

W HEN YOU ASK ANYONE to describe their concept of God, you are asking a very complex question, because there are probably as many definitions for God as there are people. Our inner visualization of what God must be like is conditioned by our religious upbringing and this is what we usually fall back on. It would be very difficult to change our concepts of not only this but all the other ticklish topics that are approached in this book. It all requires an open mind-a mind that is willing to at least listen to other ideas, even though they may at first appear to be ridiculous and preposterous. I believe the early church had to present God in as simple a way as possible in order for the people of the times to conceive Him at all. I believe that people down through the ages just accepted these early presentations of Him and a great many did not bother to question further but believed the picture the church had given them. There may have been a few even in those days, who permitted themselves a broader view of Him. When we strip aside the brainwashing and conditioning and look at these concepts with a fresh mind, it is amazing how they do not contradict at all. They are merely different ways of saying the same thing.

First we have to get away from the concept of God as an old man. If anything, he would be a woman, because women are the creative aspect. However, he is neither male nor female. He does not have a gender. He is a huge energy that is beyond belief in its power and scope.

The following is the way different individuals in deep trance answered the question of how they perceived God in the spirit state between lives.

S: We would ask that you visualize this scene. In all creation from the very edges of every universe to the center and back, there is a force, unseen but there nonetheless, which is an invisible structure holding everything together. In concrete there is rebar (reinforcing bars), invisible to the naked eye, but holding the concrete together nonetheless. Are you familiar with this?

D: *Yes, I understand what you are saying.*

S: This then is the God concept. It is the rebar of the universe which holds all together, unseen but there nonetheless. For were this to phase out for even a fraction of a second there would be total, utter, complete destruction. This is the God concept which has been given personality status on your world.

S: I am observing the structure of this universe.

D: *Can you tell me what you see?*

S: I'm not sure this language is sufficient.

I have heard this from every entity I have ever spoken to. Our English language and probably every other language on Earth is just incapable of capturing the true picture of what the entity sees. I told her I understood this and asked her to attempt it anyway.

S: Right now I'm able to see into parts of the spectrum that you cannot see with your eyes. I can see the colors and the appearance of the cosmic rays that you cannot see. I can look into the very hearts of the planets and see the scintillating network, the latticework of the atoms that hold them together. It is extremely beautiful and powerful. The narrow band of waves that you can see with your eyes are different colors, and the broader bands that you cannot see are also different colors, until it gets to the bands that you observe by hearing. But I can still *see* them and see their colors too. It's part of the same electromagnetic spectrum.

D: *These bands are so high that we can only hear them. Then does that mean that sound also has color?*

S: Yes. Sound is much, much slower than what you call "light." But they're all vibrations and energy and I can see them all; the band that you perceive as light and then beyond what you see as light. I can observe it all. It is impossible to describe it because I can also see the ether. It's very beautiful. It would be much like observing aurora borealis. Picture all of space being filled with aurora borealis interconnecting and all the different colors mixing with each other. Where you have sheets and areas of energy and colors interacting and altering each other and causing changes to come to pass. It's very complex.

D: *We picture space as being black and empty. You mean it's actually full of all these colors and vibrations?*

S: Exactly! Vibrations, colors, energy, and they go through everything, too. Just because there's a planet sitting there going around the sun, that doesn't mean it blocks or drapes the energy. The energy just goes right through. All energy that's there to be affected gets affected. The entire universe, and then this universe is connected with the other universes.

D: *What is the source of all this energy?*

S: The energy has always been there. I don't really know the source. Perhaps there was a source at one time. Yet this energy is what the universes are built out of. And when the universes have lived their lives, they'll be broken back down into this energy. And then new universes will be built out of this energy again.

This sounds like reincarnation on a massive, gigantic scale. A never-ending, constantly repeating cycle affecting the largest and also possibly the very smallest of all creation.

D: *We're so used to thinking of light coming from the sun and such as that. I thought maybe this energy was coming from somewhere.*

S: No. Energy is all there is, and it fills up the all that there is. It's all energy. And the energy, in the process of being all that there is, transforms itself into various structures, which end up being planets and suns and energy and thoughts and various universes and what-have-you.

D: *What kind of a concept do you have of this "all that there is"?*

S: (Sigh) It's too big for even me to conceive all of it at once. The only way I can put it into words is: all that there is, ever, forever and ever. All that there is: is energy. And as the energy fluctuates-as energy does-the various universes come into existence as fluctuations of this energy.

D: *I was wondering if that would fit in with our God concept.*

S: Actually that concept is rather narrow. But considering the limited scope of your minds, you do the best you can. I'm not putting you down. I'm just stating a fact. The broadest concept of God that you can possibly conceive would still be as narrow as a thread compared to this "all that there is." And then you must consider that many of your fellow human beings have narrow concepts of God, which is unfortunate but that's the way it is. They're too frightened to open up for their full potential.

D: *I was just wondering if anything was directing any of this, the making of the universe, the making of the people and all that. That goes back again to our God concept.*

S: Energy is organized. Energy has always been organized. That is part of its basic structure. It is this basic organization which goes down to the very, very tiniest limits of its structure that cause things to appear in order and to be organized.

D: *It is because of this order that people think it has to be directed by something.*

S: No, it develops the way it should develop according to its organization as regular fluctuations in the energy. There are regular fluctuations back and forth from one area to the other that affect this universe and other universes in particular ways. The fluctuations vary from the extremely large and gigantic to the very teensy tiniest fluctuation possible, which your scientists won't ever discover the limits of. They keep discovering smaller subdivisions of energy but it doesn't appear that they'll ever get down to the very basic structure.

D: *I believe it's going to be very difficult for people to get away from the idea of a God directing things. They like to think that things are out of their hands and that an overall power is in charge.*

S: Yes. One of the major things in the next stage of human development is to realize that everyone is in charge of their own fate. That what they desire to come to pass is what comes to pass. Things that appear to happen out of the clear blue are a result of past causes, past thoughts or what-have-you that were sent out.

Another entity put this back into a concept I could more readily accept. He was talking about spirits from the higher levels coming down to our level to help us here on Earth.

S: It's sometimes useful to travel backwards and help those below. Spirits from the higher dimensions sometimes return to your dimension and help those on the physical world to raise their aware-ness. There is a dispensation given to those who would do this. It is allowed, so to say, and it is done. This is not a physical type of an experience.

D: *Who or what makes this allowance or approves of this?*

S: This is done by the councils who govern the universes. Each universe has a central council, and then there are local councils.

D: *This is a new idea to me. I've always thought of just one universe. Can you elaborate please?*

S: There are many universes, many, many universes. Ours is one particular universe, or the universe we are in here now is merely one universe of many. There are many, many different universes.

D: *This is a little hard for me to comprehend. Are they outside of our universe or what?*

S: They are in physical space. The concept demands a very broad imagination to conceive of the distances involved. There are political-political is not an accurate term but it is one which can be understood here. There are governments of spiritual levels. In each universe there are governmental levels which govern the individual and collective universes.

D: *Would this be equivalent to what people call a God or an over-all Being?*

S: Of course! It is the same God for all. My God is your God, is all God.

D: *Is He the one who sets up the councils?*

S: There are councils delegated. He does not, in Himself, bother with this. He has beings underneath Him who do the work, so to say. There is a chain of command. We ask that you take a more open-minded view and consider God as merely an observer of His children in their tasks. The children are doing the tasks. God simply is. God is, period. The children are doing; God is. The concept of God is the sum of all, of everything. We are God. We are collectively God. We are individual pieces of God. God is not one, but God is all.

D: *Then the councils are set up in different parts of the universe, in different areas?*

S: Yes. Local governments, if you will.

D: *Is this true of our planet Earth? Are we under a council, so to speak?*

S: That is true.

D: *I'm trying to understand. With many universes, do you mean each one has its own God?*

S: All the universes put together make God. Each universe does have the awareness of God, although the awareness would be different in different universes as well as different areas in one universe. Their concept of God would be different. The reality of God is unchanging in all universes, in all creation. God is, we are a part of God individually. But all of us together taken as a whole is what God is.

D: *Is this the force that created everything?*

S: That is correct. This is merely a manifestation of God.

D: *What about us as individual souls? Do you have any information about how we were first created?*

S: We were merely given personalization. We are merely pieces of God, whom He has given personalization to.

D: *Why did we divide off from God, if that's a correct term?*

S: This is merely a part of the over-all plan - the grand, divine plan which only God Himself knows in fullness. Many know small details, but none except God Himself knows in completeness.

D: *You said we are all God. Yet we here on Earth all have faults, we are not perfect. If we are part of God, wouldn't that make Him imperfect?*

S: There is merely a misunderstanding of the word "imperfect." All that is, is God. But God is perfect. Therefore, all is perfect. What we perceive as imperfect is merely our perceptions. Our perceptions are not necessarily the same even on other parts of the planet, so what we perceive cannot be held as absolute. What we perceive as imperfect is not necessarily so when viewed on the God level. Imperfections are human, but God loves imperfections as surely as He loves perfections. This is to understand God. To know Him is to love Him the more, knowing that He loves us for our imperfections as well as for our perfections. The imperfections are merely imperfections to us, but not to God. We can call them what we want.

D: *You're speaking of God as though He is separate from us and yet you say it takes all of us to make up God. Can you explain? You say that he loves us. How can this be if He is not a separate entity from us?*

S: First of all, God is not separate from us. He is intimately joined with us. Perhaps it would clarify to understand the blood system in the human body, which is made up of individual cells or aspects. The system itself **could not be** whole without the individual hemoglobin's and so forth. However, each hemoglobin is not complete without being in the system. Thus all is one and one is all. Each cannot exist without the other.

JESUS

D: *Are we to believe that the man, Jesus, was the Son of God?*

S: This is a very gross simplification, for God is not human. How can He have a son? This was couched in these terms for people to understand on a very basic level. The term "son" was not meant to be taken literally. If you wish for a clarification, Jesus was an emissary from another level of spiritual reality which is much closer to God than we are. His level was not directly below God. In other words, there are levels which are more complete than Jesus. However, He was from a level which no man before had ever been from. The human mind has trouble comprehending many of these concepts. Therefore they must be couched and phrased in terms which human comprehension will accept.

D: *The Bible teaches us that Jesus was with God and a part of God before He came to the Earth. Is this in the same way that our spirits are a part of God also?*

S: That is correct.

D: *But was He not more like God?*

S: He was on a higher plane, if you would.

D: *Are there others that have incarnated that could be classified in the same; I don't know if I should say "role" but others that have come to Earth as helpers that would be considered as great as we Christians consider Jesus? Others that we may not even know about that are incarnating in the same vein?*

S: If you are speaking of *now,* then I'm not allowed to say.

D: *Have there been other emissaries like Jesus in the past?*

S: Certainly. They are well-documented. The names are not important because one tends to lose sight of the intent and focus on the individual. There were those who were, you might say, street people who were not as well-known but were from that same plane. They served their purpose admirably. They merely were not as well-known as Jesus was.

D: *What was the purpose of Jesus' death?*

S: His death was entirely His own choosing. The Bible would state otherwise and that is all right if one wishes to believe that. However, He was killed by human hands and human will, and not by divine destiny. It was His choosing to put Himself into man's destiny.

D: *You're right, the Bible does say that He Himself said that no man took His life; He laid it down of His own will.*

S: This is true.

D: *But what was the object of that?*

S: If you wish for an object notice who did the killing, the humans or the executioners in this case. This was merely to underscore the level at which human interaction was, and is still.

D: *Did He die in order to prove to men that they could live again?*

S: If that's what they need to believe. Literally, no. Figuratively, yes.

D: *What was it literally?*

S: There was no such literal translation for the need for His death. He simply placed His well-being into the hands of men and allowed them to do as they would. The outcome is well documented.

D: *Why did He choose such a horrible way to die?*

S: He didn't choose that. That was the custom at that time. He merely consented to this. He had the power to escape His death if He wished. He chose to experience it.

D: *I think we're trying to understand what He was trying to prove by dying in such a manner.*

S: His motives are His own and I will not try to second-guess them. If He were alive today a similar situation might occur where He would be falsely accused and sent through the criminal justice system and executed by injection or electric chair or firing squad or hanging. The crucifixion was simply the method "in vogue" at that time.

D: *It seems rather senseless if we don't understand the reason.*

S: Look not towards Jesus; look towards your fellow man. The answer lies in the fact that He was executed. The point here is that there is the injustice.

D: *Man's injustice to man? Is that what you mean?*

S: That is correct.

D: *Well, it has been brought down to us that He died for our sins. Do you understand that concept?*

S: These are simply rationalizations which have been put into the Bible to try to explain it on a very basic level. A much broader understanding is needed to understand the whole life and Jesus experience. Many common and accepted beliefs are harmful to a true understanding, in that clinging to these will prevent a growing awareness of

God and Jesus

the true function or philosophy.

D: *In the Old Testament of the Bible there are frequent references to the Holy Ghost. In the New Testament it is more frequently called the Holy Spirit. There is an indication that this is a spirit from God that is available to help people. I'd like to know some more about it and how it works.*

S: We would say that this would be an attempt by your consciousness to understand an aspect of the God-nature. There is a vague awareness that there are divisions of that which you call "God." And these divisions have been given these three designations: the Father, the Son, and the Holy Ghost. However, the comprehension of that which is the Holy Ghost would be as equally difficult to understand with your awareness as would be God the Father. Suffice to say, however, that this *spirit is* of an energy nature-somewhat more of a life *force* than a life *form*. Perhaps to say, more of the sustaining life. That is, the essence of life itself as opposed to the personality which is full of this life.

D: *Is it possible for a person to survive without this spirit?*

S: Not so, for how could the personality survive with-out life? Life speaks on many planes, not simply *physical* life but *spiritual* life. It is the sustaining element of personal awareness, or personality on your level.

D: *Then you're saying it is the spirit of life itself. That's the way we would recognize it.*

S: To phrase it in terms which you could understand, that would be perhaps accurate.

Thus it would seem that when the churches speak of the Triad, or Trinity, the Great Three-in-One, they are actually closer to the real concept than they realize. These are each separate, just as we are also separate from God, and yet they are all One. They are all forms of the same thing, yet their descriptions have been put into simplified terms that our

181

human minds can comprehend. It is more difficult for us to visualize God as an energy force. It is much easier for us to give Him personification. From the information I have received it would seem that the Holy Ghost and God are essentially the same thing, a life force that permeates everything. Without either one of them there can be no life because this is the driving energy behind it. Thus it would be contradictory for the church to say we should allow the Holy Ghost to enter into us, because it is already there. The absence of this Spirit would mean the absence of life itself.

Chapter 10
Satan, Possession and Demons

D: *We asked you about the concept of God. What about the concept of the Devil or Satan?*

S: The concept is merely that, it is a concept, an analogy, a rationalization which is used for purposes of understanding.

D: *Then there is no real entity?*

S: There is no such real entity, no. There is no personification.

D: *But people say the Devil is a being, a person. Is there any such thing as that?*

S: Not as one being, or one entity being evil and considered the Devil. When most people are talking of the Devil, they are talking of the being known as Lucifer, who was one at the time of the formation, and who, through his own want for power, lost all.

D: *They associate him with evil?*

S: That is because most of the elementals which have been associated with evil congregate around him.

D: *Do you think this misunderstanding, so to speak, would give these kind of forces more power?*

S: Yes, because they utilize misunderstanding to their own means.

D: *Then people give them power by thinking about them?*

S: Power is not given by just thoughts about them. It is given in the acts that people do. This is why every time someone says, "The Devil made me do it," when they have done something they know is wrong, that gives them more energy.

D: *I have heard it said that there has to be a Devil because you have to have balance. If you have good, you have to have evil.*

S: This is a rationalization or an attempt to comprehend. People need something to say, "Oh, I understand that." If we did not understand it we would not feel comfortable. These are rationalizations to make us feel comfortable so that we can feel that we understand it. We have set up many rationalizations in order to explain what we see and feel and observe around us, to the point that these rationalizations have taken on a life of their own. They should now be understood as mere rationalizations and not entities of their own.

D: *Well, is it a good or bad thing that people rationalize this way?*

S: The purpose is served. There is a feeling of security. However, it stifles growth because there is a resistance to parting with the rationalization to under-stand something somewhat more complex. It is neither good or bad, merely indifferent, as far as what is right and wrong.

D: *What about the preaching of sin and that you're going to go to Hell and burn in the fires etc.? Would you ex-plain that as a mistranslation?*

S: When you were a child your parents constantly threatened you with the belt for not eating supper or many other things. The fear of these punishments is what directed your attention or your actions away from what caused the confrontation in the first place. This is merely an adult threat in order to make you do that which is perceived to be good.

D: *Then, is there any such physical place as Hell?*

S: There is no physical. The mind will at the time of death create its own Hell if that is what it's expecting. Suppose a person lives a life of wickedness, all the while knowing that they're going to Hell for what they're doing. If they firmly believe that, then when they die that will be waiting for them.

I do not believe people necessarily have to be living a wicked life. They can be living a perfectly normal God-fearing, church going life, but the church has planted this fear in them. And being normal they know they are not perfect so they expect to go to Hell for some small insignificant sin, because this is what the church has promised. They feel they are so unworthy that there can be no other afterlife for them but Hell. This type of brainwashing does an extreme amount of damage to the person if it prepares them to expect Hell instead of Heaven. I think this is where the church is wrong and can do more harm than good. By making people fear Hell so intensely, the church succeeds in creating it for them.

S: They remain there in their version of Hell until they realize that it is a manufacture of their own mind. It may take a year or it may take hundreds, but since time has no meaning on this side it is as only the twinkling of an eye. When they realize they don't have to stay there it has no power to hold them and they are released to go where they truly belong.

D: *But there is much that we call "evil" in the world.*

S: Evil is not an accurate term. This gets back to what is good and what is bad. It's simply misguided, that would be a more appropriate term. In our perceptions the things which you call "evil" are merely energies which are misguided or misdirected. These energies are simply not evolved. They are not personifications of evil. They are not entities, so to say. There is no such Devil sitting on people's shoulders telling them to do this or that. On this side we have no concept of evil, for evil is merely a disharmony between the two forces and this has been given the term "evil," in order for your human conscious mind to be able to comprehend this dis-harmony. Please understand there is no incarnate evil. There is no such

185

thing as a Satan who is walking the Earth and snatching the souls from people. This is a fallacy and a story which was created in order to understand disharmony. I will use an analogy. There is positive and negative on a battery. If you are going to jump a car you have two jumper cables to hook up, positive and negative. And if you leave one off; well, you're going to sit for a while, aren't you? So it can be seen that both are necessary. Neither is more important, more helpful or useful for they are equal in importance and usefulness. So shed your fascination with evil and good for this is an inaccurate concept and will hinder your conceptions and understanding.

D: *Did these energies come here from somewhere else?*

S: They're energies that live on this planet. We are all energies. You are an energy; your soul is an energy. These are the energies I speak of. We could say souls.

D: *Would this go along with the idea that thoughts are things?*

S: Exactly. Thoughts are energy. Thoughts are real manifestations. Thoughts *are,* period.

D: *You mean, by people thinking about these bad things happening to the world they are actually creating these things?*

S: This is true. Thinking of hell on Earth will bring it just as surely as going out and building it by the sweat of your brow. It may not occur in the same way but it will just as surely occur.

D: *Then by thinking of these things and fearing them, people are creating a thought energy that is powerful enough to cause them. Is that correct?*

S: That's exactly right. A thought is energy. Your soul manipulates energy. Thinking is manipulation of energy. A thought is a willful act. The purpose is to counteract this disharmony by bringing in fresh energy, new ideas, hope, new directions. It's the intention of the thought itself that counts. If you send someone love, that is the intention. If you wish something in return for that, you may send them love but that is not the intention. It is entirely dependent on what is expected.

D: *And this cannot be disguised. The true feeling comes through-is that what you mean?*

S: The sender knows what the intentions are. The receiver may not.

D: *Then if it is true that there is no such thing as evil and there is no such thing as the Devil, where does our concept of evil come from?*

S: Do you really wish to know? There is one word that sums this whole concept up easily. *[He spelled out]* E-X-C-U-S-E-S. There is a lack of responsibility by blaming this unhappiness and this dread on others. It is much easier to assign the blame outward than inward. And so, voila, the Devil is there poking his three-tined prong and urging others to do that which they would not normally do. "Who, me? No, the Devil made me do it." This is heard through the centuries. This is what is meant by "excuses." This is "evil."

D: *We were thinking that evil was definitely a force and we wondered where it came from.*

S: It came from the imagination. It was conjured and so roams the world devouring innocent babes, debauching, raping, pillaging. This is evil incarnate. The excuse is to hide from responsibility.

D: *Then it comes from the mind of the persons?*

S: That is correct. It comes from the inner desires of the people and not from some outside force, for there is no such entity roaming the universe. There is simply a lack of responsibility on those who wish to assign the Devil his blame.

D: *Well, with so many people believing that there is evil and there is the Devil...*

S: Then there is the Devil.

D: *Is it possible that by believing it, people can create some kind of a thought form?*

S: They cannot create an entity, for only God can do that. They can create situations which seem to prove their existence. They set up the events which prove to themselves the validity of that which they want to believe. This is true not only in "evil" experiences, but in good and "holy" experiences also-that which you believe preprograms your experience. Believe what you want and that is what you will find.

D: *But we have heard that you can create thought forms with your mind.*

S: That is not correct, for no mere mortal has the power of creation. Only God has that right; that power. What humans are creating are these situations or circumstances which seem to prove the existence of this Devil. Can you give me a specific ex-ample of what you are asking?

D: *Well, I've heard it said that if enough people concentrated, they could create a thought form.*

S: That is not correct. They can create energy which is merely a collection of the energies being fed into it. It is simply a matter of pooling the energies. This can be done for good or for harm. But there is no creation of an entity.

D: *Then it would dissipate when the energy was released from it?*

S: There was nothing created and so the energy would dissipate and go back to the elements. I repeat, there is not the creation of any entity in this; there is simply the pooling of energies, which is a very powerful process. There is no creation of life by any creature, be it astral or otherwise. There is only energy created by God and that is all.

D: *So we don't need to fear anything like that?*

S: That is correct. Humanity has been in the chains of fear for too long and it is now time to break the chains of that bondage and release humans to accept their own responsibility. There are entities which can be considered demonic. There are entities which are just elementals which have been warped by human contact. There are also entities which are elementals which have been lifted by human contact. It's all in the exposure. The power is the same. It's how it is utilized. There are no black and white areas.

At this time I was having difficulty understanding the term "elementals." *(See also* Chapter 6.)

D: *By elementals, do you mean they are just very simple-they haven't learned anything yet?*
S: They are Earth spirits, yes.
D: *Earth-bound spirits?*
S: Spirits of the Earth. There is a difference.
D: *Are they allowed to incarnate too?*
S: No. They are what some people have come to know as when they talk of possessions, usually they are talking of an elemental overtaking.
D: *Could they evolve into a spirit like yourself?*
S: They could evolve into a higher form, but they would never be allowed to incarnate.
D: *When the Native Americans talked about trees and animals having spirits, would they be like that?*
S: This is true. They have guardians, as it were, that care for them. They're more of a feeling, sensing spirit than having much thought.
D: *Then how could they be dealt with if they cause problems? Could you reason with them?*
S: You could reason with them in the fact of letting them know that you are going to face them and telling them to go. And by telling them in the proper manner they will have to leave.
D: *Then you can't reason with them like you could another person. These are the ones that just cause trouble?*

S: Not always. There are fine examples of good us-age of elementals. There have been rude experiments in the proper usage of elementals, by gaining knowledge.

D: *Then if they are not a reasoning spirit, they can't understand whether what they do is "right" or "wrong."*

S: Right. Elementals live upon feeling energies. You will find some who live in churches. They feel the uplifting of prayer and the happiness that lives in that place, and they feed upon these emotions. And then there are those that feed upon hate and lust and things like that, and they congregate around places that generate those emotions.

D: *Is there any way humans could protect themselves from the influences of these mischievous elementals?*

S: You can always bring down a prayer of protection over yourself and over your surroundings.

D: *Is there any particular way you have to do that?*

S: Well, it depends on the way that you view the Eternal Being and the universe. You can just call down the ultimate power of what is good and ask it to protect you.

D: *Then there are no certain words that have to be said in a certain way?*

S: No. It just has to come directly from within and be said with meaning. People who are presumably "possessed" are actually examples of those spirits who have a particularly bad dose of negative energies attracted to them. It had gotten strong enough to start influencing them on the physical plane. These spirits when they cross over will have to spend quite some time in the resting place to rid themselves of this.

D: *I'm trying to understand these negative spirits that they attract.*

S: Not spirits; energies.

D: *Negative energies. I think people are always thinking of these negative energies as being similar to the Devil and demons.*

ANOTHER VERSION:

D: *When someone is possessed, is the entity doing the possession a true spirit?*

S: It is a warped spirit. More on the level of what you would term "demons." They are lower than human souls and they have been warped through touch or contact by certain entities or even people, so that they are bent and evil.

D: *But if they have not actually lived lives, where do they come from?*

S: They were at the Formation. The cases of so-called "possession" are generally caused by someone who has allowed their karma to become seriously imbalanced, leaving a vacuum in part of their karmic energies where other energies can enter in. These are usually disorganized energies, for the energy that constitutes your soul and your body are not the only energies there are. Some of the superstitious terms that used to be common in your language: Earth sprites, water sprites, elementals, and various things like that referred to collections of loosely organized energy that usually are connected to certain physical characteristics on the Earth. Because of the type of energy they are, they're attracted to certain physical situations.

D: *Then it is not normally a possession by a human spirit that crossed over?*

S: No. Usually it's an elemental type of spirit that is present on the Earth at all times because it's just simply part of the Earth.

D: *Do they really mean any harm when they do things like this?*

S: No. The reason why they enter in is because there is a serious imbalance and a vacuum there, and the vacuum needs to be filled. It is like a magnet to them and they are drawn in without their really wanting to be drawn in. They don't do it on purpose; it is just an accident. And the violence that ensues is because they are not as organized, in energy terms, as the human soul is. They are more loosely formed and so they are not able to have organized action: thus violent actions are the result.

D: *I thought they were more like mischievous-type spirit.*

S: No. There are things that they do out of mischief, but things like this generally happen because of an imbalance in the energies. It's the law of cause and effect again. These energies are drawn to this imbalance because of the interaction of that energy with their energy. It's just a matter of energies that drain rather than build up. Possession is a reality; however, elementals are drawn and not invaders as such.

D: *Is there anything that someone can do to get rid of these to expel them if they have entered in like that?*

S: It is difficult to say. Basically to realize that it was an imbalance in you that caused this. The only thing that I can see that is available at your present level of knowledge would be to meditate and get things back in balance. As things get back in balance, the elementals would have to leave just as a natural course of events. Because the polarities of the energies involved would change and they would no longer be able to stay because the energy no longer interacts in the same way.

D: *We hear of exorcisms performed by the church.*

S: That's mainly a help to the mind of the subject involved; to help them realize that something is out of balance and to help them try to put something back in balance. But usually it is like putting a Band-Aid on a deep cut. It doesn't really help the cut and you keep bleeding around the Band-Aid. The person involved must actively work with them-selves to be able to balance the imbalance. And having some water sprinkled on you and some words said over you would not correct the situation.

D: *I've heard that white light is very effective to exorcise these elementals.*

S: Yes. It is effective for protection, particularly against-or not "against," that is a bad word. It can be used for protection when dealing with people whose auras seem to clash with your own.

D: *I've heard of what they call "psychic vampires," which would be another person who absorbs your energy and makes you feel very weak or drained. That's not a very good term, but do you know what I mean?*

S: Yes. It is a good description for your language. These psychic vampires are imbalanced themselves and they need to work on that.

D: *Sometimes it is not intentional when these things happen.*

S: That is true. Sometimes it happens spontaneously. It is not that common, but still it is wise to have yourself protected.

D: *Didn't you say that a person couldn't be possessed without their cooperation? Or did I understand you correctly?*

S: A demon's only method of entering in is through stealth. Therefore they must be very stealthy in order to attain even a foothold upon another person.

D: *Can they attach themselves by finding weak spots in the aura? Wouldn't this be the same thing as the other entity said about finding a weak spot of imbalance - a vacuum or void to fill?*

S: They would attach themselves in any way. This would be one method, yes.

D: *Is it possible for those people who can read auras to detect this in others?*

S: Yes. If a person is aware of being overtaken, all he must say is, "I bid you leave in the name of Christ," and it must go. It has to obey this name; they have no choice.

D: *Who has to make that command? The person that the demon is in, or can someone else do it?*

S: If someone else does it, it is what you would term an exorcism. But if the person who is being possessed is made aware of this, they can also command them to leave. But there has to be the strength in the command.

D: *What if they don't think they are possessed? Do they have to be told what to say or do?*

S: If they don't believe that they are possessed, another may do the exorcism for them by commanding it to leave. I ask you, what harm would it do to command something to leave in the name of Christ? If there is nothing there it has harmed nothing. But if there is something there it has done great good for this person.

D: *Can you tell me if anyone ever leaves their physical body and a different spirit enters into that body and uses it?*

S: Oh, yes. Perhaps the soul has become dissatisfied with the situation and decided it cannot handle what it thought it wished to. But the body must carry on for other reasons because this person, as others know it, needs to exist. Therefore another would choose to enter into this body and live that life.

This is a typical description of a "walk-in," not a case of possession. Walks-ins are discussed in Chapter 15.

D: *Is there ever a case where a spirit is forced out of the body?*

S: No, it is the self's decision.

D: *There's much talk about these things that frighten people. They say that an evil spirit can come and force you out of your body and take possession of the body. Is such a thing possible?*

S: Perhaps if there was no desire to remain; one seeming to be high-minded could ... take over. But I have never known of this to occur. I think what you are speaking of is where others are said to inhabit the body at the same time, rather than actually the other entity leaving.

D: *Two spirits at once? Why would that be allowed?*

S: These are restless spirits more of an elemental variety.

D: *I think you told me that elemental was something that more or less didn't have any understanding. It was just a very simple...*

S: (Interrupted) It is a very basic energy. It operates more on the case of desires than the knowledge of why.

D: *Well, how could the person allow something like that to come in?*

S: By not protecting oneself. Different things. But it is always able to be thrown off at any time that the owner of the body wishes it to be done.

D: *Then they are not more powerful than the real owner of the body. If a person would perhaps be given to strong drink or drugs, does this ever open the body up to an elemental?*

S: There are those who, due to these factors, become very open. And there are those elementals who gather around these types of people, but this is a rarity. This is not something that would happen every day, as it were.

D: *Then the strong drink or other drugs don't lessen the ability to...*

S: To protect oneself? No.

D: *Okay. I thought it made them more open to these other spirits.*

S: Only if they allow themselves to be.

D: *Then as long as they protect themselves they don't have to worry about it.*

S: Simply ask for God's protection, in God's name or Jesus' name. The mere vocalization is instant protection.

D: *Could the white light be used in this way, too?*

S: That is correct-the light of protection. Merely vocalizing the name of Jesus or God and asking for their protection is the same, for instantly the light surrounds.

It apparently doesn't matter what your particular religious beliefs are. Every entity agrees that the calling upon a higher power for protection will be sufficient to keep the elementals away. They also all agree on the power of the white light. This is the personification of protection. It is very effective when you visualize this beautiful light surrounding yourself, your car, your home, or whatever.

The following is a very effective visualization for protection that was given to me by a subject in trance.

S: Vocalization is highly effective, but you should include more visualization. *See* more fully and do not rely so heavily on simply the spoken word. For, although the spoken word is in truth a creation of energies, it is much more efficient for you if you would truly visualize and see in your mind's eye exactly that which you wish. For this is, in fact, creation. See yourself enveloped in a pyramid of white energy surrounding, perhaps, the entire building you are in, or whatever you feel most comfortable with. If it is used in this way all within its space would be included in this white energy. Encourage all who participate to co-create and in so doing, the energies become stronger. It would be very simple to describe a pyramid surrounding those present, and ask that each simply visualize this pyramid of white shimmering energy, such that no discreative energies may enter from the outside. Ask that all discreative energies within be transformed and aligned into the creative energies of the universe. It would also be appropriate at that time to ask for any healing which would be required of those in the assembly. Ask that the discreative energies within the assembly, which cause these physical manifestations of illness, be turned to the white light, and aligned and turned back to the universe in a creative manner. In this way, those present will assist in the healing of whoever wishes it. Energy cannot be destroyed, but it can be converted from negative to positive. Anyone can create this pyramid of white light and surround themselves with it. If created in this way any discreative energies which come near the pyramid will be returned to the universe to be transformed into creative and constructive energies. Any discreative energies *within* the pyramid will be bathed in this white light and will automatically be converted into harmonious, constructive and creative energies. Visualize the entire pyramid completely enveloped and full of this white light. And all discreative energies within could be visualized as darkness in the light. Simply see the light changing the darknesses, raising the darkness to the light, or turning the darkness into light. In turn the dark-ness becomes light and is no longer discreative, but is again constructive energy which is returned to the universe for constructive and creative purposes. All have the ability to create this white light energy around them. They need only affirm to themselves the desire to do this. They must truly want this in order to believe it. For if the individual is not firmly of the belief of what they desire, there will be limited success with this.

D: *I have heard people say that you should ask for protection in the name of Jesus. Is this as effective?*

S: That is accurate. It is in fact entirely the same principle at work here; simply different ways of stating this principle. There are many ways this energy could be directed thusly, according to the individual's religious beliefs. However many are aligned with one particular manner more so than another. It is simply a matter of appropriateness and personal preference. It is entirely up to the individual as to how effective any one manner would be.

S: We would say again that you, yourselves, are the creators. You find around you that which has been created *by you.* Therefore that which you find is indeed real, even those things which you say are imagined. For the imagination is in all reality the pallet of your creations; therefore, that which you can imagine is indeed real. Be it physical or mental in nature, it is indeed real. These evil creatures, as you call them, are indeed real to those who would create them in their mind. There are those who do not *believe* in such and therefore they do not exist. However, it would be wrong to say that they are not real to the individuals who believe in them, for indeed they are real. It is that ability of yours to create what you wish that is even more important now than it was previously. It is essential that you be aware of this power, this ability to create what you will. For in so doing you have the very real choice of creating that which would be good or that which would be evil. It is entirely up to the individual as to the reality they create. We enjoy these times when we can commune. This was the way it was at one time before on your planet when all could converse as freely as we do now. However, there was that time of the Fall. None were spared the Fall. We are victims as yourselves of the Fall. (A somber seriousness) And we feel you know of what we speak.

We in the Christian religion have always associated the term the "Fall" with the angel, Lucifer, being cast out of Heaven by God. This supposedly gave him dominion over Earth and created the belief in Satan and evil.

S: This was the time when the knowledge was lost, and the consciousness turned down, so to say, to-wards the Earth and this higher energy plane was disregarded and discarded. So you can see from a strictly analogical standpoint there was a definite fall of consciousness from the higher plane to the more base Earth plane. There was not, as has previously been felt, a surge of evil present when this Fall occurred. It was simply that the attention of those inhabitants was shifted from the higher to the lower planes, so to say. This is what is meant by the Fall. This is not a right or wrong judgment. It is simply a fact which is in the realm of truth. So you can see that when you lose your sight of whom and what you are, then you would tend to wander, as humanity has done on this planet for many millennia now. It was simply a forgetting of the true identity. A lowering of the consciousness, so to say, and forgetting that all are truly part of the whole.

D: *I think the main thing is to get this idea of Heaven and Hell straightened out for people.*

S: That would be a most difficult task. The people have been fairly brainwashed.

D: *Were these concepts in the Bible originally?*

S: No. One reference that is used is the description that Jesus gave of Gehenna [Jewish name for Hell] and the lake of fire. He was trying to describe the condition you are in when you cross over to the spirit side and you are surrounded by negative influences. But the people listening to him took him literally and thought he was speaking of a real place. At an-other time Jesus said, "This day shalt thou see me in paradise," when he was being executed. He is referring to the fact that after they died they would transcend over to the spirit side of life, and it would be at that plane called "paradise."

D: *I was trying to think of another part in the Bible where it talks of somebody who is in Hell or something. And they were asking someone to get them out. (I was having difficulty remembering this passage on the spur of the moment.) The spirit said, "If you would just touch my lips with a drop of water..."*

S: Yes, that spirit was in the middle of mental torment which would cause a condition which on the physical plane could be likened to fever. It also means that particular negative energies were around this spirit. When he said to touch his lips with but a drop of water, he was actually asking for a bit of wisdom to help him dissipate these negative energies. And the wisdom would act as a soothing balm.

D: *So he could understand and escape from that condition. I know the churches have brought up that part of the Bible several times and say this is a permanent condition that he couldn't get out of. They use it as an example of burning in Hell.*

S: Yes, but it was not a permanent condition. He was at that time going around in a mental circle and could not break out of that chain of events so he could dissipate the negative energies. So he was asking for a bit of wisdom to help him see how he could work his way out of it.

D: *I was trying to remember if Jesus talks about Heaven anywhere in the Bible. I know there was one part about "Heaven and Earth shall pass away, but my word shall not pass away." That's the only thing that comes to mind right now.*

S: He was just speaking of the physical universe. He was saying that the teaching of His words had to do with the higher levels that would still exist regardless of the destruction of this particular universe because there are other universes as well, and the higher levels will always exist.

D: *I think it is very important that people understand that these are not real physical places that they have to go to. That concept seems so limiting, it's depressing.*

S: Yes, that is true. They do need to understand that reincarnation is not a polar opposite to their Christian religion, as they seem to believe.

D: *I try to tell them it is really just a philosophy. That's what I have been told. It is a way of thinking and not a religion in itself.*

S: Yes. People who are dogmatic about their philosophy or religion lose sight of how things really are.

Chapter 11
Ghosts and Poltergeists

D: *We hear a lot about ghosts and poltergeists. Would you have an explanation for those?*

S: Certainly, for *we* could be considered one were we to cause furniture to float and switches to go on and off. The terminology is simply applied to those spirit entities who have their consciousness focused to such a degree that they can cause manifestations on the physical level. This can be accomplished by many who are focused to that degree. Intense emotions such as anger, rage, or jealousy tend to focus the entire consciousness to such an extent that this is what happens.

D: *Are they trying to convey a message or something when they do these things?*

S: Not necessarily. Some simply enjoy the amusement and are thus entertaining themselves as well as those who are the targets of their mischief. This is not always the case for you are well aware of the less enlightened individuals.

D: *I was thinking it would not be a very enlightened spirit who would want to play games like that.*

S: Always there is the playing of games, on this side as well as yours. This is simply another form of it.

D: *Even enlightened spirits might do these things?*

S: That is correct. There is the awakening of awareness sometimes achieved through this activity. The term "poltergeist" is loosely ascribed to any spirit who manipulates physical objects. The delineation is not clarified, however, into intent. For often there is intent which is positive and helpful and good in doing this, because it enlightens the receivers of this energy to the fact that there are things which cannot be seen, which are real, as real as the physical.

D: *But sometimes these things frighten people.*

S: Sometimes people frighten these things, too. (Laughter) For we never know what the people will do.

D: *What about ghosts?*

S: The manifestation of many *ghosts is* nothing more than the projection of the energies of the individual who is seeing these apparitions. The individuals themselves are projecting these energies which could perhaps be reflections of their own former lives or awareness of other spirit planes, and they are projecting this awareness down to a physical level. We wish not to convey that *all* ghosts are these projections. However, integrate this into your awareness that these are possibilities. That not *all* are true spirits but are sometimes mere projections of the individual who is perceiving this reality.

D: *Is this in the same way that we would perceive fairies, nymphs and that sort of thing?*

S: There are indeed those energies which are perceived as fairies and nymphs; however, these are not identical to that energy of which we speak. These are separate energies perceived *by* an individual, not projected *from* that individual. These projected energies are inherent and an intrinsic part of the individual which perceives them. There are many other possibilities of projection and perception. However, we speak here only of this one particular form of manifestation, that being a projection-perception type of experience.

D: *Some people have seen what they think are ghosts in different places reenacting scenes. They seem to be trapped in a moment in time.*

S: That is an excellent analogy. They *are* trapped in a moment in time. They are earthbound entities who are trapped in their own doings, so to say, and can find no release. For they are so directed in their energies that they can perceive nothing around them except that which they have focused onto. And so they find themselves in a vicious circle, so to say, destined to repeat the same set of circumstances which put them there in the first place, until there is the awakening. The people in physical form can help and assist these individuals much more readily than we who are on the spirit. Although these ghosts are also spirit, their consciousness and awareness is locked into the physical and this is all they can perceive. So they cannot see those spirits around them who are attempting to guide them to their truth, to enlighten them and release them from their misery. This is an instance where the physical is most capable of helping the spiritual.

D: *Sometimes they don't seem to be aware of the physical people who are watching the.*

S: That is correct; for oftentimes they are so locked into their own energy they see nothing around them, even physical, except their own energy.

D: *Would poltergeist cases sometimes be this type of energy?*

S: Not true. That is not correct. For poltergeists move physical objects and are aware of their consequences. They are aware of the physical surroundings. It is true a poltergeist may be locked onto the Earth energy. However, it is not true to say that those who are locked into the Earth energy are always poltergeists.

D: *I thought maybe they were trying to get the attention of the people around them by creating disturbances in this way.*

S: That is correct. That is often the case. It is simply to get the attention of those around them, whether it be for amusement or ego gratification.

D: *But sometimes a poltergeist can harm people by its actions. I've heard of them starting fires.*

S: That is correct. We wish not to imply that all poltergeists have only honorable intentions, for such is not the case. It may be more than attention, however, that they are seeking. It may be revenge, for instance.

D: *Usually there is a young child or someone about the age of puberty in the household, and there is a theory that somehow these entities use that energy in some way. This has not been fully explained; it is just a theory.*

S: We would say that these individuals who are reaching puberty act as their own poltergeist. For they are using energies of which they are not aware. And so they create the activity themselves, as is often the case but not always.

D: *But they are not consciously aware that they are doing that?*

S: That is correct. It is simply a manifestation of their own psychic talents and abilities which are brought on by the schism of the experience of going through puberty, which is manifested by this poltergeist activity. For much energy is directed when a person goes through this puberty experience. There is much change happening in the body which is then transferred to the mental and emotional planes as well as the spiritual.

D: *Then they are not doing it out of vengeance on the family or anything like that.*

S: That is correct. It is simply a way of releasing energy. Pent-up emotions are directed and the energy is then released as poltergeist activity.

D: *It would be good to try to explain this because some people are afraid of this activity.*

S: It is understandable that they are afraid of it. For it would imply that there are spirits about who would wish them harm. As we said before, this is sometimes the case. It, however, is not always the case.

D: *If someone were confronted by poltergeist activity that was harmful, how could they make it stop?*

S: As mentioned earlier, challenge in the name of God these entities which seem to be causing this. And as in the case of possession, send them on their way by God or Jesus' name. If the entities are harmful, then there is adequate protection in Jesus' name. If they wish only enlightenment, then please accept this as such and try to remain or become enlightened.

D: *Is there such a thing as an earthbound spirit?*

S: In perhaps a deeper or yet more profound sense than is commonly held. An earthbound spirit is someone who has had many problems and does not want to admit that they can be released.

D: *Do you mean they love life so much they don't want to leave the Earth?*

S: It is either that case, or someone here on Earth is tying them so hard that they can't leave. Every time you grieve for someone who is gone, you tie that person a little closer to being earthbound. Grief has its place, but excessive grieving is bad for both the person who is doing the grieving, and the one they are grieving about. There is no reason to grieve for that person. Most of them are very happy in what they have seen on this side.

D: *Then by grieving and hanging on to them, you hold them to the Earth and this is not good. Most people would not realize that.*

ANOTHER VERSION:

D: I've *heard that there are such things as earthbound spirits. What happens in a case like that?*

S: That's a confusing matter. Usually what has happened is that they are spiritually sleepwalking. They are still conscious of the physical plane and they notice that something is different, but they can't quite figure it out. On a spiritual plane it appears that they are sleepwalking. They can sleepwalk for what may appear to be a very long time to you, in the form of earthbound spirits or ghosts or what-have-you. But after a while they'll wake up and realize that they are on the spiritual plane and they have other things to go on to.

D: *Why are they confused? Is it a sudden death or something similar that makes this happen?*

S: Usually it is because the subconscious has misjudged the amount of time left for working out a particular aspect of karma. The subconscious might have been expecting a longer amount of time, and when it is cut short it takes longer for the mind to reorient itself.

D: *Do these earthbound spirits hang around where they used to live or would they mostly travel around on the earthly plane?*

S: They tend to remain in areas they were familiar with. Probably because they are trying to figure out what is going on. Since they are sleepwalking, it is mainly their spiritual subconscious trying to straighten things out so that the spiritual conscious can switch back on, so to speak.

D: *Do they ever try to get back into a physical body while in that state?*

S: Not often. Occasionally they will try but the spirit that is there will block them and they will realize that it can't be done. It would be like bumping into somebody on the sidewalk. After that happens a few times they begin to wake up and quit sleep-walking.

D: *Can't they be helped to realize what is going on when they are in that kind of a state?*

S: When they are deep into this spiritual sleepwalking it is very difficult to reach them. Sometimes they just have to be given time until they can be contacted and helped to wake up quicker.

D: *I have heard stories of spirits that hang around taverns or around people who are drinking or using dope or things like that; I suppose it is because they want the sensations from it. Have you heard of cases like that?*

S: I mentioned earlier about the period of transition. Some spirits, especially those who have attracted much negative influences to themselves, generally have a difficult period of transition because they don't want to give up the physical sensation of things. It is usually the strong, exotic sensations such as from the various drugs that are in use in your society: alcohol, nicotine, heroin or what-have-you. So these spirits who are in transition stay around people who experience these things regularly to try to absorb their feelings, their physical sensations from it. They try to enjoy themselves vicariously.

"Vicarious" is an interesting word and especially fitting when used in this case. The dictionary defines it as: "Taking the place of another. Endured or performed by one person in place of another. Felt by imagined participation in another's experience: as, a *vicarious* thrill." He could not have chosen a more appropriate word to describe the meaning he was trying to convey.

D: *Do you think these spirits realize they have died?*
S: Sometimes yes; sometimes no. Many times, yes, they realize they have died, but they are hoping that they will be able to re-enter the physical plane immediately. They are still in the period of transition and they don't realize how things have to be balanced yet. Others honestly may not know that they have died and they are trying to participate in physical things as they did when they were alive. They don't realize that humans can't perceive them. Finally it soaks through that they have died. When they realize this, then they become aware of the spiritual plane and they finish their period of transition.
D: *They might think that what is here on Earth is all there is.*
S: Yes. Such spirits do think that at first, but the longer they stay dead the more aware they become of the

spiritual plane, simply because of a matter of vibrational attraction. During the period of transition sometimes this type of spirit cannot immediately perceive the helper who has come. They cannot immediately see or sense them because they are still too strongly attuned to the physical plane.

D: *What happens with these spirits who seem to want to stay around Earth?*

S: In those cases the spirits seem to be pulled back to Earth. They are the ones that are taking a longer time adjusting to the spiritual plane they have attained. They have their mental constructs of scenes that they are familiar with. They don't grow beyond that and they use it as a crutch. So it tends to make them stay close to the physical plane. These souls sometimes need help. Many times they inadvertently did something negative to their karma and they don't want to deal with that fact. They are afraid of what they might see when they throw away their mental crutch of these constructs.

D: *They want to stay with what's familiar to them?*

S: Right. Out of fear. If they continue to stay close to the physical plane their vibrations stay sympathetic enough with the physical plane to where sometimes there may be echoes of themselves on the physical plane. As an echo is to sound, but it would be an echo of energy. This would explain some of the ectoplasmic appearances that have been recorded on your plane-what you call "ghosts" and such phenomena.

D: *They are not really the spirit? They are just an echo of that spirit that would remain around the house or whatever?*

S: Yes, perhaps the spirit on the other side of the barrier is using a mental construct of a house. When he first crossed over, the spirit would have pictured "home," for example, to help him adjust to this new phase of life. Whenever they picture a particular house that is their home, they are just seeing it and themself being in the house. But realizing-or maybe not realizing-that spirit is afraid to go on, and so he keeps hanging onto this picture of home as a crutch because it is familiar. He is scared to leave and so he stays within this one house. That is why these spiritual echoes, which you call ghosts, are usually seen in such a limited area. Because they are using this one mental image to hang on to, much like an infant hanging onto a pacifier. Since crossing over the barrier is an individual experience they have closed their minds to their surroundings because they are using this mental construct as a crutch. In a sense, they are alone to themselves because they have closed themselves within this illusion of "home." They don't see that there are other spirits waiting there to help them complete their adjustment. It is as if they have closed their eyes and stopped up their ears, and they are only thinking about home. So in effect, they *are* alone and so the echo reflects this by being unaware of other people in the surroundings. The live occupants of the earthly house can see the ghost, but it seems oblivious of them.

D: *Does that mean they keep reliving this in their mind or what?*

S: Yes. They're holding this one picture in their mind that for some reason means a lot to them. They are just concentrating on this one picture. Usually that happens in cases when the spirit is very scared and has not adjusted to crossing over. So they lock onto this one memory, this one moment in time from their most recent life. Their mind is locked onto it and is visualizing it, and so the spiritual echo goes through the same actions over and over again, as a result of echoing what they are thinking about. It would be like, on your plane, when someone has an irrational fear and they have a lucky word that they consider to be a charm. They repeat it over and over to help ward off this fear. It is that type of situation.

D: *Sometimes the scene is a murder or something violent that has occurred, and other people see it as ghosts acting out a scene over and over again.*

S: Right. The spirit may be visualizing a particular building as his mental construct and will be hanging onto it. And he may be visualizing a particular action that took place during his most recent life. Some-times the action may involve another person and he's visualizing this other person, too. That explains why people on your plane sometimes see two ghosts interacting with each other in the same scene over and over. It is part of this memory that this soul is using as a crutch.

D: *If it is negative, does that make it more powerful?*

S: Usually this occurs when the soul is not reacting well to the transition and is interpreting it as a negative experience. It is the force of fear that causes them to do this. Usually when the soul crosses over and realizes that the level of karma they have attained this time has been in a negative direction, they don't want to complete the transition because they are scared of what they will see. Meanwhile their minds will lock onto this source of the fear, and it might be the very scene from the life that caused their karma to develop in a negative direction. That is all they can focus on. They don't realize that things are balanced on the spiritual plane. Even though they may go to a lower plane than they were before it is not designed to cause pain or torture. It is just a matter of a place compatible with them so that they can develop further.

D: *But people do have experiences with the "ghosts" or "spirits" of someone who has passed over. They come and talk to them and give them messages. Would this be the same thing?*

S: No. Usually whenever people interact with a spirit that has come back to give them a message, it is usually their guide trying to contact them. If people are advanced enough to be able to handle this aspect of life, their guides will contact them in this manner to help them and give them advice in a more direct way.

D: *You mean it is not actually the spirit of their loved one or whoever?*

S: Sometimes it is, if the loved one is on hand to help out. And they usually do want to help out be-cause people remain karmically linked across several lifetimes. Even though the loved one has already passed over to the other side for a little while, they are still karmically linked with this person because they will undoubtedly be interacting in a future life, so they are willing to try to help. Many times their guide will contact some loved one on the other end. Together they work to help this loved one cast an echo of themselves across the barrier to this person in order to deliver a message.

D: *Then they don't actually journey back themselves; they just send an echo back?*

S: Right. It is a similar process as these other spirits use who have first crossed over, but this process is under control and done deliberately. They calm their mind to get themselves in the right mental state, but it is a positive experience and they cast a spiritual echo of themselves onto the physical plane. Sometimes they have to do it several times before the person on the physical plane begins to perceive this. That is why sometimes before a person perceives what they call a "ghost" or a "spirit," other odd events will happen first. They are already projecting; they are just trying to get the person's attention turned toward that aspects of things so they would be more apt to perceive the spiritual echo.

D: *Sometimes people say spirits come back and give them some advice that they need, or they will tell them not to grieve for them - different things like that.*

S: Yes, because excessive grief can hold you back in developing your karma. You need to realize that you will be running across this person again that you miss so deeply and are grieving so hard for. You are not parted forever. It is just a temporary separation and you need to put that behind you and continue with your own growth so you will be ready for your next life.

D: *But if the person wants to give them some advice, they are able to project themselves to tell them these things.*

S: Right. The guides and these people work together on this to give them advice that they may need at a particular time in their lives.

D: *Do you mean the guide may also appear to the person as resembling the loved one?*

S: No. He will get a loved one to cast their echo. There is usually at least one on the other side, usually more.

D: *The guide never takes on this form to deliver a message?*

S: No. Sometimes the guide will deliver a message himself and the person will report having seen an angel or some other unknown celestial being.

Chapter 12
Planning and Preparation

A REGRESSED SUBJECT who was experiencing an in-between lives spirit state gave the following description of an activity at one of the schools.

S: The closest analogy is that I am attending a lecture. It is a situation of learning, where one of us who has experienced something is telling the others so we may all learn from it. I suppose you could say that I am attending a lecture.
D: *What are they lecturing about?*
S: I am not sure I can tell you because the lecture is being presented in mental concepts and images rather than in words. Some of the juxtapositions do not make any sense when you put them in words. It is quite strange. I think the best way to state it is that he is lecturing us on the malleability of the senses and how they can be fooled. To show us that you cannot depend on what your senses tell you. You must go by your intuitive feelings because your instincts are in tune with the basic heart throb of the universe and they will guide you through. Right now at this portion of the lecture the evidence he is presenting is to demonstrate how the senses can be deceived. For example, he is showing us different natural objects but they will be the wrong color and texture to show how the eyes can be fooled. Like, for example, blue, glittery okra. (Laugh) You know, things that are very bizarre. But he presents these visual images right next to other images to show how the nose and ears can be fooled, and so it is a

213

very interesting lecture. They encourage us to use our intuitive and psychic powers because it is much easier to develop them on this side. And the more you develop them here, the easier it is for them to break through when you are on the physical plane, so that you can use them there. Because the physical plane sets up a sort of barrier to them and makes it more difficult to get in touch with them. But if you have them highly developed before you return you can get past that.

D: *Do you do things on that side according to what you feel you need?*

S: It's basically what stage you are at. It seems to me what you need is what you draw to you, and that is the way it works. It is drawn to you so you learn what you need to learn or experience what you need to experience, and that fulfills that need for developing.

D: *Then the ones who want to learn the more complicated things will naturally seek these out?*

S: Yes. The ones that seek out things to learn, the knowledge will be there for them. It comes to them in the order that they need it so they can make the best use of it. There are those that... even though they may think they want to learn, basically they do not and go around wondering why they make no progress. They always come up with various reasons to explain it.

D: *Of course, many people just want to go right back into a life again and don't want to learn anything.*

S: That is true. There are some unfortunate souls that insist on keeping themselves chained to the wheel of karma. But the more development you go through when you are on this side, the more it can liberate you from past causes. Then you can go on to bigger and better things so far as your karma is concerned. Does this make sense?

D: *To other people it probably wouldn't, but, yes, it makes sense to me. I am always trying to learn things anyway.*

S: Yes, you are like one of us. *You* are a learner, too.

A SCENE describing preparatory events prior to returning to Earth.

D: *What are you doing?*
S: I am with other spirit entities. There is a group of us gathered together. You could call it a sort of discussion and planning group. The majority of us here have been linked karmically in our past lives. There is one here who is our main guide for the group in general, and our individual guides are nearby. We are discussing and planning what karmic problems we will be working on during this next upcoming life, the one that this subject is currently living. And we are discussing and planning how our lives and our karmas will interweave and interrelate and what we hope to work out karmically.
D: *These are spirits that you will be associated with whenever you return to Earth?*
S: Yes. That's one thing that influences who you have karmic links with. Another thing that sometimes influences it, is if it is found that when two particular people are together they progress geometrically in-stead of arithmetically. When they are apart they progress at one particular rate, but when they are together it multiplies geometrically simply because of the way they interact with each other. Naturally it is encouraged that they continue to cross paths in future lifetimes so they can continue to progress together. My individual spirit guide will be with me throughout my next incarnation to help guide and protect me. As an extra insurance, I suppose you could call it, and as a friend to help connect with the spirit side of things when I am on the physical plane.
D: *Is there any way you will know whenever he is there?*
S: The spirit guide? One way to tell-at least for this subject when I am incarnated - is that my visual perception of things will change, to where everything will seem to sparkle. Even things of a solid color will seem to sparkle

with intensive flashes of that color, as if the color that it is on the spiritual plane is peeping through. At those times my spirit guide will be especially close to me and we will be closely in harmony, to where my eyes begin to see things through his eyes. And there will be a particularly peaceful feeling involved, too.

D: *Will he have a name that you can call him?*

S: I am not sure. He has been known by many names. I can contact him by sending out a mental call for him, calling for my spiritual friend. He says that is sufficient. He has a name but he says that is not necessary. It might be difficult for me to remember it.

D: *So whenever you need help during this lifetime, you just ask for your spiritual friend and he will be able to advise you?*

S: Yes. He can give me advice either through directly speaking in my mind or by giving me emotions and feelings to go by, intuitions to guide me. He can also help things to come to pass by nudging them in certain directions.

D: *Some people wonder how you can know if it is really your guide speaking to you and not someone who would wish you harm. Do you know how to tell?*

S: It's hard to describe using this language. When it is your guide there is a particular warm, tingling feeling in your heart, in your chest, and you seem to see this beautiful sparkling effect of everything too. It is a particular combination that cannot be duplicated. And the feelings you have that are associated with this are generally those of comfort and confidence and security. Whereas if it is a spirit entity trying to do you harm, the feelings that you have would be insecurity, fear, and perhaps anger. If you think of doing something that feels right, do it. And if you are thinking of doing something and you are not sure whether it would be right or when you start to do it you begin to tremble or feel fear, then wait a little bit and see if any other feelings come to you. If you wait, usually another feeling will come and you will say, "Yes, that is what I'm supposed to do." Sometimes it will be something quite a bit different than what you were fixing to do, and sometimes it will be only slightly different. But it will be the better course.

D: *I've also been told that when it is your real spirit guide, he will never try to make you do anything.*

S: No, never. They'll just say, "You have asked for my advice and this is what is your best course of action. But the choice is yours. If you prefer to do something else, then we will work with that choice of action instead."

D: *I have been told that if there is any kind of force involved or if someone tries to make you do something, then it is not for your own good.*

S: That is true. These concepts are one of the underlying structures of the universe.

D: *Do you have other guides that will be helping you?*

S: Yes. He is the main one that will be in particularly close contact with me. There are others who are concerned with my progress, as they are concerned with the progress of others, also. And there are a group of guides that are concerned with our particular progress as a group. We have been linked karmically in the past many times and you might say we are progressing together as a group while each of us individually get used to things that we need to develop.

D: *Where you are right now, is it a certain place?*

S: No, no particular place. We are just ... here, gathered in close proximity. Since we are all in the spiritual form, you could say that we are floating here. It is on a different plane but I am not really sure which plane it is. Everything is very peaceful here and conducive towards thinking and planning. The one that will fulfill the role of my mother on the physical plane is here. These planning conferences are kind of rare and when an opportunity comes to have them, we do. Because usually one or the other in the group is on the earthly plane. But occasionally it overlaps to where all of us are on the spiritual plane at the same time, and we get together to coordinate things, so to speak.

D: *Yes, I suppose it makes it more difficult if someone has already returned.*

S: Right. Although we could communicate with their subconscious if need be, but it is not as clear a communication.

D: *Is there anyone else there that is going to be important in your life when you return to Earth?*

S: Yes. There is the one with whom I am karmically linked to be soul mate with. He is here. He will be returning back to Earth only shortly before I will. And there is one here that is fixing to leave fairly quickly. He is to be my grandfather and he must go back before my mother can go back. His stay on the earthly plane will just barely overlap with mine but it will be enough to make a deep impression on my life. And this impression will affect me the rest of my earthly stay. He is a very karmatically advanced spirit. It is cloudy when we look ahead but if things go the way we are working them out here and now, then that's the way it will happen. I will need to keep in mind to be patient and go by my inner feelings and not by what I will be taught as a child. I can see very clearly that what I will be taught as a child will not apply when I am an adult.

D: *That is where your free will comes in. You are supposed to think for yourself.*

S: Yes, I will need to go through some transitions that will be difficult for me. My guide will help.

D: *Then even small things are all worked out before you come back?*

S: We try to work them out. We discuss how we are going to interact with each other. We have our free will on such things from the physical viewpoint when we get there. But if we work out these things ahead of time we are more apt to be open to our spiritual guides as they try to guide us through. It is a way of not being quite so haphazard about working out karma.

D: *Otherwise it is just hit and miss, so to speak.*

S: Right. However, it all balances out in the end.

ANOTHER SCENE:

S: I am speaking with my spirit friend. The one who will be my spirit guide when I incarnate again.

D: *Can you see him?*

S: Yes. The appearance he has is that of a mature man in his late forties. The signs of age that he wears are not due to his condition but to personal choice for the mental reactions that he wants from others. He has black hair that is graying at the temples and a well-turned mustache and beard. He looks like a British doctor from the turn of the century. And he is dressed in an old-fashioned three-pieced suit, very distinguished looking with black polished shoes. That is just the image he's maintaining today. We are in a place that looks like a man's study. There is a hardwood floor with an oriental carpet and a leather-topped desk. Leather upholstered chairs and shelves of books all the way to the ceiling, and a fireplace. He has pince-nez wire-rimmed glasses. And he is very wise.

D: *I guess I have always thought of the guides wearing white robes.*

S: No, not always. It is a matter of personal choice. And he is wanting to project an image towards me. The feeling of being like a father protector or an uncle or someone who has my welfare in mind and wants to help and protect me. He knows that I am more comfortable with someone who looks like an ordinary human being rather than someone wrapped in white flowing robes. I would be more apt to feel an affinity with him. He has warm brown eyes and he is very kind.

D: *But is this only the way you see things, or is it the way other people see it?*

S: He and I are the only two in this study. This is not part of a house. It is just an image surrounding us to set a certain atmosphere. And so, were one to see it from the outside they would merely see a large piece of ectoplasm. It would look rather like a blob of mist. But they would know from the psychic feeling emanating from it that it was an ectoplasmic construct being used for a specific purpose. And they would also be able to realize that we were with-in this construct of ectoplasm.

D: *What are you speaking with your guide about?*

S: During this discussion with you he has been helping me organize information in a way that you could comprehend it with this language. But before this, we were talking-communicating I should say-about how I can help myself with my karma on the plane of incarnation.

D: *When you come back the next time?*

S: Yes. It is hard to describe in your language what he is saying so that you'll know what he means. But I understand what he is saying.

D: *But at another time when you meet him you might be in other surroundings or he may appear differently?*

S: No. Most of the time when we get together he appears like this, or rather in his face he is like this. Sometimes he is dressed differently. Sometimes he has more or less gray in his hair. But I usually identify him with a certain psychic feeling rather than with a particular visual appearance.

D: *Sometimes it helps to have a picture in your mind of what he looks like.*

S: Yes, that will help me when I am down on the plane of incarnation. But it also helps to be familiar with the psychic feeling so that I can be aware that he is nearby helping me, even though I have not specifically visualized him at the time.

When this subject awakened and I told her about the session, she said the description of the room and the man sounded like recurring dreams she had had all during her life. I suggested it would be useful if she could visualize the man and the room when she wished to talk to her guide and ask him for advice.

KARMA

S: I am looking at karmic connections.

D: *Can you explain what you mean?*

S: Through the cycle of lives certain connections between certain groups of people appear again and again in the various permutations. For example, in one life a person might be your mate, in another life one of your parents, and in another life a child or a good friend. These connections reappear in various lifetimes and are sometimes strengthened and sometimes weakened, but they are always growing. Then eventually, when we all reach the ultimate (the source), the connections have developed to the point that, if the desire is there, we can form an entity greater than ourselves with all of us being part of it.

D: *I have heard a great deal about karma. Would you be able to give a definition of it from your point of view?*

S: It is so all-encompassing and complex I would not be able to do it justice. I doubt if I could give you a good definition in your language or even mine. Karma - I've spoken before of the different universes and how they intertwine and react to each other. The energy from each individual life is like a universe in itself, and the way it intertwines and reacts to all the other energy in your universe, particularly the energies put out by other life-forms, weaves the complex tapestry that we call karma.

D: *I can tell you some of the definitions I have heard and you can tell me if they fit or not. I have heard that karma is the law of balance, the law of cause and effect. If you did something bad or if you hurt someone in another life, you had to pay it back at some time. But I have also heard it can deal with good things.*

S: Yes, that is the way it is. The law of cause and effect is one of the basic laws in effect everywhere, regardless of which universe you are in. This law is one of the underlying principles of karma that supports the entire structure. And karma applies to how the different energies interact with each other, sometimes being cause and sometimes being effect, in a complex combination of moves. This is what builds karma. And anything, any action initiated can be labeled as "cause," and anything that happens as a result of that can be "effect." The action that results can also be called cause for other effects. It is all interlocking. It would be like having a sphere made out of chain links and they are all interlinked with each other. Every chain link is interlinked with every other chain link within the sphere. You could use this analogy to picture cause and effect and how they are all connected. That is the way karma is linked with all of the life energies.

D: *I have heard it is called one of the universal laws because there is no way you can escape from the karma-you have to pay it back.*

S: It is being worked out all the time. Just the act of breathing works out karma. Regardless of what you do, you are always working out past karma and creating future karma. This is the cycle of life.

D: *Isn't there any way to get away from creating future karma?*

S: The creating of future karma is what causes the universe to go on. Your future karma does not have to be bad karma. As you are working out past karma and do the best you can in your present life, the future karma that you are creating will be good karma and it will have good effects on your future life. And you will be able to continue and improve your future lives until you reach the ultimate.

D: *There are many people that say they just want to get it all over with. They want to pay off all their debts and not create any more.*

S: When you reach the higher levels of karma you no longer have to go through physical lifetimes to work it out. You can do it on the spiritual plane and still be working towards the ultimate. And even when you reach the ultimate, your karma will be influencing and including other universes and the working out of the complex tapestry of the universes. It is not to be considered a prison. It is just a natural cycle that you can grow and develop through to become your ultimate self.

D: *Many people say they just don't want to have to come back and do it again.*

S: They are still immature. They have much growing to do in their grand cycle.

D: *I think most of the time people think of karma as: If they have hurt someone in the past, then they have to pay for it now.*

S: That is an immature view. That is only an aspect of it. To liken it to your life cycle: when you are a child, you think of punishment as always being *bad* be-cause you did something you were not supposed to do. Later you realize it was helping to teach you what you *should* do to be able to survive and live well. Later on when things good or bad happen to you, you realize it is because of a mistake that you have made in the past and you are now living through the consequences of your mistake-or because it is a mistake someone else has made. Then when you live further on and you make fewer mistakes, your life settles down into a comfortable pattern. These people who speak of karma as relating to something bad they have done in the past, are at the stage where they are looking at it as punishment. They should be looking at it as a teaching tool to help them to learn to grow and become better. They are still young in their cycles of lives.

D: *Sometimes it does look complicated. For instance, if someone has lived a good life and then they die in a very violent manner. No one can understand why such a good person has to die that way. Things like that seem so unjust.*

S: Sometimes before someone comes down for another cycle of life, they will volunteer to go through something that seems to be out of proportion to the life that they will lead. Because their going through that willingly helps to work out a major portion of karma that would take many lifetimes to work out otherwise. It is not because they are being punished for any one particular thing they have done. It is just that they felt they were ready to work out a large portion in a condensed form.

D: *But it does affect the lives of the other people they are associated with when something like that happens.*

S: That is true, but the other people can use it as a growing experience and gain wisdom.

D: *That is what I have been told. If you learn anything from an experience, then it is worthwhile.*

S: That is true.

D: *You said you were looking at the cycles of karma. Does this have to do with your own life or what?*

S: Yes, I was looking at the connections that appear to be consistent in my life cycles. And it appears that they will be consistent in future life cycles, up to what you would call the present time and into the future.

D: *You mean people you have been associated with and you will continue to be associated with in the future?*

S: Yes. They will be brought together in her present lifetime to work on some karmic things. They asked to be together again in this lifetime and it was granted.

D: *Then you are just looking at the patterns to observe them. There is nothing you can really do to influence them, is there?*

S: Do you mean in a positive direction?

D: *Well, hopefully in a positive direction. We don't want a negative direction if we can help it.*

S: I cannot influence the karma in past lifetimes because that has already come to pass. In the present lifetime, perhaps I can give it a nudge here and there. I don't know if it would have any definite effect but it would not harm anything. I could perhaps plant some thoughts in her subconscious to affect her future lifetimes and they would blossom in the future. Each life influences all the others.

Chapter 13
The General Council

I REGRESSED a subject to a period between lives and found her sitting in on a council meeting. The surroundings were ethereal, majestically beautiful and obviously located on a higher plane.

S: If you were to look at it with physical eyes it would appear that where we are gathered is suspended in midair, but it is really not. It is supported by an energy field that you cannot perceive with the eyes of your level. The energy field is a beautiful deep violet color and it surrounds all of us. There are not really any definite walls or ceilings; everything is just this deep violet and gold. And suspended in the center of this energy field is a council chamber, I suppose you would call it. There are fluted golden columns all around the sides. They really don't serve any purpose except as points of beauty, although they can also be used for focusing power. The way they are arranged, they are all evenly spaced to where the whole structure could be used as a power generator, but they are not essential for this. There are golden draperies behind these. And it is very beautiful, the gold against the violet. The furniture we are sitting on is made out of gold but has a wood grain. It is as if a tree grew that was solid gold and the furniture was made from it. It is very beautiful.

D: *Are you around a table of some kind or what?*

S: No, we are around the edges of this council chamber. There are about four or five staggered rows of chairs going up, so that the people behind can see over the heads of the people in front. They are not really chairs. It's tiers - smooth stairs going around like an amphitheater. And they surround this empty space in the center. If someone wants to come forward and speak or present something, they can do it there where all can see. It is like an oval courtroom framed by gold columns and gold drapes, with the tiers going up around and leaving an open space where there is a podium. But it is fancier than just a regular podium. It is like something ornate made out of wood, except that it is really made out of gold. It's there in case one needs to present some-thing. For example, from the podium could be projected what you could call "holograms."

D: *What would be the purpose of that?*

S: It depends on what's being discussed and what is needed to be presented. We generally come here to discuss the influence we have had on Earth and the influence we will be having in the future, and how it fits in with the grand plan of things. The things presented there in the clear space are things demonstrating the overall pattern in this particular universe. And how our karmas have interacted with this pattern and what path we need to continue to follow in order to eventually attain enlightenment. The form that we are in, we can float if we want. We don't have to sit down, but most of us are, just because it creates a more comfortable atmosphere.

D: *What form are you in?*

S: I see spiritual entities looking like white lights. It would be like miniature suns of various shapes and colors, kind of glowing out from the center. It is like having a ball of energy that is sending out rays of light. And as the light goes out from the center it has hints of other colors within the white. It is like an aurora or an opal, except that when you see an opal it is basically one color. With these entities, you see rays of other colors that seem to indicate how they feel, the mood they are in, what they are thinking and how developed they are.

D: *I was thinking the light was in the form of a person, but it is like a ball?*

S: It is like looking at the sun. You don't really see a definite outline because it is too bright. But you know that there is a center of energy there and you see all this energy going out in rays.

D: *Pulsating?*

S: It is a steady flow.

D: *Radiating?*

S: That is a good word-radiating from a common center. And each is suspended in a particular position on these tiers. Everyone is aware of themselves or self-aware, the way you and I are self-aware. It is just that they perceive on a higher level than you can perceive. And their position on these tiers is determined by some sort of energy. They are suspended in mid-air, and it depends on how their energy interacts with the energy of the surroundings. These tiers radiate energy in some sort of pattern, and it is the equivalent of sitting down in a chair. They are supporting themselves on this cushion of energy as they interact with these tiers.

D: *You said this was on a higher plane?*

S: Yes. All of us here are in-between lives now and we have been striving to raise our karma, so to speak (see Chapter 12). We have reached this level where, when we are not directly involved with a life, we can go to this higher plane to plan our future path. And to plan ways of helping others who have not advanced as far as we have yet-just as there are those who are more advanced helping us. And we all help each other. Everything is interrelated like that.

D: *You mean this is a more advanced place than other people have reached, but there are still other planes that are higher than you?*

S: Right. The highest plane of all is when you attain total enlightenment. We have not attained that yet. But we are working at it and we have been assured that we are making good progress. That is why we are trusted with helping others less advanced than we are.

D: *Is it like being a guide?*

S: Well, when we are in-between lives like this, time does not apply here like it does on the earthly plane. And people who are directly involved with a life on the earthly plane sometimes need help. We can help them from this plane without a great expenditure of energy because we are on a higher plane. I suppose you could say it is something like guides. It is rather like having a big brother or sister helping you out occasionally. Also, others who are in be-tween lives right now, but not as advanced as we are, will often need help planning for future lives so as to continue progressing their karma. We give them advice and suggestions from our experiences, and then they can make their own decisions-just as the ones who are on higher planes do for us. They tell us what they have done to attain their level of karma and whether these things would apply to our own karma while striving to attain higher goals.

D: *Then if you had questions you could not answer, you would ask the ones on the other level. Can you see those other people on the other levels?*

S: Not right now. We are in a council of this level and we are handling things so far. But if it were to come a point that we are stumped, so to speak, we can contact those on higher levels from the podium with the pillars of power and they can come and communicate with us.

D: *You couldn't go to their level to contact them? They would have to come to your level?*

S: We can contact them through a method of distant communication, like a radio on your level. But they would have to come to our level to be able to make contact with us directly, because we have only attained a certain level of enlightenment. We can't go to the higher levels because our energy level is not compatible with them yet. But we can visit the lower levels because we've already been through those levels and we know how to adjust our energy to be compatible with them. So we can go there and help the ones who are there. When you improve your karma through your lives on Earth and you come back, the ones on higher levels advise you of what you have attained. And you find that your energy is compatible to the level which you have newly attained. You remember how it was on the other levels so you can still go to those in order to help the people there.

D: *You said you can help people from your level without a great expenditure of energy. Does it take more energy on other levels, or what?*

S: It depends on the circumstances. One can help people on the earthly plane without a great expenditure of energy because we are always in repeated contact with that plane. When we are on this side, we can see how the underlying structure of energy or enlightenment links all things together. So we can, so to speak, give it a nudge here and there to help someone out in a particular direction. It doesn't have to be anything major, but it causes events to fall in another direction rather than the direction they were originally developing towards.

D: *Where does it take the most energy?*

S: It takes more energy to contact the higher levels because our energy is not compatible with those. It is a matter of concentrating our energy and refining it so it can pick a sympathetic vibration in the higher level. Another thing that takes a lot of energy is whenever you need to visit and help people who have done many negative things to their karma. The more negative a person's karma is, the more in-compatibility there is and this makes it more difficult to communicate with them and try to help them. It is like trying to push the same poles of two different magnets together. You know how they repel each other.

It is much like trying to work in that type of situation. They put up energy barriers without meaning to do it, we believe. They don't realize what they are doing to their karma. They seem to get into a never-ending circle of doing this to their karma. We usually have to watch them very carefully and try to catch them at a vulnerable point so we can break through and give them a glimmering of hope. Just the glimmering of a message to help them break out of their cycle and start making positive progress on their karma.

D: *This is much harder than working with people who are more open to your side.*

S: Right. The ones who are working on negative karma, it would be like having a hollow donut. They are running around and around on the inside of this donut and they are just staying in the same rut. Or if it is a really bad case, it is like going downwards in a spiral, and someone trying to catch them and start them going up again. Whereas, in the case of people who are working on their karma in a positive direction, it is like climbing a staircase. It is a much more open situation and it is much easier to contact them. The people who are working on negative karma - it is usually a closed-type situation where it is more difficult to break through.

D: *They probably don't even realize you are there.*

S: Exactly. They have built mental walls and walls of energy about them to block out all that they don't want to deal with.

D: *Are any of you specifically assigned to any of these people or do you just help whoever you see?*

S: It's not that we are assigned to specific people. We are rather like monitors. We are told to keep an eye on a particular portion of the overall picture, and whenever we see a part that needs a little bit of a nudge or a little bit of help, we go ahead and act on our own initiative. It may not be the same person every time that we help. Whenever we do a nudge to assist them on their way to help the overall picture of positive karma, sometimes a particular person might benefit from it. But more often it is usually an action that benefits many people.

D: *Do these people have guides assigned to them?*

S: Yes, they do. But where I am at, we are working with general events rather than with specific people.

D: *Would it be correct to say that you are higher than the regular guides? Or is there a hierarchy like that?*

S: I don't really think so. I think it is a matter of where you are in your karma as to what kind of task they give you. Task is the wrong word. When you are on the earthly plane you are working on your karma, but that is not the only place where you are working on it. When you're in-between lives and on the other planes like this plane, you are working on your karma also, but in a different way. It is hard to say; Earth languages are devoid of nuances. The ones who guide particular people are in a different place in their karma of development. They perhaps need to grow in a particular way to look at things in a broadened aspect that includes needing to guide individual people. They may have already done what I'm doing now; there's no particular order. It just depends on how you grow individually. In my case I have done a little bit of individual guiding in the past. And the ones above me felt that my karma would benefit most from being in this general council this time. They also like for everyone to have a chance to be in the general council so they can get a grasp of the overall view of things. That way they can have a pretty good idea of how they are progressing and thus continue to progress in the right direction. Usually after people have been on this general council they make pretty good progress with their karma because they have a better overview of things.

D: *You said you were mostly involved with events, but that you were also working with certain persons trying to get something through to them. Would you be able to contact their guides and give them suggestions also?*

S: Yes. We work very closely with the spirits who are acting as individual guides. We work in cooperation with each other. For they take care of helping an individual person and they also work with us. They want to make sure they are totally aware of the events so they can help these individual people to take full advantage of them for the benefit of their karma. Sometimes they will tell us that a certain person is bound and determined to do a particular thing. They ask us how that will affect the general events and will we need to alter it any, so as to have the most positive effect on the most people. So we work very closely together, all interrelated.

D: *Then from where you are you can see the possible effects of what they are doing? You can see the future, in other words?*

S: Well, we can see the general patterns of what is likely to take place, and they generally come to pass. Usually their details are different because of other individual decisions made along the way.   Sometimes at a crucial point an individual may make a totally different decision than what their guide is urging them to do, and it changes the picture a little at that point. And further down the line we'll have to give other events a nudge. But that's the way it has always been, and this is what keeps the universe alive and fluctuating.

D: *You give them a nudge to go back into the original path?*

S: Not necessarily they themselves, individually, but if they make a decision that affects an event, later on we may need to give another event a nudge to minimize any negative effects that may have occurred.

D: *That way they still have the free will to do what they want.*

S: Oh, yes.

D: *You try to keep it from affecting the overall outcome, is that what it is?*

S: Right. Everyone has their own free will to do what they wish.   But if they make a decision that is going to

234

negatively affect many other people, well, those other people did not choose to be affected that way. And that, in effect, takes away a little bit of their free will. For instance, if an individual person makes a decision that has a drastic negative effect on other people, we try to keep the events contained so they will have a less drastic effect on the other spirits.

D: *This sounds like it would be difficult to do.*

S: It is complicated, but it is part of our growth and we like doing it.

D: *It would be very far-reaching if it affected many people.*

S: It is just a matter of keeping things within the pattern. It is hard to describe to you on your plane, but here the pattern can be seen very clearly. We don't necessarily see things in visions of individual people and individual events, at least on this general council. What we see is the overall pattern, like glistening webs of energy. And if there is a snarl-up in the web of energy, we work on it with other energy and this heals it because the web is whole again. In this way it affects the events on the Earth because it is the overall pattern of energy that makes anything and everything be and come to pass.

D: *But you don't have absolute power, do you? Do you also make mistakes?*

S: We don't have absolute power, no, but we don't generally make mistakes either because the higher levels make sure that we are not given more than we can handle.

D: *It sounds like it is all interacting and so complicated that you could goof up once in a while, so to speak.*

S: Well, if it looks like we are fixing to goof up someone from the higher levels will advise us, just as we advise people at lower levels.

D: *There have been massive negative events in history that seemed to have gotten all out of control. I am thinking of wars and things like that.*

S: Yes. And those that are on this council have done their best to try to contain these massive negative decisions. Many times these things can be traced down to a single personal handful of people that are so stuck in their negative karma that nothing can get through to them. It is a matter of trying to contain the results of their decisions, in such a way so as to help keep the damage under control.

D: *But you said you are watching all this. Can you see things happening on Earth from where you are?*

I was hoping to get some information about events in our future.

S: Not right now. We are in a council meeting discussing something else that affects another plane and not the earthly plane. Usually when we're dealing with things on Earth we are concerned with the overall pattern of things. We tend to concentrate on the appearance of karmic energy rather than the individual appearance of people and things. We work closely with those who guide individual people. These guides are the ones that see things the way they appear on the physical plane, so they can help individuals.

D: *Can the individual guide see what is going to happen if a certain person does a certain type of action?*

S: Yes. We switch back and forth between lifetimes, as to whether we will work on a general council like this or be a specific guide. We do both *several* times, because there's no such thing as getting too much experience at this. And the people who are guides usually have either served on the general council before or they have worked closely enough with it so that they are aware of how it works. Whenever we are working together on something they will have opportunities to see the overall pattern of things very clearly, just as we will have a chance to focus in on individuals and see how our work with the general pattern is affecting them. So there is much interchange of information. It is just a matter of different perspectives.

D: *But you said what you are discussing now at the council deals with another plane?*

S: Yes. There are some spirits that have recently passed over to the spirit side. They have recently left Earth and they are in the process of making their adjustment now. Every spirit needs a period of adjustment when they go from either the physical plane to the spiritual plane or vice versa. To get used to the new situations before they can start working on their karma again. So, while these spirits are going through the adjustment period, the council meets and we discuss what their situation is and what they need. And how we can best serve them to help them develop their karma in this new stage they are in. There are some spirits that have been going through this adjustment period on one particular spiritual plane. We are getting the final de-tails together so when they are ready we can contact them and guide them and help them, so they can constructively use this period between lifetimes be-fore it is time for them to go back to the physical plane.

D: *When they first pass over, are they given a certain type of surroundings that makes it easier for them to adjust?*

S: Yes, depending on their spiritual development. Their personal guides work with us and we can tell by looking at the energy vibrations and their karmic development, and know at what level of spiritual development they are. When they pass over to this side, they first perceive that which they are capable of handling. And usually, when it is possible, if some other spiritual entities that were connected with them in their most recent life are still on the spiritual plane, we have them there to help them across, so to speak. To help them make the first adjustment, because the primary adjustment is always the most difficult. But after they have accepted the fact that they have crossed over and they are in a new plane of existence, then it is a matter of giving them time to adjust to this new situation of things. By that time the experiences on the physical plane are not quite so fresh on the memory so they can start thinking of things from the spiritual perspectives. Then we can help them to continue growing until they are ready to enter the physical perspective again.

D: *That way it is not quite a shock to them. Is that what you mean?*

S: Right. The transition is a shock anyway, but we try to lessen the shock as much as possible, so as to not give the spiritual entity a major setback.

D: *Then these surroundings could be anything. I've always wondered about that. People have near-death experiences and they sometimes describe the same scenes.*

S: Yes. What they're describing is what they see up to the approach to the barrier between the physical and the spiritual. The approach up to this barrier is usually very similar because you must go through the same types of energy fields to cross over to the spiritual side. But once they get past what is usually described as a bright light at the end of a tunnel - this bright light is the barrier itself - then what they see differs according to their individual development.

D: *They have described seeing scenes and people, and sometimes it is like going through a tunnel. But all these things are leading up to the barrier?*

S: Right. It is to help get them prepared in the quickest amount of time for the shock they are going through. The act of leaving the body is a very natural act; it is like breathing. But the act of passing from the physical side to the spiritual side can be a shock to the system. And these scenes that they see are to help impress upon them the fact that they are getting ready to cross over and to help them to brace themselves, so to speak.

D: *Then once they go past that light they cannot come back into the physical body at that point?*

S: That is correct. When they re-cross that light it will be for entering another body.

D: *I have been told that there is a cord that is supposed to connect the spirit to the body.*

S: Yes, and when you go through that bright light it severs the cord because you are going through an intense energy field. The cord that connects the astral body to the physical body is a type of energy. And when you go through the energy barrier, it is dissolved.

D: *Then the people who describe near-death experiences only go that far. They say they feel like they are being pulled toward the light and then they come back. Apparently they have not gone far enough.*

S: It was not yet their time to cross over. Now when they do die they will still feel the same pulling sensation, but this time they will complete the transition. And it is a very pleasant experience. It is just a big change and so it is a shock in that respect.

D: *Then these people who had these experiences really were dying, so to speak?*

S: Yes, they just did not complete the process.

D: *Then by turning around and coming back they were able to go back into the body. They say sometimes their lives are changed after an experience like that.*

S: Yes, as it should be. When such things happen it is usually because their guide has decided that they were heading towards a dead end in their karma. They were not really wanting to break out of their pattern. Something like that happens to really shake up their thinking, so they start on new patterns and can begin guiding their karma into new directions, hopefully more positive patterns.

D: *Then this is what they mean by the expression "crossing over" - they cross through that energy barrier.*

S: Yes. There are many metaphors for it in the earthly languages. "Crossing over Jordan," "going through the veil," or "passing over;" any of these metaphors are referring to this part of the experience. I am trying to use terms I think you will be familiar with. The metaphor of "shedding your old clothes to take up new garments" is referring to your energy cord being dissolved by the barrier and entering a new level of existence.

D: *Then do they see surroundings or scenes at that time?*

S: When they go through the barrier all they see is bright energy. And they feel like they are being cleansed because the energy is adjusting their own spiritual vibrations to be compatible with whatever level they have attained. This corresponds to the metaphor of "being washed clean by Jordan" when you cross over. Once they get to the other side, at first in their adjustment period they may see scenes that resemble things they remember or imagined on the physical plane, but these are much more perfect and beautiful than they could have imagined. Then as they become adjusted they realize that these are really constructs of their own mind and they start seeing the level where they are as it actually is. But it is a very smooth transition because it is guided solely by what their minds are ready for. Their minds construct these visions that they see until they are ready to see things as they truly are.

D: *How are they, truly?*

S: It depends on what level you are at. It is hard to describe how things truly are because the laws of physics don't apply here like they do on the physical plane. For example, usually when one pictures oneself as being somewhere, one pictures oneself standing on a planet with a particular set of surroundings. But on the spiritual plane this won't necessarily be true. You may be in a particular type of energy field with various properties. And various events take place due to your interacting with this energy field and with the others who are also in this energy field. So it depends on what the plane is and thus it is difficult to describe. Sometimes you will see visual analogues to help you make connections with what you are seeing compared to what you have al-ready experienced.

D: *Do you have to go back to your council? I'm not interrupting you, am I?*

S: No, not at all. Because whenever those of us on the council and on this plane are contacted by understanding spirits on your plane, it is part of our karma to help out by giving as clear of answers as we can. And it is part of *your* karma and this, your subject's karma, to help bring more knowledge of the higher planes to your plane to help other spirits in general to progress in their karma. It is all part of the pattern.

D: *That is why I have to try to put this into words that people can understand, because it is very complicated. It is very important that I present it in a way they can grasp, and that's difficult.*

S: That is one reason why I have been given this job to draw metaphors. The higher spirits tell me that I am good at drawing metaphors that can be under-stood by people on the physical plane, to help them picture things that are not pictureable.

D: *Yes, I need metaphors and analogies. They make it easier for me to grasp this. Otherwise it would just go way over my head. I always welcome any information that you can give me because I never know which way we are going. All information is important.*

S: These questions that you think you come up with on your own are actually suggestions from your guide of things to ask about. Continue to stay in touch with your creative part and stay open to these questions that pop into your mind seemingly out of nowhere, and follow up on these different questions. And from this side, I and others will continue to try to present this information to you in a way that you and others on the physical plane can understand.

D: *We think that it is time for people to know these things.*

S: Yes, it is. Your guide gave you that thought. Because we are the ones that say when people are ready to learn more about these things.

I have been told that in addition to the general councils, there are also numerous levels of councils above them. I don't know if there is any limit, as I have been told of universal councils that are over entire universes and also councils on the Creator level. The ones on that level are considered co-creators with God and work on creating new universes or whatever is needed, *ad infinitum.*

I think it would be impossible to expect our mortal minds to grasp or understand even a portion of what it is really all about. But it is fascinating to realize that there is more to it than we ever dreamed possible.

Chapter 14
Imprinting

THE RADICAL IDEA of imprinting was brought up quite by accident when I happened to ask a male subject a chance question.

D: *Have you had many lives on this planet Earth?*
S: This is my first physical life, my first true incarnation on this planet. I have had imprints from many others and been assistant to others. However, this is my first true physical incarnation on Earth.

What did he mean? This was confusing because when we first began working together we had touched on about four other lives that had definitely taken place on this planet. What was going on during those earlier sessions?

D: *Then the other ones we discussed were not real?*
S: They were imprints and assistances; they were not true physical incarnations.

I have had many startling revelations during my unorthodox pursuit of knowledge, but this really threw me. I had never heard of an imprint. In my work with regressions, either you lived a life or you didn't. The only other alternative is that the subject was fantasizing or imagining the whole thing. I have always prided myself on being able to tell the difference. In everything I have read about possible explanations for the memories of other lives, I had never heard of anything called "imprinting." I was confused. If a life is not considered to be a true physical incarnation, how would I ever know what I was dealing with?

D: *Do you mean that when some souls come into a life, rather than having lived these exact past life experiences, they take...*

S: They can withdraw information from the Akashic records and imprint this information into their soul, and it will then be their experience.

Other researchers have said that the Akashic records contain no mention of time, only the record of events, emotions, and the lessons learned.

D: *Well ... Can you tell me how I can tell the difference when I do work like this?*

S: No, because even I can't tell the difference. If I am in an imprint, that imprint is as real as if I had actually experienced it. All the emotions, the memories, the feelings, virtually everything about that life is in that imprint. So from my point of view I would be unable to tell because I would be completely absorbed in the experience. This is the whole idea of imprint. This is the ability to live thousands, hundreds of thousands of years on a planet and actually never have been there before.

D: *What would be the reason?*

S: If one has never experienced a life on Earth before, or if it has perhaps been a long time since the last incarnation, there would be no point of reference, nothing to fall back on or relate to. If one were to come to this planet without the aid of imprints, one would be totally lost. One would not understand customs, religions, politics, or how to act in a social environment. This is the necessity for imprint, if there is no previous earthly experience of human existence in their subconscious. In order for this person to feel comfortable and at ease, there must be something with which to draw on and compare those day-to-day experiences which one is encountering. For if this were not so, the feeling of total out-of-harmony would be virtually present every single day, until there arose that time when one could look back and see some semblance of history. That is, in the later part of life. However, the con-fusion and disharmony from having to experience this would negate any learning, for always there would be the disharmony which all learning would have to filter through. All learning would be colored with this disharmony and would be, in effect, no learning at all. So there must be this imprinting to allow the vehicle to feel comfortable in his new surroundings and in those experiences which would be totally foreign. For even such simple things as an argument would become so terrifying to the vehicle as to render him totally void. These innocents have no experience with anger or fear as you know it. It would incapacitate them. It would paralyze them. They would be totally traumatized.

Many people believe that all this is conditioned by the environment anyway. That a baby's mind is totally fresh and all information is learned and absorbed as it grows and lives its life. Apparently we rely more on our subconscious memories than we realize. It seems to be like a computer bank from which we constantly draw comparisons in our daily lives. According to this new idea, a spirit coming for the first time into an earthly body and facing a strange new culture must have something in their past memories to orient themselves and give them something to relate to. This whole idea was startling to me and opened up an entirely new way of thinking. It could change my whole outlook on reincarnation.

D: *But, is there any way when I work with people that I can tell if they are remembering and reliving an actual*

life or an imprint?
S: We ask why you would wish to know.
D: *Well, it is probably to help prove whatever I am trying to prove.*

I laughed inwardly, because it boiled down to: What am I trying to prove anyhow? He seemed to read my mind.

S: And what are you trying to prove?

I shook my head and laughed in bewilderment. "That's a good question."

S: We will shortly show that you will answer your own question.
D: *Well, I am trying to prove the reality of reincarnation, because many people don't believe in the concept. By having someone go through a life and being able to prove that that person did exist in that time period, I am trying to verify these things. But if someone was remembering an imprint, would we also be able to verify it?*
S: That is correct, for the experience was actually lived, even though it was not lived by the vehicle you would be presently speaking to. However, all the information would be the same, as if you had actually been talking to the very soul which had been in that vehicle at that time. Imprints become in reality a part of that soul and are so carried with that soul.
D: *Would this be an explanation for the theory that sometimes more than one person appeared to have lived the same previous lifetime? For instance, several Cleopatra's, several Napoleons. Would imprinting take this into consideration?*

I have never had this happen, but it is one of the arguments presented by skeptics.

S: Absolutely. For there is no ... (he had difficulty finding the right word) proprietorship to these imprints. They are open to all. And so it becomes useless to try to pinpoint who was actually that person, for it is meaningless.

D: *This is one of the arguments people have against reincarnation. They say if we find many people with the same lives, then it can't be true.*

S: They are being challenged to widen their scope of knowledge. They are given facts which contradict their shortsighted beliefs and are so challenged to expand their awareness.

D: *Then it doesn't matter if someone was the actual Cleopatra or whoever. We still have access to the information of their life.*

S: It can be verified as easily with the actual soul or with one of many hundred others who experience the same imprint. It makes no difference.

D: *But would different people perhaps perceive the imprint in a different way? If one person was questioned who had the life as Cleopatra, and another having the same life, would their concept possibly be different?*

S: A very good question. We would say that human experience is like a filter and colors these perceptions which pass through it. So if an experience in that Cleopatra incarnation was found objectionable to the conscious of the person relating that, it would either be deleted or changed in order to present it in such a manner as to not cause the disruption of the entity.

That sounds like self-editing. Could this then explain errors that sometimes crop up? Wouldn't this be similar to the way people understand and use research for their own purposes and to prove their own various points of view?

D: *It would nonetheless be true; it would just be different ways of looking at it.*

S: That is correct. It would be presented in as accurate a portrait as possible, but in the most comfortable one also.

D: *Would this also explain the question of parallel lives, two lives apparently occurring at the same time or overlapping each other?*

S: Yes, this is how the paradox or the contradiction arises about parallel lives. It is simply a matter of acquiring societal experiences, laws, regulations, customs, in order to carry out effectively in one's incarnation.

D: *Then it doesn't really matter if it can be proved or not, does it?*

S: Exactly. What is the point? One could go for millennia in tracing ones "past lives," and in this respect it would be totally useless. However, there is much that can be learned from these recalls. Not only from a personal point of view for the regressee but for those who read and hear of this. Much knowledge can be shared so there is much use for everyone.

D: *By reliving past lives, some people receive much benefit in their personal lives, such as understanding their personal relationships with others.*

S: Yes, that is true.

D: *How is it decided what imprints you are going to have or someone else is going to have? Are certain imprints chosen for certain individuals?*

S: The imprint is determined by what the incarnation's goals are to be. If one were to become a leader, a president, for example, one might have imprints from various levels of leaders, from tribal leaders on up through possibly past presidential leaders, maybe a mayor, maybe a leader of thieves. If the emphasis is on leading, many imprints of a leading nature could be used so that the entity is familiar with the aspect of or the idea of what the job of leading is. There is also the secondary and even tertiary advantage of learning humility, patience, fun and entertainment. All of the multitudes of experiences are in these imprints. The *method* of imprinting is beyond me. The effect is to experience multiple lives, maybe simultaneously, maybe serially. But the effect is to learn lessons from other people's experiences. The lessons are shared. The experiences each of us are having in this lifetime now will be available at the end of these lifetimes to be imprinted for use by anyone who would have a use for them. It is simply borrowing books from a library if you would consider each life a book and reading and understanding it instantly.

D: *Are you saying then that the energy of life is as though stored in a book and placed in a library and is available to be imprinted into other people's lives if they so desire to use that information?*

S: That is accurate. There is no limitation on how many can use one particular life. Thousands of people could imprint the same experience simultaneously.

D: *So it would be possible for me to regress more than one person to a particular life if it just so happened that the imprint was available to both individuals.*

S: This is true. The imprints are chosen before the incarnation. There is a method which is far too complex to understand. But you can say that there is a computer, a master computer which has access to all the lives, every one previous. And so the information is fed in of what is to be expected of this life, and the appropriate imprints are then selected and overlaid. There is a hierarchy of spirits whose job it is to do this. There is a council which oversees this. They assist the soul. This computer or council is given all the information regarding the mission and the past experiences of the vehicles with which to draw from. And so there is the choosing between that previous lifetime which has been deposited into the records, and a match between that which pertains and the experience which is about to begin. All memory, all thoughts, all senses, everything that a real existing life would have is there intact. It is a hologram, a three-dimensional summation of that lifetime. All experiences, remembrances, emotions are imprinted into that soul and become a part of that soul. This information is then carried after the in-carnation is over and is a gift from having lived in this realm of existence and so then becomes part of the permanent record of that soul.

D: *Wouldn't it be proper to say the imprint is like a pattern? Would that be another word? That you pick these patterns and use them to try to pattern your life after?*

S: That could be used.

D: *I just had an interesting idea. It is rather like doing research in a library, isn't it?*

S: Yes. You are given books on many subjects and with that knowledge in hand you carry forth.

D: *But when a person really lives a life they gain much from the day-to-day experience of living that life. Would they gain the same value, so to speak, from the imprint?*

S: You speak from a karmic point of view and we would say this is not accurate. For the imprint simply gives reference from which to draw. It does not assist in working off any karma. It simply is an added tool with which to work off karma. Were every-one to receive imprints then there would be a standstill in which no one would be experiencing true lives. And there would be nothing, eventually, relative to imprint from. So there is or must be real actual lives being lived with which to add to this record library.

D: *Yes, after a while the soul would prefer the shortcuts to the actual experience.*

S: For some souls the shortcuts are appropriate; for others they are not. For this vehicle is now living a lifetime which is appropriate. It could be said that he could have simply waited for someone else to have experienced an incarnation at this time and then received that imprint, could it not? However, the actual experience would not have been learned. The free will of the soul is here, in that the imprint is made by the free will of the soul and not some-one else's free will. All relative information is given into this computer and those appropriate incarnations are then given for imprinting. The imprints are available from this source but the individual makes the final decision. The soul has the power to reject if he finds an imprint which is not acceptable to him, for whatever reason. If he simply decides to use his authority to say, "I do not wish to have that one," then so be it.

D: *This is causing me a little confusion. Are you saying then that there is no such thing as reincarnation as we know it?*

S: Let me say, there is the progression from body to body. There are also the imprints. Someone may have lived actually five lives, but yet have the experience of five hundred. It's a combination of effects.

D: *In other words, that is information you have at birth and it is utilized by you during your life.*

S: The imprints are complete at the time of birth. But extra imprints are also available whenever necessary. This would be similar to packing luggage for a trip and finding during the trip that one has forgotten something. And so, there are stores along the way. Are you familiar with map overlays? For example, you might have the physical boundaries of the United States with no political boundaries such as states or counties. But these would be on transparencies. Each transparency is then laid down in succession and a complete picture is given. This could be used as an analogy to imprints. The imprints may be overlaid in many different ways, one being in a dream or a physical experience of some sort. It can be a traumatic experience such as a death in the family or a loss of one's

251

job or any time where one is open from within by some experience. Be it joyous or grievous or anywhere in between, the opening of oneself is the key here. And that imprint which is necessary will be neatly fitted in, with no notice whatsoever by the entity. But the fact is you can also actually live many lives without ever having an imprint. Imprints are simply aids. They are not necessary for everyone.

D: *The idea just occurred to me, is the life of Jesus available to be imprinted by the average person?*

S: The life is available and has been used throughout history. This is an extremely exceptional life which has been made available. The life embodies all the ideals that humanity is striving for.

D: *These would be the principles of Jesus' life, is that what you mean?*

S: That is correct.

D: *Then it would be very admirable to be imprinted with those.*

S: It would be most useful. It would correlate as a friend to a friend in the inner planes at this lifetime. The experience could also be overlaid on a person. Many who are incarnate have this imprint now. Jesus came as the foundation for this present evolution, to imprint this particular life for the healing of this planet. That is what is called the "Christ Consciousness." And each person who walks this path as the friend to the friend or as the healer, as Jesus was, has this imprint. And they are able to call upon this imprint when they have reached a certain state of consciousness in their own development.

D: *I was wondering, would this experience go along with what the Christians term as being "born again" and the entire changing of the person's life? Would that be what happens if they take on the Christ imprint?*

S: It is an awakening to this imprint, and is perceived as being "born again." Many describe it as Christ entering their life, when in fact it or He has been there all the time. It would be like finding a jewel in the closet.

D: *In this way it changes their life when they are awakened to this?*

S: This is definitely correct.

D: *When there is a true change brought about, does a change in their level of consciousness take place so that they are then operating from the Christ consciousness?*

S: They are operating *with* the Christ Consciousness through their inner planes. The Christ Spirit is then brought into the eternal flame within the heart and bums as unconditional love.

D: *Then this is a* real *experience; one experienced by many religious people?*

S: That is correct. It is a most profound experience, as sure as a light being turned on in the darkness.

D: *I have always thought there would be some way I could correlate the work I am doing with these experiences that Christians have had, and show that there really is no conflict at all.*

S: There is simply the terminologics involved. Much conflict is created from arguments over what to call these experiences. It is merely a matter of semantics or labeling, and the way people are attracted to their own religious orientation. Each will experience and call it something else and therein arises the argument. Each person is attached to his concept or perception as being the more correct one. Much work must be done to assure these people that their beliefs are valid, even without their labeling. For the labeling becomes the crutch, so they can hang on to that which is unseen. The labeling then be-comes more important than that which is labeled.

D: *Are these experiences unique to the Christian religion?*

S: There are similar experiences throughout *all* of humankind from the beginning, and they will continue for as long as humankind exists. It is in all religious aspects and evolution through all cultures. As I said, thousands of people could imprint the same experience simultaneously. The incarnate body of Jesus was not the only incarnation on this planet of the Christ consciousness. This planet has had many of those who have embodied these concepts, such as Gautama (Buddha), Mohammed, Moses, Elijah etc.

D: *I think it boils down to "truth is truth" no matter what you call it.*

S: That is correct.

D: *This would help explain that there really isn't as much difference as people think.*

S: There is merely labeling and the controversy that goes with such labeling. The effort has to be directed at allowing these people to see what is beneath the labels and to accept the labels for what they are.

Chapter 15
Walk-ins

T HIS EXPERIENCE WITH A WALK-IN happened with totally unexpected spontaneity. It would be impossible to predict something like this anyway. When taken through the birth experience the majority of my subjects relive coming into this life in the conventional manner. Thus I was not prepared for this radically different way of entering the physical body.

The young girl who was my subject had told me the story of her birth into this present life. She said that she had been born dead during a home delivery. The doctor tried, but had been unable to do anything for her, so he had put her limp body aside to care for her mother. It was only through the intervention of the girl's aunt that she is alive at all. Although the doctor told them there was no use trying, her aunt had worked with the lifeless body for several long minutes until finally a feeble cry was heard. This young woman had been told this story all her life. The family fully believed that if it had not been for the aunt's perseverance, she would not be here today.

I wanted to take her through the birth experience to see what had really happened. Subjects have benefited greatly from regressions such as this. They especially have received greater insight into the feelings and attitudes of close family members, because it has been proven that the entity is fully aware of everything occurring during pregnancy and preceding their birth.

I have taken enough subjects through their birth experiences to be sure that this young woman was not even in the baby's body at the time, but had delayed entry for some reason. Perhaps she was still conversing with her teachers and masters at the school on the other plane and had almost not made it in time. Perhaps she had been having second thoughts about entering into this life and the teachers had to use stronger persuasion. Often the entity tries to take on too much karma to be worked out as they plan their curriculum in this earthly classroom. They begin to wonder whether they are taking on too heavy of a load. It is very similar to signing up for college. There are often courses that are required which are more difficult than the easier extracurricular courses. Often a student realizes he is taking on more than he can comfortably handle. This is similar to coming into a life. It always looks easier during the planning stage. But often the plans have gone too far with karmic relationships already arranged etc., and it is too late for the entity to back out.

I have discovered with my work at least two main ways that the entity is born. They may enter the body while it is still in the womb and go through the actual birth if they wish to experience this. They may also remain outside of the baby's body but in close proximity to the mother and merely watch. They have freedom during this time to still go back and forth to the spirit planes as they are not totally tied to the baby yet. The main requirement, no matter which way they choose to do it, is that they enter the baby's body at the first breath. Failure to do so can result in stillbirths.

Because of the circumstances of her birth, instead of asking her to go to the time she was born, I asked her to go to the time she first entered this physical body to whom I was speaking. Maybe it was this wording that triggered the incident. I counted her there and asked what she was doing.

S: I'm watching.

I was not surprised because I knew she would not be in the baby's body.

D: *Where are you?*
S: At the foot of the bed. (A deep breath) I'm preparing to enter into the body for the final time. Up to this point it has been for ... short periods only.
D: *Do you mean the infant's body?*
S: No. It is not the body of a baby. It is an adult body.

This was a shock and one I was totally unprepared for. What did she mean?

D: *You mean you are not coming into an infant's body that has been born?*
S: No.
D: *This is not a normal thing, is it?*
S: No, but it is becoming more normal than a lot of people would be led to believe.
D: *You said you have entered this body for only short periods up until this time? What did you mean?*
S: There has been an exchange of souls. A trying-out period, as it were, to decide whether or not the relinquishment would be made. Whether or not she would accept what she had asked for.
D: *She asked for this?*
S: Yes. It is something that has been wished for and the other entity felt her time was over.

I was having difficulty accepting this. It sounded very much like what is called a "walk-in." This is a term that originated in Ruth Montgomery's writings and has come into popular usage. It loosely means a spirit that "walks-into" a living body instead of being born as a baby. I had encountered this phenomenon only once before in regressive hypnosis. That experience involved an entity that entered the body of a young child who was very ill. An exchange of souls was made when the occupying soul wanted out. That experience happened during a session conducted in the 1960s, long before the term "walk-in" had even been coined. (This was reported in my book *Five Lives Remembered.*)

D: *Why? Did something happen? Was there a reason for this?*

S: The decisions that affected the life. She thought that she would be able to handle the problems that she had put upon herself and when she found out that they were too strong, she asked to be returned home.

D: *Will you please explain what you mean?*

S: (A deep breath) She did not have the strength she thought that she had; therefore she is asking to be relieved of the situation.

D: *Couldn't this occur with the death of the body?*

S: Yes, but why cause the body to die when another can take its place and do much good. It was the soul that decided she could not deal with the karma she had chosen to deal with, and decided to leave the body. This body ... it is not time for it to die. It *must* continue on. In these cases the body is left operating so that another soul may enter.

D: *And doing something like this is not frowned upon?*

S: It would be frowned upon if she took the life of the physical body.

D: *You mean like suicide?*

S: Yes. But in just relinquishing it to another who would do good, there is no harm and there is nothing badly thought of this entity. This is a trade that is made with both parties agreeing.

I think one thing that was confusing me was that this sounded so much like possession. We have had so many movies lately like the *Exorcist,* that the idea was frightening.

S: There is no similarity whatsoever. A possession is when a warped spirit would try to *control* another. In a walk-in situation there is no control. There is but one entity in that body. The only way that entity can step into that body is that the other one willingly relinquish it. There is total permission. With a possession, it is exactly that-it is possession with-out right.

D: *Where is all this decided? Where is it worked out?*
S: On the spirit side. We discuss this with the masters and the decisions are made.

I wondered if the physical personality had anything to say about it. This girl certainly was not consciously aware of a decision of that magnitude.

D: *Does she go somewhere at different times to discuss it?*
S: Yes, when she is in a state that appears as sleep to others, she would journey.

This was a disturbing thought to me. To think that as conscious human beings we have so little to say about what is going on in our own lives. It is as though our consciousness is but a thin veneer covering an extremely complicated interior.

D: *Has the discussion been going on for quite a while?*
S: For about two months.
D: *How old is this physical body that you are going to enter?*
S: Twenty-one.

Twenty-one? This was another shock. I had met this girl shortly after her twenty-second birthday. This means that this exchange occurred just before I met her. Yet she seemed no different from anyone else I came into daily contact with.

D: *She stayed with that body a long time.*

S: Yes. There were a lot of things that were cleared up. There was just too much karma that had been accepted that it could not be carried out.

Was this the reason for her delay in originally entering into the physical body at birth? Was she having second thoughts about her ability to carry out all the assignments she had given herself? She had already had many problems in her young life and by all outward appearances she had faced and solved them admirably. Had she really lived her life with reluctance and only reached the age of 21 through perseverance?

Does this mean we can never really know a person? Does it mean we can never really know ourselves? This situation impressed upon me quite strongly for the first time the separateness of the different parts of a human being and how little control we truly have over these other parts.

D: *Who made the decision as to who would enter the body?*

S: The masters decided that there was enough like-ness of selves that the change would not be greatly noticeable.

D: *Did you know the other entity?*

S: Higher? Yes. We have also shared other lives together.

D: *You said this occurrence is becoming more frequent. Why? Are the pressures of living on Earth becoming too great?*

S: Yes. Plus the fact that those who are walking-in have not gone through the trauma of childhood or birth and they are more open to the influences from *this* side. At present and in the future there is a great need for this openness. These are people who shall guide others into the times to come. One of the reasons for the walking-in is that there is a short-age of *time* and a shortage of vehicles. There must be those who have an ear open, as it were, to the other side. And what better way than if they didn't have to go through birthing and childhood and forget all of the memories of before? Therefore much good can be done through them. The energy that we bring with us when we are walking-in influences those around us also-in many ways that are not always noticeable on the surface. Much important work is being done.

From the work I have done with regressions, I have developed a theory about children and memories of past lives. When the soul enters the body the memories are still very close to the surface. It must be very frustrating to suddenly find oneself entrapped within the body of a baby unable to communicate. No wonder they cry so much. They are trying to get the thought through to people that they are really an intelligent old soul that knows more than we can possibly imagine. During the first two years the spirit becomes so involved in learning to make this new body work and learning to communicate again that the memories are muted and pushed into the background. The few children who do still remember and try to tell people are usually criticized or ridiculed until they stop trying, and resign themselves to being "normal." I believe if such children were encouraged, instead of being made to feel different, they would learn to use these abilities to their advantage. The walk-in, on the other hand, enters the body fresh without the trauma of birth and without spending years trying to get the body to function. Thus they are very psychic because the memories and abilities carried over from the other plane are highly developed and very fresh and active.

D: *Will the physical body notice any difference when the exchange is made?*
S: No, the heart-rate and breathing will be continued on. In many cases this exchange is done at the point of death where a person would seem to die and then begin again. But this is not always the case. Many times there is just a going to sleep. And when they wake up, they... you are

that person and the other one has gone. But all of the memories have been absorbed, so you are that person.

D: *What about the other entity's karma? Do you continue this for them?*

S: Yes. In the agreements made, I must finish certain things that the other person stipulated must be finished.

D: *You work out the other person's karma.*

S: Not so much karma as, there are certain things that this original takes on when a body is begun. There is so much interaction with other souls that if certain obligations were not completed it would affect too many lives. Therefore the bargains must be made so these obligations can be met.

D: *Do you mean that the soul who comes in knows all the obligations that the previous occupant of the body had? And is totally aware before they come in of what they have...*

S: (Interrupted) What it is they must do, yes.

D: *So you have your own memories and you are absorbing her memories also?*

S: I have her memories of this life, but no past.

D: *Then you don't carry the records of her other incarnations?*

S: No. Only my own.

This opened up another intriguing idea. Does this mean that if I had regressed her a few years earlier I would have gotten the memories of totally different lives than she had given me during the year I worked with her? This has happened to other researchers and it is a point that is often grasped by psychiatrists and skeptics to disclaim reincarnation.

D: *Why doesn't the person, the physical entity, know that something like this has occurred?*

S: Sometimes it would be too traumatic to know at that time. Some walk-ins go for the rest of their existence never knowing. But they live better and happier lives than previously, doing much good to others and for others. The remembrance is not always important. The good they do is.

D: *I was thinking, if the physical body sometimes doesn't even know that anything has happened, does this mean the physical body is a separate entity?*

S: Is it not such? If you are born into a body, the body would continue on for some time without the soul being in it. Therefore it has a separateness.

D: *You mean when the spirit goes back and forth, whenever the body is a little baby?*

S: Yes.

This was a point that has been brought up in many regressions, that the soul leaves the baby's body continually for long periods of time when the baby is little. This most often occurs while the baby is asleep and everyone knows babies sleep a lot. It continues until the child has reached the age of around two years old. The soul is usually conversing with the masters at the school during this time and making last-minute decisions. This is also a possible explanation for crib deaths. The soul stayed away too long or decided to renege on its contract. So in this way the body can be separate and continue to exist for periods of time without the life force within it. I believe this is also what happens to people in comas. The body continues to live but the soul has gone on elsewhere. This is why I think it is wrong to keep a clinically dead body alive. When the body has been vacated too long, there is little likelihood the soul will choose to reenter. The body may also be damaged to the point that reentry of the original occupant or by any other soul is impossible. In such cases the body may be incapable of being reactivated.

Between Death & Life

As she talked, her voice sounded tired and her responses began to dull. She no longer had any interest in answering or couldn't remember the answers to the questions. I have witnessed this before sometimes when the entity entered a baby's body. When they were cut off from the other side, the knowledge was also cut off. They were no longer thinking in spiritual terms but were becoming involved in the physical.

D: *I know you are tiring because when you enter the body you are beginning to absorb. Have you entered the body now?*
S: Yes.
D: *And the physical body is asleep at night when it is happening?*
S: Yes.
D: *And the other entity has gone on?*
S: Yes.

Her responses were slowing down more and more, as though she was falling asleep.

S: (Softly) It is strange to feel the heart again. To feel the body.
D: *Had you intended to come back this quickly, or were you going to stay on the other side?*
S: It was to be soon. I much prefer this way. I do not have as many problems to deal with as growing up. There is much work to be done now. 'Tis much easier this way.
D: *Well, I'll allow you to rest then because it must be quite an ordeal to do something like that.*

Not to mention the ordeal she had just put me through.
When this young woman was told upon awakening what she had said in trance, she was startled, to say the least. She said, No! She could not believe that. She felt no different; she knew she was still the same person. Her conscious mind

rebelled at the idea and she had the same difficulty that I had in absorbing something of this magnitude. I told her if she did not want to accept the idea, she did not have to. She could just treat the information as an interesting curiosity. She did say that her parents had remarked that she seemed different, that she had changed in the last year or so. But that could have been merely part of the natural maturing process. None of us stay the same; we are constantly growing.

Since the story of her birth was a well-known fact and had been retold many times within her family, it was obvious this information about being a walk-in was the last thing she expected to come out during the regression.

Later I received very similar information about this topic from other subjects.

D: *Have you ever heard the term "walk-ins"?*
S: That is correct.
D: *Can you explain that for me?*
S: As we mentioned earlier, there are more souls waiting to incarnate than there are bodies to accommodate them. Sometimes there comes a time in an individual's life when he finds that he truly no longer wishes to be in the physical. He has reached a point where the physical weights and cares have dragged the soul to a level from which it cannot sustain itself. And so the individual is given the option to pass over to the other side. There is then made available the opportunity for an individual on the spirit side to come and inhabit that body. So there would be a mutual exchange of places, so to say. This is very beneficial for both. For you can see the original soul is released to his true home. And that individual on the spirit side is then allowed a vehicle on which to work karma.
D: *If the spirit wanted to go back, why couldn't the body just die?*
S: There would be the loss of the vehicle, the physical body. And there is often a time frame which must be reckoned

with. For example, assume the original host entity or soul had a relationship to work through with his wife. The situation developed so that the husband found he could no longer continue in that condition, and so was released to the spirit side. The entity entering into the body then would be charged with the responsibility of working through that karma with the wife. Thus after completing various tasks agreed to beforehand, the entering entity is then allowed to begin work on its own tasks and karma.

D: *Then it has to agree to finish whatever the vehicle started?*

S: That is correct. There is no exchange without consent from both sides. That is, for the one to relinquish the karma and for the other to assume the karma.

D: *How is it decided who will enter this body that still has to be kept alive?*

S: It is decided in the same manner that the decision is made of who will enter in the first place. It depends on who has karma to work out with these people. Whether or not it is felt that they can handle what *must* be done. And whether or not the person is advanced enough to not need the lessons of childhood and birth and to enter into an entity with full memory.

D: *That makes it more difficult, doesn't it, to not lose those memories at birth?*

S: (Emphatically) One does not lose the memories at birth. Children still have them. They can be seen in some of the games they play that parents and adults call "make-believe." We, as adults, silence them in many ways whether it is intended or not. But the memories grow quieter as one grows older because of these outside influences, more so than anything *in* the entity.

D: *I thought maybe the trauma of birth and growing up, learning to use the body, might push the memories back.*

S: Some of them, yes, but not all.

D: *Then I suppose as they grow older if this memory is not exercised, they forget. I am beginning to understand this better, but I think the reason why it always bothered me is because it sounded so similar to possession by a spirit.*

S: As we said, there is no exchange without the expressive consenting agreement between both souls. It is agreed upon beforehand and oftentimes a schedule is arranged between the two. An orderly schedule in which the procedure is to be accomplished. And so it is not an unwilling and unknown act at all. It is a partnership agreement.

D: *But what about the conscious vehicle? Is the person aware of any changes that have taken place?*

S: Oftentimes the vehicle will not know that owner-ship has traded hands, so to say. For there is with the implant of the new spirit the possession of all past remembrances of that vehicle's life. And so from the physical point of view there is no apparent change of ownership or custodianship.

D: *Then the conscious vehicle has nothing to say about it. It is not consulted, in other words.*

S: The consciousness is never interrupted. The sub-consciousness changed hands, so to say. There is no discomfort and no interference. Sometimes when it is necessary or desired there will be the realization and remembrance of the actual transfer. And oftentimes with time there is the gradual realization and possibly remembrance of the exact time of the transfer.

D: *I think that is what is bothering me. It seems you have so little to say about it.*

S: It is not that we have nothing to say. We simply have more to say than can be received.

He obviously did not understand my remark. I was referring to the physical person not having anything to say about it. He thought I meant, he, as the communicator, was not supplying enough information. This demonstrates how literally the subconscious interprets remarks that are made while in the trance state.

S: We simply do not know what your questions are until you ask them.

D: *That is true. You said before that the questions are as important as the answers.*

S: That is correct. There must be a void before there can be the filling of the void.

D: *Then this is not frowned upon whenever a soul wants out, so to speak, or they want to renege on the deal?*

S: It is not a renege; it is simply a situation in which a soul finds itself. For it is well observed and well known on this side that all does not go as planned. And so it is simply a situation which has an ideal solution. We find favor in this transfer for it is quite admirable and noble. It is much more useful and effective than allowing the vehicle to die, in which no further use or goodness or work can be had from the body.

D: *I was trying to figure out the difference between a walk-in and a suicide. Is it because the suicide destroys the body?*

S: That is correct.

D: *That is what is frowned upon?*

S: That is correct. Not simply because the body has expired without someone to fill it. There is the disruption of the soul harmony because of this. It is an act which is inexcusable.

D: *Then that body had things to accomplish and it interrupted the order of several things?*

S: That is correct.

D: *Under normal circumstances, can you tell me at what point or at what time in the progress of the human physical development does the soul or spirit inhabit the body?*

S: It is at that point at which the spirit chooses to inhabit. It could be at the precise moment of fertilization or conception, or perhaps some time removed from the birth experience, so as not to *have* to experience the trauma of birth. It is entirely up to that individual spirit's choice. It is also determined by what lesson the spirit needs to learn.

D: *So what you are saying is that a person could have life for a period of time without having a spirit or soul?*

S: Not so, for there would need to be the life force given. However, the residency is not a requisite of the life force concept, in that the life force would perhaps emanate from the mother. However, the residency of the spirit into that form would be optional or up to the individual spirit as to when that spirit would assume the custodianship of that life form and thence integrate it into its own reality, and begin nourishing it with its own life force.

D: *So what you are saying is that we would not be able to define at what point life really begins.*

S: That is accurate. And so abortion should not be criticized in the sense of killing a soul because it is not possible to gauge at what point that physical life form had indeed taken a soul.

D: *If I understand what you are saying, in all probability an abortion would not actually take a life. Is that true?*

S: It perhaps might be best understood to know that in deciding whether to carry out an abortion this responsibility is shared by, not only the mother, but by that life force which would inhabit the vehicle which is aborted. It is done on a somewhat deeper level of awareness than subconscious but not completely on the inner realms. There is some conscious communication which is inherent in this decision making process. It is of a level that is somewhat inner and yet somewhat outer at the same time or simultaneously.

We have already discussed that the incoming soul has chosen the parents and environment during the planning stage before entering the fetus. The spirit does not like to be confined within the developing baby because it has been used to being free, so it does not remain in the baby's body during the entire pregnancy. It can still go back and forth between the spirit worlds if it chooses. During this time the baby is being kept alive by the life force of the mother, so the incoming soul does not have to be present. If the pregnancy is interrupted by abortion or miscarriage it cannot harm the soul because that part is eternal and incapable of being harmed. If the incoming soul still wants to be connected with that family it will simply wait for the next opportunity. Maybe the next time the mother becomes pregnant she will be better able to handle the responsibility of the child. In the meantime many lessons have been presented to be learned. So in the case of an abortion the incoming soul just says, "That's okay. I'll catch you next time." In the case of a miscarriage the baby's body was not developing correctly and would not have been an appropriate vehicle to carry out the plan the soul wanted to accomplish. So the same thing happens, the soul simply waits until the next appropriate opportunity to come into the same family environment.

I had one client who said, "I wish you could have told my mother that. She miscarried a baby before me, and she grieved for that child all her life." I told her there was no reason to grieve because the mother didn't lose anything. That first baby had returned as my client, the second baby. We have even had this happen in my own family. One of my daughters had a baby boy that was born dead and almost to the day a year later she had a second boy. We have never grieved for the first one, because we know it returned as the second one. Apparently the first time he was not quite ready to make the jump to enter this chaotic world. He had to be persuaded, "You signed a contract. You made a deal and now you have to go through with it."

D: *Another question along that same line. On the other end of life, are we justified in trying to maintain life in a body that has lost its ability to function?*
S: Again this decision would be shared. Those who are of the decision making process should go inside, into their own

consciousness and in so doing attune themselves, not only to *themselves* but to that individual which would be making this choice for themselves. This decision making process, that is the inner turning, is an attunement to that life energy which would be involved in this decision.

D: *Going back to the spirit taking over the life form: Is it conceivable that a spirit for some reason might reject that particular life form?*

S: That is accurate.

D: *What would happen to that vehicle or body?*

S: That, in your terms, could be described as crib death. That is, the life force simply vacated the vehicle and took with it the life energy.

D: *Would this be the* primary *reason for crib deaths?*

S: That is accurate. There was a reverse decision or need to withdraw. Perhaps some occurrence from the physical level or on some spiritual plane necessitated that energy withdrawal. Perhaps a karmic connection for that infant was lost. Perhaps one whom that infant had bargained and contracted with to meet at some point in that future life had either been killed, perhaps through accident or disease, or had decided not to incarnate. Then perhaps the life force would choose not to incarnate because the contract, as it were, could not be consummated.

D: *Are there also cases where the spirits just change their minds?*

S: That is accurate.

D: *If the planned spirit does not take over the vehicle...*

S: (Interrupted) Yes, the vehicle would then be available for another to inhabit that form. It is possible for another spirit to swap places. In such cases the baby would revive by seemingly miraculous means. It is entirely up to all the individuals involved. It can often include very complicated karma which is beyond your present ability to understand.

Apparently we, as conscious human beings, are the *least* informed participants in the whole earthly scenario.

Chapter 16
The Return Trip

BEFORE BEGINNING THE RETURN TRIP into the physical life the spirit not only goes through the planning sessions with the masters and teachers and consults with the other people they will be trying to work karma with, but they also check out the family they are considering being born into. One woman I told about this thought the idea was very eerie. "Do you mean my baby was watching me the whole time I was pregnant?" she asked, her eyes wide with astonishment. The idea is a little creepy but apparently it is all a part of the plan, and shows that the spirit is in total control of his birth circumstances. The following are a few examples of a spirit checking things out before being born into a family again.

D: *What are you doing?*
S: I am watching the family that I will be born to.
D: *You haven't come back to Earth yet?*
S: No. I am studying and learning about them so I will know how to deal with them.
D: *Where are you watching them from?*
S: I am here.

She described the place where the family lived. She was about to be born into a peasant life in China.

D: *Do you know why you have picked this family?*

S: We have known each other before and I have things that I must accomplish. They are people which I have things to work out with, and in that manner they will help me to accomplish much.

D: *What do you do? Just wait here until it is time to be born?*

S: No. We watch and learn and sometimes go back with the masters and they teach us things.

D: *Then you don't have to stay right with the family. Well, when do you enter the new body?*

S: Sometimes before birth, sometimes at birth, sometimes a little after.

D: *Then you don't have to be in the baby's body before it is born?*

S: No. Some do not enter until days after the baby has been born. It depends on the lesson that must be learned. This time I shall probably choose to enter before birth.

D: *Do you mean the spirit just kind of hangs around the baby?*

S: Yes. Or some of those who entered will leave for short periods of time. Perhaps they are not wanting to stay; they are arguing. In most cases there is al-ways a choice for the first short while about whether or not one must stay, or whether one decides that, for some reason, it is not right and decides to leave.

D: *Would there be reasons for them to change their mind?*

S: Yes. There may be certain things that have changed since they decided to enter that body. Maybe they decided the parents were not ready for them, or not ready to give what they would need. Or that they themselves were just not ready.

D: *Then it is not really a foolproof system. There are ways of backing out. You said sometimes they can leave for a while and go back and forth. Is this safe for the body?*

S: Usually it is done when the body sleeps and there is no great harm, unless one stays gone too long. This could cause harm; the body could die.

D: *But most of the time they can leave and come back?*

S: It is a new experience. Not new in the essence that they have never done this before, but it is perhaps long forgotten. Especially if they have been in the spirit existence for any length of time. They now feel entrapped.

D: *I can see why they would. So they are allowed to leave for a while when the baby is very young and no harm is done that way. Is there any certain age that they have to stop this and just stay in the baby? Are there any regulations about that?*

S: It is preferred that it stop at about age one. But there have been cases where people have done it until three and even five years old. There are those who remember longer than others what it was like on this side.

D: *But the body doesn't know what is going on, does it?*

S: No. It keeps on with its own existence for that period of time.

D: *Do you know what you have to learn in this life you are coming into?*

S: I will have to learn the meaning of ... not wanting so much. Learning how to deal with people on a one-to-one basis and not coveting, as it is said in one book.

D: *One book? What do you mean?*

S: One of the things we learn by, it is a guide. Hopefully I will be able to master these things.

D: *In the past have you wanted too much?*

S: Upon occasion, yes. It is one of the things that is perhaps a little harder to learn than others. Because if you have nothing and you see that those around you have things, you long for it. Because you say, "Why is this person any better than I and they have so much more." This is something that must be learnt and dealt with.

D: *That is very human. You don't need it but you want it.*

S: You must learn the difference between needing and wanting, and strike a happy medium between.

D: *That is one of the things that you are going to hopefully learn in this life?*

S: I shall strive to.

D: *And you think this family can help you.*

S: It can be hoped.

D: *Okay, but right now you are just watching them, getting ready for the time when you will come back. Are you more or less assigned to that family?*

S: Yes, the choice has been made.

D: *It must take a while to get all these things together and all these different factors working, right?*

S: Yes, and also the time of birth must be right.

D: *It all sounds complicated. To me, anyway. I guess it is not to the ones that are in charge.*

S: At least it seems to work.

It was ironic that this life did not turn out the way the entity had programmed it before entering the body. His main lesson was supposed to be not to covet, but while living the life the pull of the flesh was too strong, and of course, he had no memory of the carefully laid pattern his soul had worked out on the other side. He became a very shrewd Chinese trader. I considered him to be a thief, or at least a "con" man with a lively gift of gab. He just considered himself a smart businessman. His downfall came when he coveted a black pearl and succeeded in obtaining it. But it caused his arrest and death by flogging. As another entity said, things look so simple on the spirit plane, but when you are in the physical body things become more complicated, and you lose sight of your goal.

Another example of pre-birth:

S: I watch the woman who is to be my mother. In this manner I will know what to expect.

She described the family and the house.

D: *What do you think of the family?*

S: I am very unsure. They are very demanding. They have definite ideas of what they wish to do. The final decision hasn't been made.

D: *When will it be made?*

S: Soon. I have a choice. I have to decide whether the lessons I feel I need to learn can be taught in this particular existence.

D: *How long do you watch them before the decision is made?*

S: Sometimes a few days, sometimes longer.

D: *If you decided you didn't want to be born there, would another spirit come?*

S: Yes. But there is a need for me in this situation. I could learn much from this.

D: *What do you hope to learn in this life?*

S: Humility. And dealing with relationships with people on a day-to-day level, learning tolerance of others. I must learn to give more freely of myself. To not hold back, working and having good bonds with others instead of being too self-sufficient.

D: *Is that what you've done in the past?*

S: Yes, and I must learn to correct this fault in me.

D: *Are there people in this life that you are going to have karma with?*

S: Yes. There were problems in my relationship with the soul that is to be my mother. We must work these out and learn to love in spite of faults.

D: *Are there other people in this life that you've already made arrangements with?*

S: Yes, there are those who will be there with me. I see someone who will look to me for guidance, that I must strive to give. There was failure and there is a need to repay this.

D: *Do you know what you're going to be in this life?*

S: I will be a priest. It is needful for me to follow that path in order to pay debts that I owed.

D: *I suppose they are debts you have incurred in past lives. Has the life already been planned?*

S: To an extent that things are planned it has been ordained. There is still free will that must be involved.

D: *I have heard that there are some things that* have *to happen. That there is no way they can be changed?*

S: If you need it in order to accentuate your growth, this will occur no matter what the desire.

D: *But they say the best laid plans often go awry. Does that happen? Do you know what I mean?*

S: Of mice and men? Someone will say that... But, this is not a *man-made* plan; therefore not everything that is planned can be changed. If it has been shown to be needful, it will occur.

D: *You couldn't make things so foolproof that there would be no way out. That wouldn't leave you any free will. So even though you plan things very carefully, they can't always work out the way you want, can they?*

S: Sometimes not.

D: *But you can hope, I suppose.*

S: You must not *hope,* you must *believe.* Hope has no power or strength, but believing does. With belief we can work toward our ultimate destiny.

It is again ironic that the plans for this life became more complicated in practice than in theory. He indeed did become a priest, but it was not his own choosing. During the time period in which he lived, if a family had many children a son was often given to the monastery to become a priest, rather than have another mouth to feed. This was the fate of many within the church at that time, and since they had not entered religion because of a desire to help humankind, the superiors were often bitter and wielded a power over the monks that amounted to cruelty. Thus the entity became a priest, but not in a helping capacity. He lived a destitute, lonely, and unhappy life until he escaped by having an early heart attack. Again the best laid plans of mice and men had gone awry.

I HAVE TAKEN many regressed subjects through the birth experience. It verifies what has already been explained, that the spirit will at times choose to observe the birth and enter the baby's body after it has been born. Or they may decide to enter the baby while it is within the mother's body and experience the physical birth. They do not like to be within the developing fetus; it is a cramped, uncomfortable feeling. They have the sensation of feeling warm but being in the dark. They can also describe all the emotions that the mother-to-be is experiencing. I have had some sad regressions where the mother did not want the baby and the spirit was very much aware of this. But they felt there was no backing out and maybe they would be able to rectify the situation once they were born. They still felt the necessity of being born into that family for some reason, probably karmic.

It is very strange to watch someone go through the actual birth process. They often experience strong pressure about the head and shoulders. Sometimes they gasp as though experiencing difficulty breathing. It is at these times that I must try to minimize any physical discomforts. They do not see anything until they come out into the bright light. Then they feel very cold and totally confused. One subject saw the people wearing white, but said they were dressed differently than the people at "home" who also wore white. They are aware of everyone's thoughts and they don't like being separated from the mother. Their first cries are in frustration at being unable to communicate with these strange creatures in this new environment. Then softly a wave of forgetfulness seems to sweep over them as their responses dull and the memories of the other planes and other existences fade away.

MANY PEOPLE have wondered about what is called the "population question." They say there are more people on Earth now than the total accumulated population that has ever lived on Earth, and yet it just keeps increasing. If these are only the same souls coming back over and over again, how do you explain the increase in population? The people who ask these questions are obviously hampered by a narrow outlook. They think the souls that have been incarnating since historical times, as we know it, are all the souls that there are.

S: We understand your question. Where are all these new souls coming from? We would ask that you understand that there are many more souls than there are vehicles available. For were the re-verse true, can you imagine bodies walking around without souls? This would be an interesting situation. However, as we said, there are more souls available to incarnate than bodies to incarnate in. And so there is the waiting process for the correct vehicle to come along.

D: *I think their argument is that we have more population now than we have ever had. And if this is all the people who have ever lived...*

S: That is not correct. For were everyone to incarnate, there would be no one left in the spirit world to tend to the store, so to say. There must always be those on this side to assist and guide and direct. For there is work to be done here in a bureaucratic sense or governmental sense just as surely as on your planet.

D: *That is what I've tried to tell them. That all the souls that have been created have not incarnated.*

S: That is correct. For there has never been a total influx of all the souls on this planet. Were that to be, you would surely be standing several feet deep in people, shoulder to shoulder over the entire Earth.

D: *We don't want that.*

S: Neither do we. So we merely say that the souls are being incarnated now at a rate which is compatible with the amount of vehicles available.

THERE ARE many lessons to be gained on Earth. If certain ones are learned, it makes the others easier.

S: We shall speak to you now of unconditional love. We would say that in order to experience this concept one would necessarily be required to experience a *lack* of this same energy we call unconditional love. So, in the scheme of things, in the grand design, one finds oneself returned out of the dark-ness and lack of love and understanding. And thence into the light again on this side and surrounded with those who provide this unconditional love. Then one can easily remember the lack of it and relate in a most harmonious way to an abundance of it. This is a lesson this planet as a whole is now learning. The confusion and disharmony pre-sent on the planet has clouded and distorted this love to such a degree as to make it almost unrecognizable. This transition from one of conditional to unconditional love is now in its later stages.

D: *Can you define unconditional love for me?*

S: This would be somewhat impossible to accurately define in your system of concepts and wordings, as there are no concepts available to do justice to this. It can be described; however it cannot be defined.

D: *Then could you describe it or give me an analogy?*

S: We would say that the most accurate portrayal or example of this on your planet would be that of a mother's love for her child because she loves this child regardless of its meandering into and out of social conforming. When one finds one's child has transgressed the laws of society and must pay the penance, then more love is given, more understanding is poured out. And this is exactly as it should be, as there is from the child's point of view a much greater need for this love and understanding. So this love is given unconditionally regardless of the circumstances of the transgressions.

This love is given simply because of the bonding nature between the two. This is an example of unconditional love.

D: *This is what we have to learn from each other?*

S: That is accurate.

D: *But you know how people are.* Love *is very difficult for some people, let alone unconditional love. That is a very hard concept for some people to understand.*

S: That is accurate. That is the wisdom shown in using this as a lesson because this is such a difficult one to learn.

D: *Wasn't this what Jesus was really trying to teach when He came to Earth?*

S: That is an undisputed fact! His incarnation was the personification of unconditional love. Many are now attuning to this fact and are becoming aware of the subtleties in the Christ's teachings. There are many more lessons on a subtler plane than could ever be hoped for in the literal.

D: *Is there another lesson you wanted to present?*

S: We would say that tolerance and patience are like twins, in that each is a compliment to the other. For without one there could not be the other.

D: *Are these some of the lessons that we should try to learn when we come to Earth?*

S: That is accurate. A well-rounded and wholesome personality would not be found lacking in these qualities.

S: We would speak to those who feel that perhaps there should be more to life than what they have experienced. You desire more yet you seem not to find the door, perhaps, to go through to experience it. Your door, if you choose to use that analogy, is your own mind and simply nothing more. The ultimate goal on the physical plane is to know yourself. You shall be offered many lessons which will challenge you to know yourself. And oftentimes these will be painful. We would ask you to examine the rose and see that in such beauty there is always some element of hurt. For to truly enjoy the rose it must be plucked from the stalk. And so there is the danger of sticking one's finger on the rose thorns. This could be used as an analogy of life on the physical plane. However, in those times of distress and urgency, we would ask that you always remember that your experiences are given to you by yourself. You, yourself, choose that which is to be experienced, so that you may learn those lessons which you need. Thus through these painful experiences you will indeed begin to know yourself. And if you learn something from these experiences, then they will not have been in vain. You are truly the master of your own fate and destiny. You, yourself are in complete control of what you call your lifetime. You are the one who is making decisions as to when and where and how. We, from our point of view, can see all the options spread out before you. But it is you, yourself who must make the final decisions. You al-so cannot help but influence other individuals while you are living on this plane. You influence individuals continuously.

D: *I thought we were not supposed to influence another individual.*

S: It is one thing to dominate, but yet something all-together different to influence. For would it be possible for you to teach if you were not able to influence? Influence is not bad. For each person has the ability to discriminate between that which is good and that which is not. *You* simply put your pieces on the board and allow others to decide which they choose. There always seems to be so much turmoil on Earth. This is quite natural in the cyclic nature of events which are destined to occur on this planet. However, from your perspective this is quite unnatural, for you would seem to prefer that period in which all is as it should be, so to say. However, were all to remain as it should be, nothing would ever change. It would be as it should be forever. That is not the purpose of Earth. For Earth is a testing ground, a battleground, a play-ground, and many more concepts. So in order to accommodate these many varied experiential manifestation; for lack of a better terminology; it is necessary to occasionally shift the realities such that the emphasis is less on one and more on the other. Per-haps it will be less of a playground and more of a battleground and so forth. The priorities are simply shifted around when needed. And that which you perceive as upheaval is in fact merely the physical manifestation of the reshuffling of priorities. We would say that you should follow your own intuitive guidance while on Earth. This would be most appropriate. For that which is highly undesirable to one may in fact be highly desirable to another. There is no set or firm reality. No real truth, for all is in fact relative. So one must be careful in assigning truths and realities, to see that those realities and truths do not impinge on another's. Thus when creating realities it is important to always remember to include the disclaimer, that only that which is most appropriate will be manifest. We would say, that which is necessary is that which will be manifest.

D: *It is very difficult for us here on Earth to see the anguish, heartache and pain of other people, and recognize that it is evolution.*

S: That is true given the perspective of the mortal experience. We feel this is perhaps one area which is not quite understood by many who are working now on your plane. It would not be beneficial to describe that point at which you on Earth now stand in this evolution. For were we to say it is the beginning, then there would be a great heaviness of heart, which there should not be. And were we to say it is at the end, there would be an eager anticipation of that which may not be for some time. So it would be most appropriate to simply accept that we are in this upheaval and turmoil at whatever point we are in. And to work in this period we are now in and to allow the cycle to continue on its own. The most important period to work on is the present. And if your reality is now only in the wash cycle or the spin cycle, it is irrelevant. For the laundry will surely be done.

D: *(Laugh) But we don't know which cycle we're in.*

S: The souls who decide to go down and have another cycle of life in your time are either foolhardy or brave, depending on their viewpoint. Some of them do it just out of duty because they know they need to go through a certain number of lives to be able to develop to a certain point. Most of these are the ones that are rather dull and plodding and conventional on your world. Other souls who are more advanced do it with both eyes open, knowing full well it will be difficult. But they know that it will advance their karma since they are going into that life already advanced and they know they will be able to do two or three lifetime's worth of advancement in one lifetime. This is possible by going down at this particular time when it is difficult to advance spiritually in the materialism of your world. These more advanced souls are able to stay in touch and keep in tune, and they do much spiritual advancement because of the work they have to put into it. Due to the resistance of the general world trend this causes them to become that much stronger, to where it is the equivalent of two or three life-time's worth of growth. When they cross back over to this side, they are extremely advanced, and they are usually asked to stay on this side for a while to help prepare those of us who wish to go back. Then after a while, they say, "Well, gee, you know I'd like to go back, too, and do some more advancing," and so they do. And that is the way it goes in the pattern of things. We would say to you now gathered in this room, that each of you can, in your own particular way, now see in some form or another a journey which lies ahead of you. We would say that actually in very simple terms, everyone on this planet has this same journey. However, many are more aware of it than others.

D: *We're all on the same path, just going in different directions.*

S: That is accurate. However, all paths will eventually converge and meet in one single place.

D: *It just makes many more twists and turns along the way.*

S: That is accurate.

IT IS AMAZING that all the information in this book was obtained from many different people who did not know each other. They were of various religions and occupations. Yet in spite of their differences, the information they gave while in deep trance does not contradict but rather compliments each other. In many places it fit so well when combined that it almost sounds as though it came from one person instead of several. This is an amazing phenomena in itself, that when put together it creates a solid book of cohesive information. To me this is proof that they were seeing and reporting similar scenes when regressed to the so-called "dead" state. If they all see the same things, then I believe the afterlife must be a very real, identifiable place with definite rules and regulations and a hierarchy that keeps it all in order.

I don't claim to have all the answers; the questions about such a subject as life after death are far too deep and complex. The reader will probably be able to think of many questions they would have liked to have asked that I did not even think of. But such is the way it is when you open the door to search for knowledge, and hunt for the answers to questions that most people refuse to acknowledge even exist. The information I have received in my work is probably only the barest skimming of the surface. It does give us a glimpse of what lies in that other world that we all must someday visit. There can be no accident that similar information came from many subjects while in deep trance. In order for their descriptions to resemble so closely what each other have said, they must truly be picturing the same places and circumstances. It isn't always easy to accept another way of thinking that partially or completely disrupts the pattern laid down for us since childhood. But if it contains the ring of truth, then it is worth considering and exploring. Again, this information is merely hearsay and we will never know until we actually make the journey ourselves. But if we can find out this much knowledge from those who have already made the trek and carry the experience within their soul's memories, then we are at least one step closer to understanding the frightening realm of the unknown. I believe all of us carry these memories and maybe they will be awakened at the time when we most need them.

I think my research is much like reading in a geography book about a strange and exotic country which lies far across the seas. It is a real place which we know exists because the book describes it and shows us pictures of it, and tells of the activities the inhabitants are involved in. But until we actually go there and see for ourselves, the information remains only words and pictures in a book. Maybe the author exaggerated, maybe the author minimized, maybe he only reported from his own point of view while another geography book would have reported the facts differently. Any time we travel to a foreign country we see it through our own eyes and we may notice something that completely escaped the notice of someone else. Everything that happens to us is colored by our own thoughts and experiences.

Thus we will never actually know until we leave our body for the last time and journey toward the brilliant light that marks the barrier between this world and the next. Even with the knowledge I have gained through my work I am not anxious to make that trip. At least, not yet. I feel I have much to accomplish yet here on this plane. For in my study of death, I have found the celebration of life.

But I think when the time comes the journey will not hold as much fear as it once would have. Because I know I am not going into a strange, dark, forbidding unknown. I am merely returning *home* and there will be as many familiar people and sights on those planes as there are on this one. Maybe the information I have found has allowed us to lift the veil a little and peer beyond, and allowed us to glimpse through the glass into the shadows and what we see is not as dark as it was before. It is the awakening of memories long buried. And the memories are truly wonderful, because what we see is a beautiful sight to behold.

I am grateful that I was allowed to have these conversations with the spirits. What they have told me encourages the shedding of fears and doubts and brings the realization that what lies beyond the barrier is only a joyous "homecoming."

About the Author

olores Cannon, a regressive hypnotherapist and psychic researcher who records "Lost" knowledge, was born in 1931 in St. Louis, Missouri. She was educated and lived in St. Louis until her marriage in 1951 to a career Navy man. She spent the next 20 years traveling all over the world as a typical Navy wife, and raising her family. In 1970 her husband was discharged as a disabled veteran, and they retired to the hills of Arkansas. She then started her writing career and began selling her articles to various magazines and newspapers. She has been involved with hypnosis since 1968 and exclusively with past-life therapy and regression work since 1979. She has studied the various hypnosis methods and thus developed her own unique technique which enabled her to gain the most efficient release of information from her clients. Dolores is now teaching her unique technique of hypnosis all over the world.

In 1986 she expanded her investigations into the UFO field. She has done on-site studies of suspected UFO landings, and has investigated the Crop Circles in England. The majority of her work in this field has been the accumulation of evidence from suspected abductees through hypnosis.

Dolores is an international speaker who has lectured on all the continents of the world. Her seventeen books are translated into over twenty languages. She has spoken to radio and television audiences worldwide. And articles about/by Dolores have appeared in several U.S. and international magazines and newspapers. Dolores was the first American and the first foreigner to receive the "Orpheus Award" in Bulgaria, for the highest advancement in the research of psychic phenomenon. She has received Outstanding Contribution and Lifetime Achievement awards from several hypnosis organizations.

Dolores has a very large family who keep her solidly balanced between the "real" world of her family and the "unseen" world of her work.

If you wish to correspond with Dolores about her work, private sessions or her training classes, please submit to the following address. (Please enclose a self-addressed stamped envelope for her reply.) Dolores Cannon, P.O. Box 754, Huntsville, AR, 72740, USA or email her at decannon@msn.com or through our Website: www.ozarkmt.com

Other Books By Ozark Mountain Publishing, Inc.

Dolores Cannon
Conversations with Nostradamus,
    Volume I, II, III
Jesus and the Essenes
They Walked with Jesus
Between Death and Life
A Soul Remembers Hiroshima
Keepers of the Garden.
The Legend of Starcrash
The Custodians
The Convoluted Universe - Book One,
    Two, Three, Four
Five Lives Remembered
The Three Waves of Volunteers and the
    New Earth
Stuart Wilson & Joanna Prentis
The Essenes - Children of the Light
Power of the Magdalene
Beyond Limitations
Atlantis and the New Consciousness
The Magdalene Version
O.T. Bonnett, M.D./Greg Satre
Reincarnation: The View from Eternity
What I Learned After Medical School
Why Healing Happens
M. Don Schorn
Elder Gods of Antiquity
Legacy of the Elder Gods
Gardens of the Elder Gods
Reincarnation...Stepping Stones of Life
Aron Abrahamsen
Holiday in Heaven
Out of the Archives – Earth Changes
Sherri Cortland
Windows of Opportunity
Raising Our Vibrations for the New Age
The Spiritual Toolbox
Michael Dennis
Morning Coffee with God
God's Many Mansions
Nikki Pattillo
Children of the Stars
A Spiritual Evolution
Rev. Grant H. Pealer
Worlds Beyond Death
A Funny Thing Happened on the Way to
    Heaven
Maiya & Geoff Gray-Cobb
Angels - The Guardians of Your Destiny
Maiya Gray-Cobb
Seeds of the Soul
Sture Lönnerstrand
I Have Lived Before
Arun & Sunanda Gandhi
The Forgotten Woman
Claire Doyle Beland
Luck Doesn't Happen by Chance

James H. Kent
Past Life Memories As A Confederate
    Soldier
Dorothy Leon
Is Jehovah An E.T
Justine Alessi & M. E. McMillan
Rebirth of the Oracle
Donald L. Hicks
The Divinity Factor
Christine Ramos, RN
A Journey Into Being
Mary Letorney
Discover The Universe Within You
Debra Rayburn
Let's Get Natural With Herbs
Jodi Felice
The Enchanted Garden
Susan Mack & Natalia Krawetz
My Teachers Wear Fur Coats
Ronald Chapman
Seeing True
Rev. Keith Bender
The Despiritualized Church
Vara Humphreys
The Science of Knowledge
Karen Peebles
The Other Side of Suicide
Antoinette Lee Howard
Journey Through Fear
Julia Hanson
Awakening To Your Creation
Irene Lucas
Thirty Miracles in Thirty Days
Mandeep Khera
Why?
Robert Winterhalter
The Healing Christ
James Wawro
Ask Your Inner Voice
Tom Arbino
You Were Destined to be Together
Maureen McGill & Nola Davis
Live From the Other Side
Anita Holmes
TWIDDERS
Walter Pullen
Evolution of the Spirit
Cinnamon Crow
Teen Oracle
Chakra Zodiac Healing Oracle
Jack Churchward
Lifting the Veil on the Lost Continent of
    Mu

For more information about any of the above titles, soon to be released titles,
or other items in our catalog, write or visit our website:
PO Box 754, Huntsville, AR 72740
www.ozarkmt.com

Other Books By Ozark Mountain Publishing, Inc.

Guy Needler
The History of God
Beyond the Source – Book 1,2
Dee Wallace/Jarred Hewett
The Big E
Dee Wallace
Conscious Creation
Natalie Sudman
Application of Impossible Things
Henry Michaelson
And Jesus Said – A Conversation
Victoria Pendragon
SleepMagic
Riet Okken
The Liberating Power of Emotions
Janie Wells
Payment for Passage
Dennis Wheatley/ Maria Wheatley
The Essential Dowsing Guide
Dennis Milner
Kosmos
Garnet Schulhauser
Dancing on a Stamp
Julia Cannon
Soul Speak – The Language of Your
    Body
Charmian Redwood
Coming Home to Lemuria
Kathryn Andries
Soul Choices – 6 Paths to Find Your Life
    Purpose

For more information about any of the above titles, soon to be released titles,
or other items in our catalog, write or visit our website:
PO Box 754, Huntsville, AR 72740
www.ozarkmt.com